204

24 HOURS AT
THE CAPITOL

24 HOURS AT THE CAPITOL

AN
ORAL HISTORY
OF THE
JANUARY 6th
INSURRECTION

NORA NEUS

BEACON PRESS, BOSTON

BEACON PRESS
24 Farnsworth Street
Boston, Massachusetts
www.beacon.org

Beacon Press books
are published under the auspices of
the Unitarian Universalist Association of Congregations.

28 27 26 25   8 7 6 5 4 3 2 1

This book is printed on acid-free paper that meets the uncoated paper
ANSI/NISO specifications for permanence as revised in 1992.

Text design and composition by Kim Arney

*Library of Congress Cataloguing-in-Publication
Data is available for this title.*
Hardcover ISBN: 978-0-8070-2062-3
E-book ISBN: 978-0-8070-2063-0
Audiobook: 978-0-8070-2213-9

The authorized representative in the EU for product safety and
compliance is Easy Access System Europe 16879218, Mustamäe tee 50,
10621 Tallinn, Estonia: http://beacon.org/eu-contact.

For my grandparents:
Marion, Donald, Vivian, Linsy, and Ursula

"This is not a rally and it's no longer a protest. This is a final stand where we are drawing the red line at Capitol Hill."

—Post on the right-wing social network Parler, emailed to the FBI on January 2, 2021

CONTENTS

INTRODUCTION

In the early morning hours of January 7, 2021, I got home from my overnight shift at CNN's New York bureau, hung up my face mask, and went straight for my journal. It was—and is—how I best make sense of things.

As I wrote, I began to process what we'd all seen on our screens: thousands of armed American civilians besieging their own Capitol building. A president inciting them to violence. That same president clinging to power like a fascist autocrat. I kept circling back to one persistent thought:

"It's hard to believe it was real and not some make-believe movie scene," I wrote. "But at the same time, nothing about this is shocking. We knew this was coming. It was literally scheduled." On December 19, President Trump had announced that a "wild" protest would take place on the day Congress was to certify the electoral college votes: January 6.

I'd felt this way only once before. Three and a half years earlier, on August 12, 2017, hordes of armed white supremacists had taken to the streets of my adopted hometown of Charlottesville, Virginia. We'd known that was coming, too. The hate groups had scheduled that rally weeks ahead of time, ostensibly over the removal of a Confederate statue. As the rally date approached, antiracist activists had pointed city officials and local law enforcement to the specific and credible threats that these extremists were making online. Yet the city had failed to listen, prepare, or protect their citizens. I tell this story at length in my previous book, *24 Hours in Charlottesville*. The inactions of those in power allowed a white supremacist protestor to murder an antiracist counter-protestor, Heather Heyer.

We as a nation did not learn our lesson from that tragedy. President Trump had responded to it by claiming there were "some very fine people on both sides" in the streets of Charlottesville, and during the rest of his first term, the threat posed by the far right and white supremacists only increased.

It often felt like a runaway train—we could see that we were heading for disaster, yet we were unable to stop it. Shortly after January 6, 2021, I wrote in another journal entry: "Where are the adults? Who do we call when it's the president?" (I laugh now at my naivete: I understand now that there *is* nobody to call, and that *we* the citizens are the adults in the room.)

In the years since, many commentators have offered their version of the January 6 story. Too often, it is told as a self-contained arc: It begins in the months leading up to the 2020 election, with Trump seeding suspicions that voting would be "rigged" against him. It escalates with Trump's attempts to invalidate the results once President Biden won, and it culminates with the insurrection at the Capitol. This is the story of "Stop the Steal." But in reality, the story of January 6 begins all the way back in Charlottesville in 2017.

"We will never be able to unsee what I saw in Charlottesville, nor will I be able to unsee the aftermath watching these groups grow," antiracist counter-protestor Constance Paige Young told me. "For a lot of people, it was like this big fuss around like, 'Oh, Trump is so terrible and Trump is so bad.' And it's like, sure. We all understand that. However, there are these movements that are growing in real time that are very real and extremely dangerous. And somehow Trump is legitimizing them."

Activists like Young watched in horror as the 2020 election approached, and then with an eerie sense of déjà vu in the weeks ahead of January 6, 2021.

"If you lived in Charlottesville, you didn't see these things as disparate events. You saw it all as one movement, all sort of one trajectory, one time-line," another Charlottesville-based antiracist activist told me. "You started to see the exact same storm clouds gathering, for lack of a better term. It was like we were seeing the same lead-up that happened before August 12th[, 2017]. We kept saying, 'They're coming to town, they're gathering, they're planning something. There's going to be a larger event here. There's going to be a culmination that is going to be violent and dangerous.'"

And so the attack on January 6 was both shocking and not at all surprising. It was the fault of one man—Donald Trump—and also encompassed a growing extremist movement.

Jacob Glick, investigative counsel for the House Select Committee to Investigate the January 6th Attack on the United States Capitol, summarized it well. To create the conditions leading to January 6, he told me, "You need the paramilitary movement to exist. You need the white power movement to exist. But you also need Donald Trump to be seen as an ally. *And* you also need Donald Trump as that ally to tell them to do something. And without all of those things happening, January 6th wouldn't have happened."

The opening three chapters of this book will tell that story of how January 6 was years in the making. The rest of the book will reconstruct the twenty-four hours of January 6 itself—a day that has gained even more significance since Trump won a second term in 2024. Many of the witnesses I interviewed see January 6 as the turning point that wasn't: a moment in which the American people could have demanded accountability from the man responsible for an armed insurrection on our own Capitol. And briefly, it seemed possible. Congress convened the House Select Committee to Investigate the January 6th Attack, which released a final report on December 22, 2022, ascribing primary responsibility for the attack to Donald Trump. And the Department of Justice pursued charges against more than 1,200 rioters, sending many to prison. But in the long run, accountability has been hard to find. In 2024, the public went on to reelect Trump with millions more votes than he received the first time. After that victory, special counsel Jack Smith—who had been appointed by Attorney General Merrick Garland to investigate Trump's role in the insurrection—dismissed the charges against the president, knowing that he would claim presidential immunity once he was back in office.

Much like my previous book, this narrative will tell the story through the voices of the people who were actually there. Their quotes have been condensed and edited for clarity and flow. I've removed many filler words, including "um," "like," and "you know." I have at times edited quotations for clarification. I have also granted anonymity to a few sources who feared retribution, be it from the far right or from employers. In some cases, I gave a source a pseudonym (e.g., Jane, Larry, etc.), and in other cases, the source allowed me to use their real initials.

I chose not to interview any of the rioters who stormed the Capitol. Best practices in combatting the rise of hate groups include not conducting new interviews with their members—such interviews could be repurposed as propaganda or held up as a sign of legitimacy. I am still able to tell their story in their own words due to the work of the congressional January 6 select committee, which did interview insurrectionists and made the transcripts and sometimes recordings available. The insurrectionists are also quoted in the tens of thousands of pages of court documents, which include some of their private communications and messages. Already, many of these documents—once freely available online—have been taken down by the Trump administration, making books like this one even more important. I am indebted to two organizations for granting me permission to quote from their own collected oral histories of January 6: the United States Capitol Historical Society, a consortium of historical institutions in Washington, DC; and Co-Equal, a Washington, DC, nonprofit dedicated to preserving Congress as a co-equal branch of government. I thank them for the work they have also done in preserving the stories of this historic day and am grateful for their permission to access their recordings. I am also incredibly grateful to the many individual sources who were at the Capitol on January 6 and were willing to share with me their time-stamped text messages, photos, and videos—including raw and unpublished material from photojournalists—so I could better reconstruct the day.

Finally, I am incredibly grateful to the interviewees who trusted me enough to retell and relive what was for many of them one of the most traumatic days of their lives. I take seriously the weight of what I am asking them to do in these interviews. Sometimes I don't even know how difficult it is for people to speak to me. When I reached out to photojournalist Jason Andrew, he responded quickly with what seemed like an easy yes. But weeks later, as we wound down an intensely emotional interview that had lasted for more than two hours, he told me what receiving my initial request had been like.

"I mean, when I got the email from you, I was on an assignment and I was up in New York," he said. "And I literally called my wife crying. I was like, 'I can't do this.' And she was like, 'you don't have to.'" They talked through the decision, and ultimately Jason chose to speak to me in hopes that it would help him to process the experience more thoroughly.

Many people decided not to speak to me, and others simply did not respond to my emails. I have the utmost respect for their decisions. And I know there are even more people out there—both in Washington, DC, and around the country—who likely would have spoken to me if I'd asked, but there was simply no way to interview everyone. In that way, this book is just a sampling of experiences; I know that there are many more stories out there.

CAST OF CHARACTERS

Note: Names and titles reflect those as of January 6, 2021.
   ★ denotes name changed
   + denotes original interview conducted by the author

MEMBERS OF THE TRUMP ADMINISTRATION

Michael Flynn, former national security advisor
Rudy Giuliani, attorney for Donald Trump
Greg Jacob, counsel to the vice president
Christopher C. Miller, acting secretary of defense
Mike Pence, vice president of the United States
Jeffrey Rosen, acting attorney general
Donald Trump, president of the United States
White House security official

MEMBERS OF CONGRESS

Rep. Mo Brooks (R–AL)
Rep. Ruben Gallego (D–AZ)
Rep. Paul Gosar (R–AZ)
Sen. Mitch McConnell (R–KY)
Rep. Jim McGovern (D–MA)
Speaker Nancy Pelosi (D–CA)
Rep. Jamie Raskin (D–MD)
Sen. Ben Sasse (R–NE)
Rep. Chuck Schumer (D–NY)
Rep. Eric Swalwell (D–CA) +

CONGRESSIONAL STAFFERS

Senior Black Democratic aide

Bruce,★ congressional staffer

Craig,★ congressional staffer

Leah Han, aide to Speaker Nancy Pelosi

Michelle,★ congressional staffer

Richard,★ congressional staffer

Shane Smith, aide to Speaker Nancy Pelosi

Cierra Stewart, aide to Sen. Sherrod Brown +

JOURNALISTS

Hannah Allam, NPR reporter

Jason Andrew, freelance photojournalist on assignment for the *New York Times* +

Sandi Bachom, filmmaker +

Olivia Beavers, *Politico* congressional reporter +

Igor Bobic, *HuffPost* reporter +

David Butow, freelance photojournalist +

Alan Chin, freelance photojournalist on assignment for *Business Insider* +

Anderson Cooper, CNN anchor

Julio Cortez, Associated Press photojournalist

Lisa Desjardins, *PBS NewsHour* correspondent

Jon Farina, freelance journalist on assignment for Status Coup News +

Adam Gray, freelance photojournalist on assignment for the *Daily Mail* +

Andrew Harnik, Associated Press photojournalist

Ron Haviv, freelance photojournalist on assignment for the *New Republic* +

Jane,★ staff photojournalist for a major mainstream outlet +

Frank Lockwood, *Arkansas Democrat-Gazette* reporter +

Evy Mages, *Washingtonian* photojournalist +

Alex Marquardt, CNN correspondent +

Louie Palu, freelance photojournalist on assignment for *National Geographic* +

Mark Peterson, freelance photojournalist on assignment for the *New York Times* +

Nick Quested, documentary filmmaker +

Boris Sanchez, CNN correspondent +
Jake Tapper, CNN anchor
Stephen Voss, freelance photojournalist on assignment for *Politico* +
Chris Wallace, FOX anchor
Judy Woodruff, *PBS NewsHour* anchor

LAW ENFORCEMENT

Jimmy Albright, DC Metropolitan Police officer
Michael Byrd, US Capitol Police officer
Caroline Edwards, US Capitol Police officer
Michael Fanone, DC Metropolitan Police officer
Eugene Goodman, US Capitol Police officer
Aquilino Gonell, US Capitol Police officer
Daniel Hodges, DC Metropolitan Police officer
Larry,★ US Capitol Police officer +
Gus Papathanasiou, US Capitol Police officer +
Steven Sund, chief of the US Capitol Police
Maj. Gen. William Walker, DC National Guard commander

DC FIRE AND EMERGENCY MEDICAL SERVICES (FEMS)

Craig Baker, assistant fire chief of operations
Timothy Bennett, sergeant paramedic
Kevin Cole, firefighter paramedic
Gary Dziekan, firefighter
Rocco Gabriele, firefighter paramedic
Glenn Hanna, firefighter paramedic
David Hoagland, lieutenant
Christopher Holmes, battalion fire chief
Jon Hope, firefighter
Mitchell Kannry, fire marshal
Ellen Kurland, EMS captain
La'Kisha Lacey, EMS captain
Danny McCoy, area commander
Sean McGee, firefighter paramedic
Angelo Westfield, battalion fire chief

RIOTERS

Stephen Ayres, rioter

Eric Barber, rioter

Joseph Biggs, Proud Boy

Janet Buhler, rioter

Thomas Caldwell, Oath Keeper

Daniel Herendeen, rioter

Joshua James, Oath Keeper

Saundra Kiczenski, rioter

Roberto Minuta, Oath Keeper

Dominic Pezzola, Proud Boy

Stewart Rhodes, Oath Keepers founder

Robert "Bobby" Schornak, rioter

Kevin Seefried, rioter

Justin Winchell, rioter

John Wright, rioter

CONGRESSIONAL SERVICE EMPLOYEES

Black service worker

Congressional food service employee

OTHERS

Jeremy Bertino, Proud Boy

Blaire Boyland, Rosanne Boyland's younger sister +

Cheryl Boyland, Rosanne Boyland's mother +

Lonna Cave, Rosanne Boyland's older sister +

Rev. Gini Gerbasi, Episcopal pastor

Ricardo Mitchell, Labor Division of the Architect of the Capitol

Alexandra Pelosi, Speaker Nancy Pelosi's daughter +

Christopher Rodriguez, director of the Homeland Security and
   Emergency Management Agency

Craig Sicknick, Brian Sicknick's brother +

Enrique Tarrio, leader of Proud Boys

Paul Vos, Speaker Nancy Pelosi's grandson

Jeff Walters, Architect of the Capitol carpenter

Constance Paige Young, activist +

Karlin Younger, DC resident who found a pipe bomb near the Republican National Committee headquarters

EXPERTS ON FAR-RIGHT DOMESTIC TERRORISM

Titles as of time of writing

Amy Cooter, militia and extremism expert, Middlebury College

Jacob Glick, investigative counsel for the House Select Committee to Investigate January 6th (as of January 6, congressional staffer) +

Mary McCord, executive director of the Institute for Constitutional Advocacy and Protection at Georgetown University +

Sandeep Prasanna, investigative counsel for the House Select Committee to Investigate January 6th +

Jacob Ware, Council on Foreign Relations research fellow +

24 HOURS AT THE CAPITOL

PART ONE

"A YEAR IN THE MAKING"

CHAPTER 1

"IT'S TIME FOR FUCKING WAR IF THEY STEAL THIS SHIT"

SANDEEP PRASANNA, *investigative counsel for the House Select Committee to Investigate the January 6th Attack on the United States Capitol*: It wasn't a secret that hundreds of thousands of people were coming to DC January 6th because Trump called them all there. What was surprising to most people was what happened after that.

LOUIE PALU, *freelance photojournalist on assignment for* National Geographic: January 6th was a year in the making.

JACOB WARE, *Council on Foreign Relations research fellow*: There were a lot of warning signs.

2019

HANNAH ALLAM, *NPR reporter*: The chatter just became increasingly violent online. And these "Stop the Steal" groups, other sort of self-described patriot groups—you know, just sort of this right-wing soup.[1]

JACOB WARE: 2019 is really the year where those of us who were working in counterterrorism, or far-right terrorism specifically, realized that we were kind of in an emergency situation. We'd seen the warning signs, we had seen violence, but things spiraled out of control all of a sudden.

MARY MCCORD, *executive director of the Institute for Constitutional Advocacy and Protection at Georgetown University*: In 2019, during the first impeachment, Trump starts retweeting things about this is going to be a "hot civil war."

DONALD TRUMP VIA TWITTER, SEPTEMBER 29, 2019: If the Democrats are successful in removing the President from office (which they will never be), it will cause a Civil War like fracture in this Nation from which our Country will never heal.[2]

MARY MCCORD: That's when you first started seeing militias and in particular Oath Keepers saying, raising their hands, "Hey, we are here for you, Trump, to basically be your military if you need your own military."

OATH KEEPERS VIA TWITTER: This is the truth. This is where we are. We ARE on the verge of a HOT civil war.[3]

MARY MCCORD: And so this notion of a president actually deputizing or calling forth an unlawful, unauthorized private militia starts kind of creeping into at least—I'm not saying everybody was paying attention to this—but I mean it starts creeping into something that you've got to be paying attention to if you're worried about the power of militias.

2020

That creeping concern only grew when the COVID-19 pandemic started.

JACOB GLICK, *investigative counsel for the House Select Committee to Investigate the January 6th Attack on the United States Capitol*: Trump immediately embraced vigilante activity in 2020, particularly around COVID lockdowns.

DAVID BUTOW, *freelance photojournalist*: That context, we've sort of forgotten about it, but it's very important.

MARY MCCORD: So then you have, of course, Trump being very opposed to governors' shutdown orders. And again, he used words that were very much a permission structure, right? When he said, "Liberate Minnesota, liberate Michigan, liberate Virginia," tweeted those things. And that's really, I think, a pretty thinly veiled call to arms.

DONALD TRUMP VIA TWITTER, APRIL 17, 2020: LIBERATE MINNESOTA![4]

DONALD TRUMP VIA TWITTER: LIBERATE MICHIGAN![5]

DONALD TRUMP VIA TWITTER: LIBERATE VIRGINIA, and save your great 2nd Amendment. It is under siege![6]

MARY MCCORD: And that's the way the militias saw it, right?

FACEBOOK POST IN A FAR-RIGHT GROUP UNCOVERED BY RESEARCHERS: This Has Been A Long Time Coming: Stand-By For Instruction[7]

TELEGRAM MESSAGE FROM A FAR-RIGHT ADHERENT: [Trump] did just say you can start shooting and hanging your state politicians[8]

MARY MCCORD: And that's when we saw armed assaults on the State House in Lansing, Michigan, and in multiple other places.

APRIL 30, 2020

LANSING, MICHIGAN

Like governors of forty-two other states and territories,[9] Gov. Gretchen Whitmer issued a stay-at-home order in an effort to stop the spread of COVID. In response, about eight hundred anti-lockdown protesters swarmed the Michigan State Capitol in an organized action they called the American Patriot Rally.

PROTESTERS: Tyrants get the rope![10]

PROTESTERS: Make treason punishable by hanging![11]

Inside the state capitol, which is open to the public, protesters demanded entry into the House of Representatives' chamber.

PROTESTERS: Let us in![12]

PROTESTERS: Tyranny![13]

MICHIGAN STATE SENATOR DAYNA POLEHANKI VIA TWITTER: Directly above me, men with rifles yelling at us. Some of my colleagues who own bullet proof vests are wearing them.[14]

The protesters were allowed to stay and watch the proceedings. Only one "highly-intoxicated" person was arrested, according to the *Detroit News*.[15]

THE *NEW YORK TIMES*: A handful of them, wearing camouflage fatigues with semi-automatic rifles slung over their shoulders, watched ominously from the gallery above the Senate chamber as the elected officials did their work.[16]

AMY COOTER, *militia and extremism expert, Middlebury College*: Given the general lack of consequences . . . this becomes normalized and legitimate and made it easier to scale up.[17]

MARY MCCORD: And then add to that the murder of George Floyd [on May 25] . . . racial justice protests kicking off all across the country.

ALAN CHIN, *freelance photojournalist on assignment for* Business Insider: In Portland, in Richmond, in New York City, in Philadelphia, in Atlanta. I mean, in Louisville, Kentucky. I'm just listing the number of cities I was in 2020 where I was at different protests and rallies, some of which turned violent to one degree or another.

ADAM GRAY, *freelance photojournalist on assignment for the* Daily Mail: I'd been working with a group of journalists the whole year. We were always working in the groove. We'd watched each other's backs. It was really nonstop. We'd been driving around the country, we'd been reacting—you know, there would be a Proud Boy protest, or the police would kill someone somewhere, and we would go and we'd be there the next day or the same day, depending on how far it was.

MARK PETERSON, *freelance photojournalist on assignment for the* New York Times: You saw a lot of the Proud Boys at a lot of those demonstrations, the anti-vaccine demonstrations and that. So there was a connection and they saw it as a way to attack the "woke" mentality.

JACOB GLICK: Once you got to the Black Lives Matter [BLM] protests, there was a sense that Trump's enemies were also enemies of these paramilitary organizations.

ADAM GRAY: And then the two things started to come together. People from lockdown protests would then start countering the BLM protests.

SUMMER 2020

In the days after George Floyd's murder, antiracist groups held protests near the White House, on Lafayette Square, and on the newly created adjoining Black Lives Matter Plaza. The Metropolitan Police—the police force of Washington, DC—were dispatched to the site daily.

CONSTANCE PAIGE YOUNG, *activist*: The militarized police, they had long guns. Sometimes it felt like we were just waiting on a massacre.

DANIEL HODGES, *DC Metropolitan Police officer*: 2020 was just constant protests and riots and stuff like that, so we were activated all the time.

LOUIE PALU: It kept escalating every night. I think law enforcement felt like, "This is the White House and no one can do this in front of the White House. We can't have the perimeter of the White House breached." [Every night] I could feel the anger in the crowd, and it was combined with what was happening in the world. People weren't going to take it anymore. That's how it felt.

The nightly protests continued until June 1, when police aggressively cleared all protesters from Lafayette Square—regardless of affiliation or actions—to make room for a photo op for President Trump.

STEPHEN VOSS, *freelance photojournalist on assignment for* Politico: No one in the crowd knew what was happening.

LOUIE PALU: I got hit by a couple of rubber pellets. They hurt a lot. There was so much tear gas [that] it looked like the set for a haunted movie.

Suddenly there's a line of horses. And I know when horses show up, it's not good. That means they're going to clear. So all these horses start charging, everybody panics and runs and the police chase them and they're hitting people, journalists, everything. And I'm like, *What the hell's going on here?*

CONSTANCE PAIGE YOUNG: It was just really fucking scary, honestly. It was just pretty terrifying. It was terrifying.

GINI GERBASI, EPISCOPAL PASTOR VIA FACEBOOK: We were literally DRIVEN OFF of . . . Lafayette Square patio with tear gas and concussion grenades and police in full riot gear.[18]

STEPHEN VOSS: And then only as I had pulled back, a friend of mine in the White House texted me saying, the president's coming out. And I was like, *Oh, that's why we're being cleared.* I had no idea. But that was very unexpected, very, very sudden.

AUGUST 2, 2020

DONALD TRUMP, IN AN OHIO CAMPAIGN SPEECH: I'm afraid the election is going to be rigged, I have to be honest.[19]

JACOB WARE: The big thing that was causing alarm was the claims of electoral fraud, the pre-bunking, right? It unlocks a confirmation bias. If you've already said that it's stolen, then when you then lose the election and you claim that it was stolen, people don't look at you as a sore loser. They look at you as psychic.

MARY MCCORD: He's starting to seed the false narrative. It builds throughout the election season. You layer that on top of what is already an escalating involvement of militias in our civic life, it was the granddaddy dog whistle really of them all, right? *What's happened here has been a fraudulent election and we need to do something about it.*

SEPTEMBER 29, 2020

With Proud Boys across the country holding widely covered protests against both the lockdowns and Black Lives Matter, FOX anchor Chris Wallace asked President Trump during a presidential debate to condemn the group.

CHRIS WALLACE, *FOX* ANCHOR: Are you willing, tonight, to condemn white supremacists and militia groups and to say that they need to stand down and not add to the violence . . . ?

DONALD TRUMP: You want to call them? What do you want to call them? Give me a name, give me a name, go ahead—who would you like me to condemn?

CHRIS WALLACE: White supremacists, white supremacists and right-wing militia.

DONALD TRUMP: Proud Boys, stand back and stand by. But I'll tell you what: somebody's got to do something about Antifa and the left. Because this is not a right-wing problem—this is a left-wing problem.[20]

JACOB WARE: The Proud Boys Telegram channel blew up. They took it as an instruction.

PARLER MESSAGE BY JOSEPH BIGGS, PROUD BOY: Trump basically said to go fuck them up! This makes me so happy.[21]

TELEGRAM MESSAGE BY A PROUD BOY: Leftist fags are seething right now lol. It's glorious.[22]

TELEGRAM MESSAGE BY ANOTHER PROUD BOY: Standing down and standing by sir.[23]

MARK PETERSON: He was telling them what to do. To be ready to be his vanguard when he would call them up.

JEREMY BERTINO, *Proud Boy*: I was in awe. We reveled in it for a little bit. You know, like, holy crap, the President just mentioned us. . . . And then there were thousands and thousands of thousands of emails every day [from people] about wanting to join.[24]

| **President Trump faced no consequences for his statement.**

LOUIE PALU: I mean, you can't even write that in a script for a movie where some fascist, right-wing comic character says that he basically tells a right-wing paramilitary group of a gang to, "Hey, just don't do anything but be ready when I call you." And nothing happens!

MARY MCCORD: So that's the sort of stew we're in as we're coming into the 2020 election.

NOVEMBER 4, 2020

ELECTION NIGHT

| **By 2 a.m., the race still had not been called. Multiple states were still counting the unusually high number of mail-in ballots that had been sent in due to the pandemic. President Trump nonetheless declared victory while also continuing to spout electoral fraud theories.**

DONALD TRUMP, IN A SPEECH FROM THE EAST ROOM IN THE WHITE HOUSE: This is a fraud on the American public. . . . Frankly, we did win this election.

| **Right-wing extremists immediately responded to his statement online.**

POST BY JOSEPH BIGGS, PROUD BOY, NOVEMBER 5, 2020: It's time for fucking War if they steal this shit[25]

| **A group of Oath Keepers started a private group chat on the secure messaging app Signal. It was called "Leadership intel sharing."**

MESSAGE FROM STEWART RHODES, OATH KEEPERS FOUNDER, TO OATH KEEPERS' LEADERSHIP INTEL SHARING, NOVEMBER 5, 2020: We aren't getting through this without a civil war. Too late for that. Prepare your mind, body, spirit.[26]

NOVEMBER 7

| **Joe Biden was officially declared the winner of the election.**

VICE PRESIDENT MIKE PENCE VIA TWITTER, NOVEMBER 9, 2020: It ain't over til it's over . . . and this AIN'T over![27]

PRIVATE SIGNAL MESSAGE FROM STEWART RHODES TO LEADERSHIP INTEL SHARING, NOVEMBER 7, 2020: We must now do what the people of Serbia did when Milosevic stole their election. Refuse to accept it and march en-mass on the nation's Capitol.[28]

ALAN CHIN: I kind of knew, like, okay, what's going to happen next?

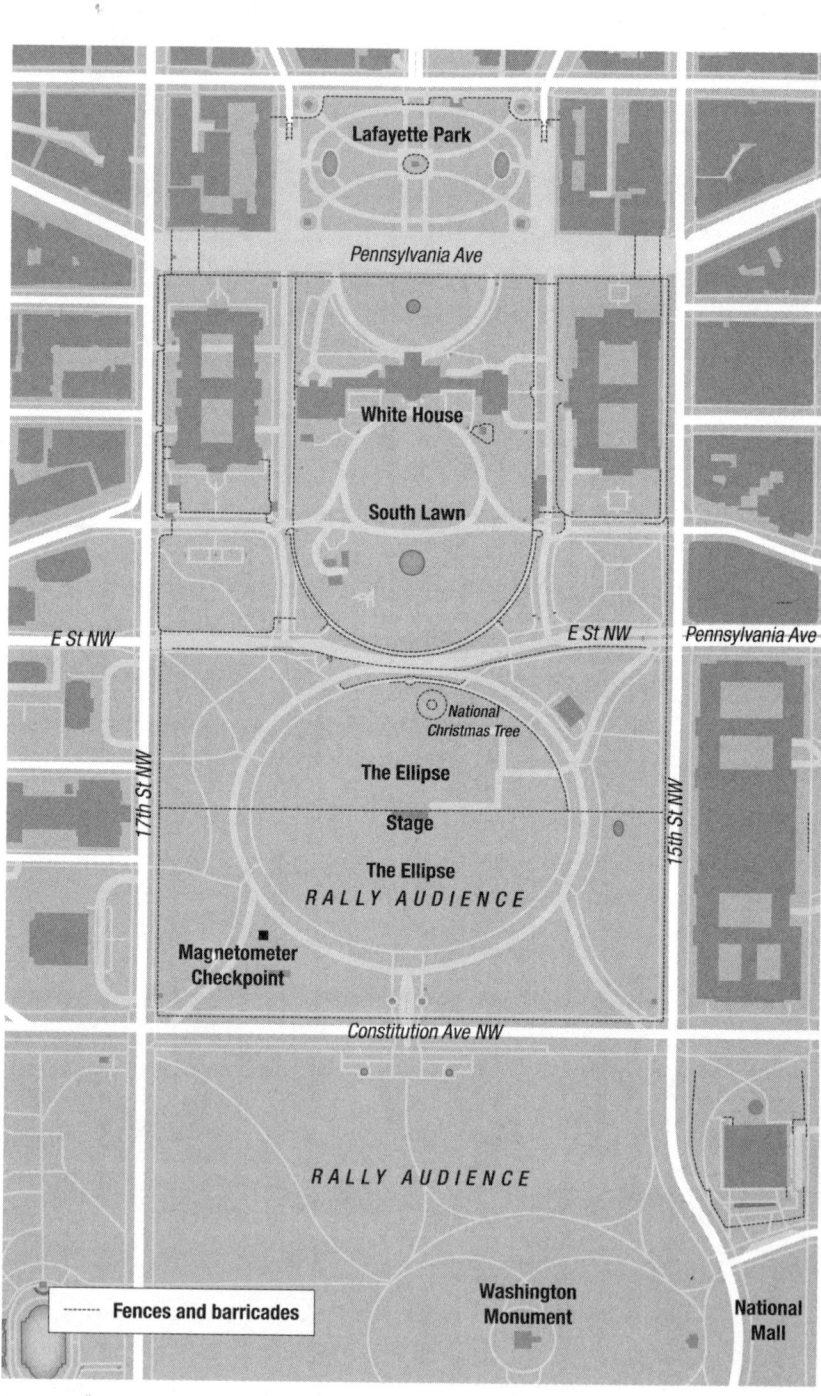

Lafayette Park

Pennsylvania Ave

White House

South Lawn

E St NW   E St NW   Pennsylvania Ave

National
Christmas Tree

The Ellipse

Stage

The Ellipse
RALLY AUDIENCE

Magnetometer
Checkpoint

17th St NW

15th St NW

Constitution Ave NW

RALLY AUDIENCE

------ Fences and barricades

Washington
Monument

National
Mall

CHAPTER 2

"WILL BE WILD"

Immediately after Election Day, Trump supporters and militia groups began planning a series of "Stop the Steal" rallies in DC.

JANE, *staff photojournalist for a major mainstream outlet*: "Stop the Steal"—it was a movement. You could watch it building all this momentum on Twitter, on social media, in chat rooms.

Trump was upset with anybody, any outlet that was pushing back on his belief that he had won the election. And so he was pushing his followers underground to kind of a closed media ecosystem, from FOX News to OANN to Newsmax, and then even off Twitter to Parler.

If you look at that timeline, it was probably one of the biggest, most accelerated mass radicalization events, because all these people are suddenly in this space, Parler. That's where they were openly talking about all this violence that they were planning on committing. They were giving each other pointers about what kind of things they could bring that were still legal, like wasp spray, for example, that would fuck people up.

They informally named the rallies after the "Make America Great Again" acronym.

ALAN CHIN, *freelance photojournalist on assignment for* Business Insider: "MAGA I" was in November.

SATURDAY, NOVEMBER 14: MAGA 1

ALAN CHIN: The daytime protest was pretty much what we had come to expect.

LOUIE PALU, *freelance photojournalist on assignment for* National Geographic: There were thousands of people there. I could tell no one cared that everybody said the election was not stolen. They're like, "No, it was stolen."

As I walked down to Pennsylvania Avenue, it was just thousands of people with flags and banners and the chanting. And I know people don't like it when people liken it to the '30s in Germany. But it felt like Nuremberg, like it was ominous and dark. It felt so nationalistic in such an extreme right manner that it kind of frightened me.

The crowd was a mix of mainstream Trump supporters, far-right hate groups, and militias.

DAVID BUTOW, *freelance photojournalist*: There were the Proud Boys, and you could see they're the ones wearing yellow somewhere, and a lot of them had their combat vests on.

LOUIE PALU: Oath Keepers were a little more subtle—Proud Boys were not. I'm like, *Wow, that's like a lot of Proud Boys.* I remember seeing the "Stand Back and Stand By" shirts. A lot of the Proud Boys were wearing those.

According to multiple reports, President Trump asked his US Secret Service (USSS) motorcade to drive by the protest on his way to his golf course.

STEVEN SUND, *chief of the US Capitol Police*: In a highly unusual maneuver, President Trump had the USSS drive his motorcade through the thick crowd of supporters gathered around Freedom Plaza.[1]

The supporters cheered loudly.

CHIEF SUND: I can only imagine the "pucker factor" that the Secret Service agents were experiencing as they made this drive and as the motorcade was being rushed and surrounded by hundreds of unscreened individuals.[2]

DAVID BUTOW: The fact that here's the sitting president contesting the results of the election and trying to energize his supporters to show up for something like that was just—I'd never heard of anything like that ever happening in the United States before.

During the day, the protest stayed mostly peaceful. But then, night fell. Proud Boys and other militia members began to fight leftist counterdemonstrators in the street.

ADAM GRAY, *freelance photojournalist on assignment for the* Daily Mail: The violence kind of always came at night.

SANDI BACHOM, *filmmaker*: At night when the sun goes down, there's skirmishes.

LOUIE PALU: And there were all these pitched street battles all over downtown DC. It was like '30s Germany, like the Marxists against the fascists. The protesters had ax handles, they had helmets on, and they all wore body armor like a uniform with their Proud Boy hat, their Proud Boy patch, that kind of thing. Very militaristic. And all the police were doing was trying to keep them separated.

EVY MAGES, Washingtonian *photojournalist*: I was shocked that the Proud Boys could, undisturbed, roam through downtown Washington, DC. It was shocking. It was shocking. Nobody was holding them back. There was no kind of accountability. I'm from Austria. So it definitely reminded me of Nazis. I mean, not the discipline or anything, but just they had the ear of the president! It was dangerous.

LOUIE PALU: I guess some people got arrested, some people got hurt. I took some photos and I thought, *Oh, okay, here we are. This is over.* Then they plan another protest.

DECEMBER 12: MAGA 2

LOUIE PALU: This time it's less of just the general protesters and way more of the paramilitary-looking guys.

JACOB GLICK, *investigative counsel for the House Select Committee to the January 6th Attack on the United States Capitol*: You had the Oath Keepers and you had the Three Percenters and [other groups]. And they were standing beside these MAGA traditional [supporters]. And so there was this idea that a rally could have an accompanying armed [contingent] that was normalized by people up from Trump all the way down.

| **Stewart Rhodes, leader of the Oath Keepers, made a speech.**

THE ANTI-DEFAMATION LEAGUE: In his speech, Rhodes called on President Trump to invoke the Insurrection Act to help him remain in power, adding that if he does not do so, groups such as the Oath Keepers would have to mount a "much more desperate" and "much more bloody war" to ensure that outcome.[3]

Then former national security advisor Michael Flynn, whom Trump had pardoned for lying to the FBI during the Russia investigation, took the stage. While he spoke, President Trump took the concept of a "drive-by" to new heights.

JACOB GLICK: Trump actually flew over it [the crowd] in Marine One.

CHIEF SUND: At 1:34 p.m., two Marine Sikorsky helicopters (the one carrying Trump designated Marine One) took flight from the south grounds of the White House. The crowd on the plaza could clearly see the helicopters as they cleared the tree line. The two massive aircraft slowly passed over Freedom Plaza, eliciting loud cheers from the crowd. They flew in tight formation around the Capitol and the Supreme Court, making several passes over the energized crowd.[4]

MICHAEL FLYNN, FORMER NATIONAL SECURITY ADVISOR, FROM STAGE: There he is! He's a sneaky guy. But he's a fighter.[5]

SANDI BACHOM: There was [also] so much of this Christo-fascism. I come up on this group at Freedom Plaza and they're all wearing MAGA hats, and they're chanting, "America First." And they're chanting, "Christ is King." So that's how they got all those people—there was the Christian thing that Trump was sent by Jesus.

DAVID BUTOW: I heard on several occasions through these megaphones, people say, "Donald Trump is not my God, but he is my president." Which sounds a pretty strange thing to say. Why would you think to even come up with something like that? So I mean, that tells me that there's—this is not just the people who are supporting him politically. This is some other level of—I mean, there's some very, very deep-seated psychological connection with this man that's kind of hard to understand for many of us. And then you begin to think, well, *I wonder what these people are really going to do. How far are they willing to go to support his cause at this point?*

| **Again, the violence started once the sun went down.**

SANDI BACHOM: There were thousands, it seemed, of Proud Boys. And the other thing to remember is the whole city was in lockdown. The streets were barren except for the protesters.

LOUIE PALU: It was kind of like little pockets of battles all around downtown DC. I remember there were these three Proud Boys and I was beside the cops and I was taking photos with my flash and they were so pissed. They're like, "We're going to fucking kill you." And one of them had a can of mace in his hand. I kind of thought, *Whoa, the police aren't even taking the mace away from them.* They have bats and axes and they're not being disarmed. They're not like, "Hey, you're all under arrest." They're just, "Hey, stay away from the armed protesters and don't fight." That's all the cops were doing. I thought, *How are they not arresting these guys?*

And so that night when I got those death threats right to my face, the cops were like, "Hey, you should get out of here. You should take off." I kind of felt scared. The cops knew it was going to explode.

ADAM GRAY: People were using bear spray, baseball bats, anything they could get their hands on, and they were kind of chasing each other. That was kind of the biggest street fight that I saw before January 6th, I think.

9:48 P.M.

| **The Proud Boys tore down a Black Lives Matter banner from a Black church and burned it in the street.[6]**

10:02 P.M.

ADAM GRAY: You just spend so much time in protests, in crowds, you kind of get a really good sixth sense of when something's happening, when they change their focus. And I kind of noticed people looking to the side and a lone guy was walking down the street, and the Proud Boys went over to him.

| **He was a person of color.**

ADAM GRAY: He kind of ended up surrounded. I'm not sure why he decided to come down the street and he got surrounded and then it just descended into a fight. A Proud Boy pulled something over his head so the guy couldn't see, and the guy pulled a knife out and stabs him whilst he has this thing over his face.

SANDI BACHOM: I didn't hear until after it happened. There was just so much hate. All that hate had to go somewhere.

| **The same attacker went on to stab at least three other people.**[7]

LOUIE PALU: I rode my bike home that night and I took the most circuitous route possible so no one could follow me home. That's the first time where I thought, *What if one of these guys follows me home?*

JACOB GLICK: You have to assume, at that point, Trump was told there was violence in DC by some of the people who were at this event. But [two days later], Monday the 14th, is when the Electoral College met all around the country to actually vote. And that's a huge blow to Trump's efforts. And then there are several court cases that Trump loses that week of the 14th. And McConnell comes out and says the election's over. It was a bad week.

Then, the 18th, that Friday, Michael Flynn is in the Oval Office. So you have people in the room who were also at that rally on stage with Stewart Rhodes on the 12th, and then you don't really know what happens, but Trump sends [a] tweet out that morning, the 19th, after meeting with Michael Flynn and other people who have been at this event on the 12th.

DECEMBER 19

DONALD TRUMP VIA TWITTER, DECEMBER 19, 2020: Big protest in DC on January 6th. Be there, will be wild![8]

JACOB GLICK: He again calls out for the crowd, knowing that just a week before, they had basically engaged in vigilante violence on the streets of DC.

JANE: I remember when he tweeted that. It was not a surprise because I was kind of waiting for him to do something like that. I mean, I was waiting for it. So when I saw that tweet, it was like, *Okay, here we go.*

CHAPTER 3

"ONE MILLION PATRIOTS"

DECEMBER 19

Trump supporters immediately responded to their leader's call to gather on January 6. At least a dozen permits were filed for events on January 5 and 6 in DC, including an approximately five-thousand-person rally at the Ellipse on the morning of January 6. On the far-right online forum TheDonald.win, users took Trump's tweet to heart.

THREAD ON THEDONALD.WIN: TRUMP TWEET. DADDY SAYS BE IN DC ON JAN. 6TH.

MRMCGREENGENES: Well, shit. We've got marching orders, bois.

BUTTFART88: He can't exactly openly tell you to revolt. This is closest he'll ever get.

LISTROPOE: Then bring the guns we shall.[1]

TELEGRAM POST: We should march into the capital [sic] building and make them quake in their shoes[2]

ERIC BARBER, *rioter:* Trump had never asked me personally for anything. He never asked conservative America for anything, really. And he personally asked for us to come to DC that day. And I thought for everything he has done for us, if this is the only thing he is going to ask of me, I'll do it. . . .

The other part was that, it kept being promoted to me as it "would be wild." And I didn't know what that meant, but as someone who likes to drive race cars—I like high-risk activities, I like really hardcore things—the notion of something being wild and hardcore and fun really appealed to me.[3]

Bobby Schornak, a thirty-nine-year-old Trump supporter from Roseville, Michigan, also answered the call.

ROBERT "BOBBY" SCHORNAK, *rioter:* We believed something great was going to be revealed or happen that day. I wanted to be there for that.[4]

TEXT FROM BOBBY SCHORNAK TO HIS BROTHER: We can't stay home n watch our republic be stolen. They want a fight let's have it.[5]

TEXT FROM BOBBY SCHORNAK TO HIS FRIEND: I'm going to DC on the 6th and I don't expect it to be peaceful.[6]

Schornak asked his friend Daniel Herendeen, a forty-four-year-old construction worker from Chesterfield, Michigan, to go with him.

FACEBOOK MESSAGE FROM BOBBY SCHORNAK TO DANIEL HERENDEEN: Cant stay home, I would not be able to live w myself[7]

DANIEL HERENDEEN, RIOTER: That's how I feel. . . . I heard it might be hard to get to DC. I go regardless.[8]

BOBBY SCHORNAK: Hard, nothing easy ever worth doing. Just call me bro.[9] Wanna make a plan? I have next two weeks off work. Just worked every day from Thanksgiving till this Thursday.[10]

DANIEL HERENDEEN: Well, the president asked us to come. . . . And I thought it'd be fun. I planned on going and seeing the city and everything, making a little trip out of it.[11]

Stephen Ayres, a Trump supporter and carpenter living in Ohio, found out about the rally from his friend Matthew Perna.

STEPHEN AYRES, *rioter:* He's like, "If you want to go, we've got room." I'd never been to a Trump rally before that. And I figured that was going to be his last one, him leaving from the Presidency.[12]

Janet Buhler, a middle-aged Trump supporter from Utah, agreed to attend the rally with her stepdaughter's sixth husband. She wanted a chance to bond with her new son-in-law, who was also a former cop.

JANET BUHLER, *rioter*: He called me, like, two maybe three days before the rally—and he said, "Listen, I really want to go. And I don't have anybody to go with. And so will you go with me?" And out of the idea of creating better relationships in the family, that's why I went, because not everybody gets along with him. So I just thought, *Okay, this will be a good way to kind of bond with him and bring the family closer together*, that kind of thing.[13]

In the back of my mind, I wanted Congress to understand, like, how many people were there that were concerned about the election.[14]

Other families weren't so thrilled that their loved ones were going to DC on January 6. When thirty-four-year-old Trump supporter Roseanne Boyland of Georgia announced her plans to go, her parents and sisters were concerned.

LONNA CAVE, *Roseanne Boyland's older sister*: Roseanne was five years younger than me, so growing up we didn't really have too much in common because of the age difference. Honestly, I always just kind of thought of her as my annoying younger sister until we got older. Then we could start going to concerts together and everything.

She's always been super sweet and caring and helpful, just always the first one to jump if you need help moving or something, to help somebody else and not gain anything from it.

BLAIRE BOYLAND, *Roseanne Boyland's younger sister*: She was older than me by three years, so we were pretty close growing up. And then when we became teenagers, she got a little too cool for me [*laughs*] and kind of didn't let me hang around her and the neighborhood friends as much.

She wasn't afraid to tell people how she felt about things, and me being a very shy person—very introverted, especially growing up—I just always looked up to her for that.

CHERYL BOYLAND, *Roseanne Boyland's mother*: She had a background as a drug abuser and worked very hard to get herself off of heroin, and succeeded, which is very rare. And swore she would never ever do that again. She knew that if she ever did anything like that she would die, because so many of her friends had in the past, and she didn't want to put anybody through that.

Boyland's family says she got clean around 2014.

LONNA CAVE: When Roseanne was having all of her problems, I actually stopped talking to her for over a year just because I couldn't take all of the back and forth and the drama. And then my husband's twin brother overdosed, and that's kind of when we started getting close again. And then when I got pregnant, then we were all in together. I think it was right then. That's when she was like, "I'm done."

BLAIRE BOYLAND: I feel like Lonna getting pregnant definitely cemented her staying clean too. She was so excited, just knowing she'd be an aunt and get to watch, not only Lorelei, but also Lonna's other daughter, Annily, grow up. She was so excited to be the cool aunt to them.

CHERYL BOYLAND: Roseanne had cervical cancer and so she knew she wasn't going to have kids. Lonna's were her only outlet.

LONNA CAVE: Yeah, she did better than me at writing down milestones and stuff. Roseanne was always the one that wrote down stuff—"lost her first tooth"—and she was always asking after their checkups, "How tall is she? How much did she weigh?"

But then COVID hit.

LONNA CAVE: During Covid, everybody was doomscrolling on their phone. Nobody knew what was going on. Everybody was by themselves. There were no [AA or NA] meetings that she could go to. She was on Facebook a lot. I was over there swimming one day and she was talking about some Wayfair [conspiracy theory] thing. The kids were getting smuggled in these expensive furniture items, like armoire that cost like twelve thousand bucks and stuff. I kind of talked to her about it and I left, and then she texted me the next morning and was like, "Call me when you are awake." And she had been up the whole night, just rabbit-holing through all of this: Adrenochrome, Wayfair, all of the children, Pizzagate, all of the QAnon children's stuff. She had just gone deep. And honestly, I think Facebook is really what made it worse for her.

BLAIRE BOYLAND: The whole "Save the Children" was circulating around online, and I know there was Save the Children protests. That kind of added to the content being shared online. Coincidentally, stuff [was] going on in Roseanne's personal life with people in real life she knew being affected by stuff like that.

Roseanne's family members say that two of her close friends had children who had been physically and sexually abused.

BLAIRE BOYLAND: And then Lonna having our two nieces, she was just really worried about them too. So it all kind of was this perfect storm of things.

LONNA CAVE: I looked at all the hashtags that she was doing, and at the beginning it was all Save the Children, Pizzagate, blah, blah, blah, all stuff relating to kids. And then somewhere along the line it turned into Trump is the only one that can save all these kids.

I just don't know how all of a sudden it happened, but there's definitely a point in time when it switched from being all innocent about "saving the children" to Trump is now our savior, and he's the only one that can save the world from these—

CHERYL BOYLAND: Pedophiles.

BLAIRE BOYLAND: And that part happened overnight, it felt like just all of a sudden.

LONNA CAVE: And that's when she got more standoffish about it and more— not necessarily aggressive, but she didn't want to talk about it. And we got into a couple arguments because we just couldn't see eye to eye. I actually did some research on how to deal with people in a cult because that's what I was worried about. If we try and probe her and try to tell her all the things that are wrong, it's just going to push her further and further in.

CHERYL BOYLAND: She wanted to go on January 6th because she thought there was going to be mass arrests of all these pedophiles at the Capitol, and I don't know where she got that from.

LONNA CAVE: That's all the QAnon stuff. I was talking to her and saying it was a bad idea, blah, blah, blah. But there's really no telling her what to do.

CHERYL BOYLAND: And my husband—all three girls and my husband have severe crowd issues. I just couldn't imagine that she even wanted to go there. But one of the things she told me was, "Mom, I've done so many stupid things in my life and my president has asked people to be there, and I want to go. And if something happens to me, God forbid, at least it will be something for a cause that I believe in instead of stupid heroin or something."

In addition to mainstream Trump supporters, the extremists were making plans, too. The militia groups were gearing up for more illicit activities. They explicitly talked about their plans to bring weapons.

OPEN LETTER FROM STEWART RHODES, OATH KEEPERS FOUNDER, PUBLISHED ONLINE, DECEMBER 23: Tens of thousands of patriot Americans, both veterans and non-veterans, will already be in Washington DC, and many of us will have our mission-critical gear stowed nearby just outside DC. . . . [We may have to] take to arms in defense of our God given liberty.[15]

Privately, the messages among Oath Keepers were even more explicit in planning where that "mission-critical" gear would be stowed. They planned for a QRF—in military parlance, a Quick Reaction Force—of fighters with multiple guns, including an AR-style assault rifle and a shotgun.

SIGNAL MESSAGE FROM JOSHUA JAMES, OATH KEEPER: We have a shitload of QRF on standby with an arsenal.[16]

SIGNAL MESSAGE FROM STEWART RHODES: We WILL have a QRF. this situation calls for it.[17]

They discussed the logistics of transporting and activating those weapons.

MESSAGE FROM THOMAS CALDWELL, OATH KEEPER: Can't believe I just thought of this: how many people either in the militia or not . . . have a boat on a trailer that could handle a Potomac crossing? If we had someone standing by at a dock ramp (one near the Pentagon for sure) we could have our Quick Response Team with the heavy weapons standing by, quickly load them and ferry them across the river to our waiting arms . . . if it all went to shit.[18]

There's no evidence that the boat plan materialized. Instead, they rented hotel rooms.

COURT DOCUMENTS: The Comfort Inn Ballston, in Arlington, Virginia, [was] the location that the QRF would use as its base of operations for January 6, 2021.

| The Proud Boys also coordinated their operations.

MESSAGE FROM A PROUD BOY IN A GROUP CHAT: What would they do [if]
1 million patriots stormed and took the capital building. Shoot
into the crowd?[19]

RESPONSE, UNKNOWN PROUD BOY: They would do nothing because they
can do nothing.[20]

DECEMBER 21

Amid this planning process, the Proud Boys along with other demonstrators stormed yet another state capitol building, this time in
Salem, Oregon. They carried firearms and bear spray.[21]

SANDEEP PRASANNA, *investigative counsel for the House Select Committee to
Investigate the January 6th Attack on the United States Capitol*: Militia groups
interrupted a COVID legislative session, literally hand-to-hand combat with
Oregon State police officers, militia members spraying bear spray on police
officers and beating them with flagpoles.

Most of the protesters were not able to enter the building, but some
gave speeches outside during the six-hour standoff.

DAVID KLAUS, PROTESTER SPEAKING TO THE CROWD: I'm very proud of
everybody that showed up today. . . . We put the fear of God in
the citizens of our state. They know we're not messing around
anymore.[22]

MARY MCCORD, *executive director of the Institute for Constitutional Advocacy and
Protection at Georgetown University*: It very much showed, hey, you could do
this. You can shut stuff down by going armed and busting through doors to
get into the hearing rooms and, in Lansing, basically scaring legislators into
fleeing or coming in bulletproof vests to their own legislative sessions. You
can have this real impact. . . . Or Oregon, what have you.

And then the escalation and it not being condemned by people in power.
Not only Trump, but lots of people in positions of power were not con-
demning it. That just leads to more and more, I've got permission. I'm not
getting prosecuted. Nothing's happening to me.

TIERZEROLEAD, IN AN OATH KEEPERS CHATROOM INFILTRATED BY MARY MCCORD'S TEAM: From the looks of it Oregon is the start of it now so we either take our capitols or join them[23]

With so many right-wing groups openly planning for January 6, there was plenty of intelligence about what would likely happen.

MARY MCCORD: As we started seeing planning for January 6th, that's when I started thinking we should be sharing this with law enforcement. I would routinely share things.

Because private researchers can do things that law enforcement can't. Law enforcement, at least the FBI, by their own internal guidance, can't just decide, oh, I'm going to go undercover and start mucking about and infiltrating private forums. They need to have a predicate for it, right? Some reason to believe that some illegal conduct or violence or something like that is going on. They have to open investigations and justify them. I don't have any of those constitutional restrictions.

I've got the information I can give them. They have no restrictions on receiving information and considering it for what value it is.

EMAIL MESSAGE:

On Dec 22, 2020 6:06 a.m., Mary McCord wrote:

Good morning, Brian [FBI contact],

Sharing this in case you haven't seen it.

Best, Mary

There has been a noticeable tone shift among participants in the Oath Keepers chat room. Many are frustrated at the political situation they are facing and the lack of organizing.

Top Points

- User says that "fucking bullets" are the only way to achieve their goals

- Same user says they are ready to die for the cause as "sacrificial lamb" and calls on others to join him

- Different user calls for getting teams together in Oregon[24]

Federal and local law enforcement—including the Capitol Police, who are charged with protecting the many buildings that make up the Capitol campus—also received a significant number of anonymous tips about January 6.

ANONYMOUS TIP SUBMITTED TO THE FBI, DECEMBER 26: They think that they will have a large enough group to march into DC armed and will outnumber the police so they can't be stopped. They believe that since the election was "stolen" that it's their constitutional right to overtake the government and during this coup no US laws apply. . . . Their plan is to literally kill people. Please please take this tip seriously and investigate further.[25]

ANONYMOUS TIP SUBMITTED TO CAPITOL POLICE, DECEMBER 28: I'm an internet expert of sorts who has been tracking online far right extremism for years. For weeks I've seen countless tweets from Trump supporters saying they will be armed on January 6th. Even when told of the gun laws, their response is "They can't stop all of us."

Ive also seen tweets from people organizing to "storm the Capitol" on January 6th. Often these threats never amount to anything, but January 6th will be the day most of these people realize there's no chance left for Trump. They'll be pushed to what they feel is the edge. . . .

To whoever is reading this email: Even if you decide not to respond, PLEASE be careful on January 6th. Many of these people will be carrying. I've been tracking online extremism for years and this is the first time I've been truly worried.[26]

Evidence suggests the intelligence was also raised in meetings with DC mayor Muriel Bowser.

CHRISTOPHER RODRIGUEZ, DIRECTOR OF THE HOMELAND SECURITY AND EMERGENCY MANAGEMENT AGENCY, TALKING POINTS WRITTEN AHEAD OF MEETING WITH MAYOR BOWSER, DECEMBER 30: Our greatest concern is: Some groups have expressed intent to come armed on social media. . . . Others are calling to "peacefully" storm the

Capitol and occupy the building to halt the vote. Not sure what
"peaceful" means, but they are calling to occupy the building.
Due to the convergence of many diverse groups . . .
Accelerationists and pro-Administration supporters. Neo-Nazis
and militia groups . . . and their intent to bring weapons to
demonstrations, we assess there is likely to be violence on
January 5 and 6.[27]

**Mayor Bowser asked the public not to gather in downtown DC
on January 5 or 6 and to avoid engaging with demonstrators. She
also activated the district's emergency operations center beginning
Monday, January 4.[28]**

**As the New Year dawned, right-wing groups issued more threats of
violence.**

ENRIQUE TARRIO, LEADER OF PROUD BOYS, SOCIAL MEDIA POSTS, JANUARY 1:
Let's bring this new year with one word in mind . . . Revolt.
New Years Revolution[29]

Trump supporters began to arrive in DC.

BORIS SANCHEZ, *CNN correspondent:* Going back to that weekend, there had
been people showing up across town. My apartment building is across the
street from a hotel and it's about ten minutes' walking from the White House.
There were people that would put up decorations on their hotel room wall
that said TRUMP. And I remember somebody had printed out signs that
said "Stop the Steal" and that sort of thing.

And a few days before January 6th, there was a huge brawl. Some folks
that were very clearly Trump supporters and people on the street exchanged
blows. Police broke them up. So I got the sense that when he invited these
folks to DC, that was going to be a moment of tension, release, a number of
different ways to describe it, but that was going to be the height of the anger
and the aggression that had been building for months.

Within that window of a few days before January 6th, there were brawls
outside the gates of the White House. There were Proud Boys marching
through the street. I could see from my apartment these packs of young men

roaming in this amateur military chic attire. You can paint a picture of what that looks like. And there was obviously something building.

JANUARY 4

An assistant United States attorney in DC discovered threatening posts on Parler, made by user "1776(2.0) Minuteman." He forwarded the posts to his bosses, who in turn forwarded them onto the investigations unit of the Capitol Police.

1776(2.0) MINUTEMAN: We are acting 1/6 . . . choose wisely
congress . . . your very lives do depend on it. Not a
threat . . . it is a fact. We are not coming to play games. We
will not leave empty handed. . . . We are going to execute the
worst of the traitors on the spot and you know exactly [w]ho they
are. . . . That will be their last day in office and for many last
day on earth.

THE BULLET IMPACT MARKS AND BLOOD STAINS ARE NEVER TO BE REPAIRED.[30]

On the same day, reporters around the country were also deciding to make the trek to DC. Alan Chin was with two fellow freelance journalists in Georgia, where Trump was holding his penultimate rally as president.

ALAN CHIN, *freelance photojournalist on assignment for* Business Insider: The three of us were in our motel after that Trump rally on January 4th. And one trick we learned in 2020: when you're covering America and you're driving these long distances, and especially during COVID when restaurants were not open, the trick is to buy these airplane-size bottles of whiskey or vodka or gin or whatever your poison is, because that way you're not driving with an open bottle.

So there we were outside in the courtyard of this motel in rural Georgia, drinking our little single servings, and we said, "You know what? There's going to be another rally in DC in two days, January 6th. What do you think?" And we all kind of looked at each other. We were like, "Yeah, I think we need to be there."

Ellipse rally organizers soon realized they should expect more attendees than they'd put in their original estimates. They requested that the National Park Service amend their permit's attendance estimate from five thousand to twenty thousand people.

JANUARY 5

Drawing from the same playbook as his election "pre-bunking," Trump began to warn his followers about potential Antifa action on January 6.

DONALD TRUMP, JANUARY 5, 2021: Antifa is a Terrorist Organization, stay out of Washington. Law enforcement is watching you.[31]

Most leftist activists had already decided not to attend.

JANE, *staff photojournalist for a major mainstream outlet*: All of the local protesters, which I covered for years, told each other to stay the fuck away from that space. They were smart and they knew exactly what was coming. They were not calling for their people to be there.

CONSTANCE PAIGE YOUNG, *activist*: Me and people with similar values, we said, "We are not going anywhere near this. This is not us. We are not involved. I don't want to be involved in something that has to do with treason." They were going against the government. Why would I insert myself there?

RON HAVIV, *freelance photojournalist on assignment for the* New Republic: I arrived in DC on the 5th of January and went straight to the site just to do a little preliminary survey. We went to the Capitol and saw these kind of bicycle gates. Literally nobody was there. There were some MAGA people walking around with flags and so on. It was totally calm the day before, but it just seemed odd and very open.

I remember going, "This is strange. There's going to be 25, 30, 50,000 people here who are angry at Congress. You think there would already be some preparations." It seemed like somebody was missing something on the protection side.

JASON ANDREW, *freelance photojournalist on assignment for the* New York Times: I just felt it was going to be bigger than what everybody was expecting. There was just something in me; everything felt like it was a recipe for disaster. Everything leading up to it. I had called my friend who worked for US Customs. He knew nothing. I called my friend who worked at the FBI as an analyst. She was not assigned to it, and she said, "We have nothing." This was on the 5th. I was sitting at a coffee shop and she called me and she's like, "What are your spidey senses going?" And I'm like, "My spidey senses say it's going to be bad."

That night, the FBI Norfolk Field Office in Virginia sent a Situational Information Report to other law enforcement. It summarized the most serious and specific threat warning yet discovered.

FBI REPORT, JANUARY 5, 2020: An online thread discussed specific calls for violence to include stating "Be ready to fight. Congress needs to hear glass breaking, doors being kicked in. . . . Stop calling this a march, or rally, or a protest. Go there ready for war."[32]

Attached to the report were screenshots from unnamed social media sites. They included a map of the Capitol with access tunnels highlighted and the caption "Create perimeter." [33]

Around the same time this report was circulated, the Oath Keepers were unloading their firearms and ammunition at a Comfort Inn in northern Virginia for the QRF they had planned.[34]

As the sun set, Trump supporters gathered at Freedom Plaza to hold what seemed almost like a pep rally for the next day.

JANE: The night before just really set the tone. Or, it didn't *set* the tone. We already knew what the tone was, but it underlined the tone, I guess.

Some of us went down there to just kind of see the temperature, see what was going on.

There was a lot of praying.

SANDI BACHOM, *filmmaker:* All the speeches were about holy war. Holy war!

FRANK LOCKWOOD, Arkansas Democrat-Gazette *reporter:* You had people who believed that President Trump was God's anointed leader, that his reelection was preordained and that it was inevitable and unstoppable, that he would be the next president. These weren't predictions, these were prophecies.

7:40 P.M.

On the other side of the National Mall, an unmanned security camera in a Capitol Hill neighborhood filmed a person wearing a face mask, black gloves, and a gray hoodie pulled up around their head. They were carrying a backpack. Ten minutes later, they sat down on a bench outside of the Democratic National Committee (DNC) offices. They stretched their shoulders, as if they were sore from the heavy backpack. They then appeared to take something out of the backpack, place it in a nearby bush, and walk away.

About twenty minutes later, they walked down an alleyway a few blocks away, near the Republican National Committee (RNC) offices.[35] Finally, they walked away, stretching out one shoulder again.

Left lying in the shadows beside the DNC and RNC headquarters were two pipe bombs. Each was affixed with a timer.

Meanwhile, the rally at Freedom Plaza was ending.

EVY MAGES, Washingtonian *photojournalist*: Then they went on to Black Lives Matter Plaza and antagonized Black people. I mean, it was just crazy.

WASHINGTON POST, JANUARY 5, 2021: Late Tuesday, there was another skirmish. A group of about 200 Trump supporters marched to the police line at Black Lives Matter Plaza just before 10:15 p.m. Punches were thrown at the line and a woman was bloodied.[36]

BORIS SANCHEZ: The night before, I wrote a letter to this girl that I was dating. We lived together, and I said, "If you're reading this, something has gone horribly wrong." And I outlined what to do with money, what to give to my family, my nephew and nieces, what she should do. And then I basically told her what to tell my mom. And then I started packing my day bag. I had a flak jacket ready, that sort of helmet hat that they give you that looks like a regular baseball cap, but it's plastic or whatever it is. I basically went to bed that night thinking, *Who knows what's going to happen tomorrow?*

JACOB GLICK, *investigative counsel for the House Select Committee to Investigate the January 6th Attack on the United States Capitol*: I lived with my now fiancé, then boyfriend. And there was a Hyatt right across the street. And a lot of the night before, there were a lot of people who rolled up to the hotel with Trump flags and placards saying "Fuck Biden" and "Stop the Steal." And they were really loud the entire night for a long time, chanting those things. I remember being quite scared. I mean, I thought about a lot of these really deeply rooted stories of pogroms and mob violence against Jewish people that are a big part of my lived experience. I am a gay Jewish man. And I thought about Charlottesville too, which is a recent part of our national experience. We had a Biden flag up on the window and we had a Pride flag, and I was scared. I closed the windows, and it was a really frightening tableau. . . . I was hoping the next day they'd just leave. I was hoping it'd get better in the morning.

JOHN WRIGHT, RIOTER, FACEBOOK MESSAGE TO A FRIEND, 10:57 P.M.: WE ARE GOING TO HAVE TO FIGHT THE BLUE TOMORROW[37]

11:05 P.M.: FROM WHAT I SEEN TONIGHT THE TEMPERS WILL BE UP TOMORROW AND POLICE LINES WILL BE BREACHED[38]

11:07 P.M.: THE FIRST MISTAKE THEY MAKE IN CHAMBERS WE ARE GOING IN AND DRAG THEM OUT[39]

12:27 A.M.: ALMOST WAR TIME[40]

HANNAH ALLAM, *NPR reporter*: I remember texting my editor the night before saying, you know, I'm really dreading this one. This one felt less like a rally and more like a last stand.[41]

PART TWO

THE INSURRECTION

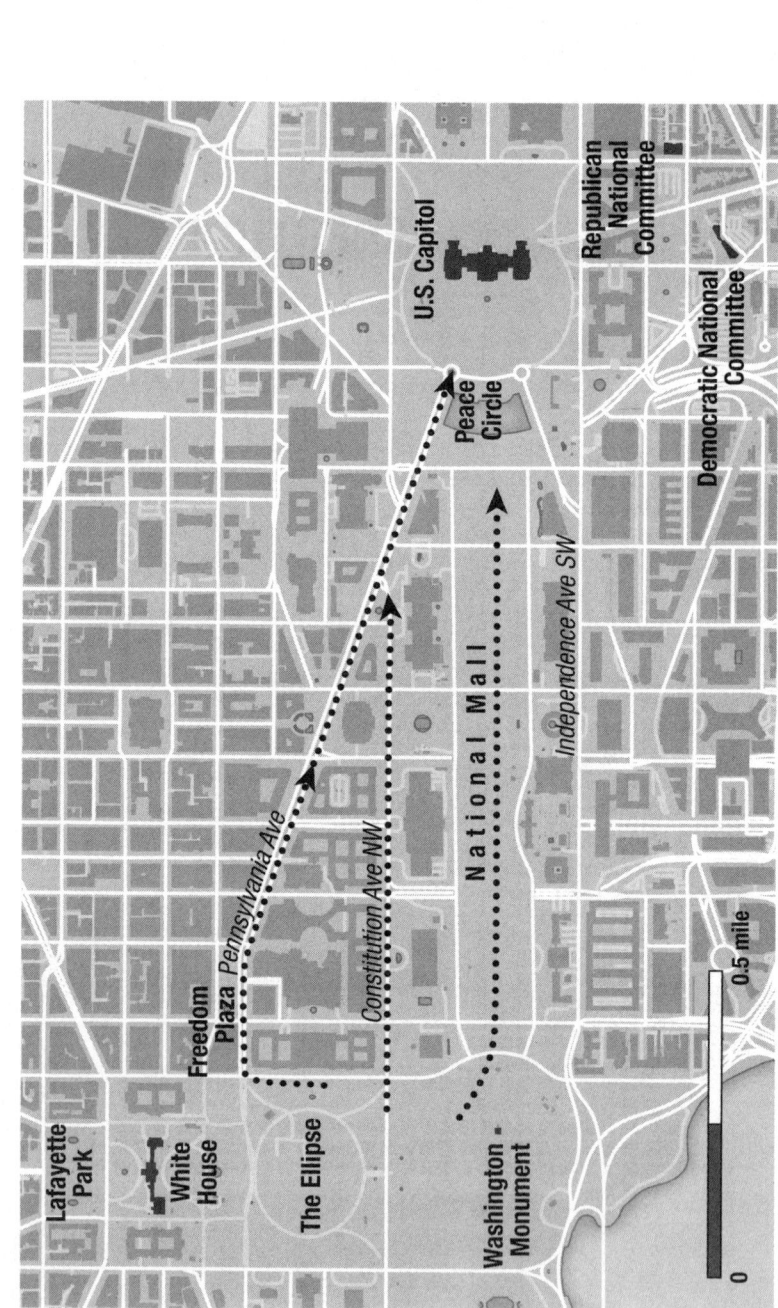

CHAPTER 4

"THAT'S EXACTLY HOW CHARLOTTESVILLE BEGAN"

JANUARY 6

THE ELLIPSE

THE *NEW YORK TIMES*:

WASHINGTON GIRDS FOR A PRO-TRUMP RALLY, AS LOCAL OFFICIALS WARN OF POSSIBLE VIOLENCE

Thousands of President Trump's supporters are expected to gather in Washington on Wednesday to hear him rehash false claims of voter fraud in the November election, just as Congress begins formally counting the Electoral College vote.[1] With a grand stage, video monitors and a planned presidential appearance, pro-Trump demonstrators will condemn Joseph R. Biden Jr.'s victory with a planned show of force.[2]

4 A.M.

BORIS SANCHEZ, *CNN correspondent*: I got up at four in the morning. I remember walking to the Ellipse, and that to me was one of the inflection points where I thought, *If something's going to happen to me, it might be now.* Because I was completely alone. It was very dark. And again, there were these packs of young men that looked like they were looking for conflict. They were walking with purpose in seemingly random directions. And at four in the morning, I'm wondering, *Where are they going? They're not walking to the Ellipse, to the speech, so where are they going?* So as I'm walking over there, my head is on a swivel, I'm wearing the flak jacket underneath a giant parka.

6:45 A.M.

BORIS SANCHEZ, LIVE ON CNN: Good morning, Alisyn. Yes, an enormous line at the Washington Monument, gathering since before three a.m., and waves of supporters for the president are still arriving now.[3]

BORIS SANCHEZ: I remember getting to the riser between the White House and the Washington Monument. I faced the camera. I could see the Washington Monument and it was pretty dark. The sun hadn't come out. And it was immense, the crowd—I could see it was an ocean of people and the movement of it in the darkness. You couldn't see faces, but you could catch glimmers of signs and flags and just the enormity of it. I thought, *This has the potential to go horribly wrong.*

Once the sun came out and you could see the mass of people, the riser shook, was shaking, vibrating because of people walking, because it was a massive crowd. And then when they would yell, it was deafening. I was sweating like crazy because I had so many layers on, and that flak jacket was moist on me.

Roseanne Boyland was already in the crowd. She had come with a relatively new friend, Justin Winchell.

JUSTIN WINCHELL, *rioter:* We got there about 7 a.m., right by the National Monument and the Ellipse. Everything was peaceful. A lotta children, people sellin', you know, their T-shirts. And, I mean, there was even food vendors. . . . Everybody was just happy to be an American. You know, I think there's a person or two in the United States that doesn't think that the election was fair and honest.[4]

CHERYL BOYLAND, *Rosanne Boyland's mother:* Justin Winchell called my husband first during the day just to introduce himself, which was very mature of him, I thought. And [Justin] told him, "I'll take care of her." He sent a couple pictures.

DC Metropolitan Police officer Daniel Hodges started his day around 7:30 a.m. Usually he was a patrol officer, but when needed, he worked in the CDU, or Civil Disturbance Unit.[5]

DANIEL HODGES, *DC Metropolitan Police officer:* I stood on foot as the crowd poured down the street and into the park. There were a significant number of men dressed in tactical gear . . . wearing ballistic vests, helmets, goggles, military face masks, backpacks. They appeared to be prepared for much more than listening to politicians speak in a park.[6]

Some 28,000 rally goers passed through metal detectors to attend President Trump's speech—far more than the estimate of 5,000 to 20,000 attendees. As they passed through, the Secret Service confiscated 269 knives, 242 cans of pepper spray, 18 brass knuckles, and 18 tasers.[7]

JASON ANDREW, *freelance photojournalist on assignment for the* New York Times: A truck with Pennsylvania plates had gone by, and there was three guys in full military fatigues, helmets, backpacks, faces covered. Red Chevy pickup. And I remember returning and taking a picture of it, and [my colleague] goes, "Why did you photograph that?" And I said, "Because that's exactly how Charlottesville began."

On the other end of the National Mall, staffers, reporters, elected officials, and law enforcement were all arriving at work and preparing for their busy days.

CONGRESSIONAL FOOD SERVICE EMPLOYEE: I got up, went to work, but my son, he was like, "Ma, you shouldn't go to work." So I'm like, "No, I got to go. I got to go to work, I got to go." So I went.[8]

REP. ERIC SWALWELL (D-CA): I had two little kids, one who was three and one who was two, and so I was up pretty early. I knew it was going to be an intense day. And I had been up late the night before. I had hosted a bunch of colleagues at our home to watch the Georgia returns,* so [US representative] Ruben Gallego [of Arizona] had been at my house. He's my best friend. His wife is my wife's best friend. So we see them a lot. We both have little kids

---

* No candidate for US senator from Georgia had won a majority of the vote in November, so a second runoff election was held, per state law.

who are close in age, and yeah, we're incredibly close with the guy. And we were just up late watching the Georgia returns.[9]

So I figured I'd knock a run out pretty early.[10] I ran from the residence I have in Washington, DC, to the Capitol and then back. It's a run I do often. And I recall on the run back from the Capitol, actually running up North Capitol [Street], seeing dozens of individuals carrying signs that read, "Stop the Steal," and wearing body armor and military fatigues.

And I remember pulling down the cap that I was wearing; it was pretty cold, so kind of pulling it over my face because I didn't want to be seen by this crowd or recognized by this crowd. But it certainly just gave me an unsettling feeling about the direction the day was headed.[11]

After his run, Representative Swalwell joined other members of Congress in receiving his second COVID vaccination. They were lucky— the shots were still not available to most of the public at this stage.

Meanwhile, DC-based reporter Olivia Beavers was three days into a new job covering Congress for *Politico*, and four days into finding out that her recent ex-boyfriend was seeing someone new. She hadn't slept well the night before, but she'd been assigned to cover the certification of the election, and so she headed toward the Capitol building.

OLIVIA BEAVERS, Politico *congressional reporter*: That morning I was driving, and I was talking to a friend's husband who was saying, "Be careful." And I was sort of dismissing him like, "Oh, nothing big is going to happen. People are hyping stuff up." There's this feeling that the building was so safe that nothing could happen.

IGOR BOBIC, HuffPost *reporter*: I kind of walk up [to the Capitol building] and the first thing I noticed are people milling about already. There was kind of a little bit of nervous energy in the air. A lot of Trump supporters, the flags, the red hats. The [other] thing that struck me that was unusual was the barricades the Capitol Police had set up. Usually you don't encounter barricades as you go up the Capitol. It was very rare. So I find it unusual that they had this sort of maybe four- or five-foot-tall barricade set up that

I had to walk through. So walking in, I already thought that this is going to be a weird one.

Capitol Police used a few different types of barricades, but most were flimsy metal crowd-control barriers that resembled bike racks.

DANNY MCCOY, *DC Fire and EMS (FEMS) area commander:* We started the morning out like every morning. We had our briefing, and we went over what the plan was.

Most first responders would stage close to the event down at the Ellipse. They say they had no idea the crowd planned to march to the Capitol.

DANNY MCCOY: I remember at one point I said we'd be fine as long as everybody stays at the Ellipse and they don't march to the Capitol—or something like that. It was just a random thought.

SGT. AQUILINO GONELL, *US Capitol Police officer:* Inside the Capitol Police office, I revised the daily schedule. The coronavirus had severely weakened our force. Dozens were either working remotely or out sick. I covered the vacancies as best as I could with members of my Civil Disturbance Unit.

After the attendance check, everyone went to the cafeteria to get coffee and carryout. In the hallway, I saw my colleague Officer Brian Sicknick heading to the break room, wearing his blue mountain bike jacket. He was also a veteran and introvert who was my age. Whenever he worked under my command and I asked him to do overtime or volunteer for anything, he'd jump in and never complain, the type you wanted on your team.[12]

Sicknick was often described as reliable and dedicated to his job, including by his older brother.

CRAIG SICKNICK, *Brian Sicknick's brother:* I hate using the overused clichés, but he was just nice. He always felt like he had to do the right thing no matter what. . . . He was ten years my junior, he looked up to me when we were growing up. He kind of worshipped me, tailed me, wanted to be with me whenever we went places.

The last few years, I was kind of looking up to him. It's like, wow, look what he's doing. Look at the people he's around. My whole family was very happy when he got that job because he came back from [serving in the armed forces in] the Middle East. God forbid anything horrible was going to happen—we figured more than likely it would've happened over there. He comes home, he's got a job with one of the safest police forces in the United States, as far as line of duty deaths over its history.

He was a Trump supporter at one point until he realized what a piece of crap that Trump was like. [Trump] promised the world, and then look what he did. [Brian] never just came out and said, "Oh, I don't like this guy." But he didn't talk about him nearly as much the last few months.

That morning at work near his home in New Jersey, Craig was thinking about Brian, knowing his brother was apprehensive about the demonstrations.

CRAIG SICKNICK: My brother said he was concerned. Just from what he heard from the grapevine that he works with, he said they had some idea that it was going to be a little crazy. Exactly how, they didn't know.

The day started off perfectly normal for me. I just woke up super early, got into work, had to dress up in my fire-resistant clothing. I used to work in an oil refinery. It was a high-stress, high-adrenaline job. On a good day, it was boring. I'd come home, my wife would ask me how my day was, and I said, "Boring," which was a good thing. If something went bad at a refinery, it went *really* bad. If I did something wrong, I could blow up half of New Jersey as well as a lot of the other people that work there.

DEMOCRATIC NATIONAL COMMITTEE HEADQUARTERS

8:30 A.M.

Ahead of a planned visit from vice president–elect Kamala Harris, two Secret Service canine teams swept the inside and outside of the DNC offices. They didn't find anything out of the ordinary. The teams gave the all clear. But lying in the shadows under a bush was one of two pipe bombs the person in the gray hoodie had planted.

THE VICE PRESIDENT'S RESIDENCE AT THE NAVAL OBSERVATORY

8:30 A.M.

JANUARY 6 REPORT: On the morning of January 6, 2021, Vice President Michael R. Pence gathered his staff to pray. Vice President Pence and his closest advisors knew the day ahead "would be a challenging one." They asked God for "guidance and wisdom" in the hours to come.

THE ELLIPSE

9 A.M.

ANDERSON COOPER, CNN ANCHOR, LIVE ON CNN: I'm Anderson Cooper. Welcome to CNN's special coverage of a monumental day in America.[13]

The rally at the Ellipse officially began at 9 a.m. with a speech from Republican representative Mo Brooks of Alabama. As he shouted at the crowd, they heaved pro-Trump signs and religious symbols, including crosses, toward the sky.

REP. MO BROOKS (R-AL): Will you fight for America?[14]

CROWD: (*Roars*) Yes!

BORIS SANCHEZ, ON CNN, 9:15 a.m.: Right now, we're hearing from Alabama congressman Mo Brooks and he was just riling up the crowd, asking them if they're willing to do what it takes to save the country. I've been to a lot of Trump rallies, a lot of them high in tension and animosity from some of the president's supporters. This is up there with some of the most charged events that the president has ever held.[15]

ALAN CHIN, *freelance photojournalist on assignment for* Business Insider: I had to park pretty far because there were a lot of people in town. And in my lack of sleep, I actually did not bring my N95. I left the flak jacket and the gas mask and all that in the trunk. I didn't think I would need it. I thought, *I'll just go. I'll check out the rally. I'll come back to the car. I'll file, and then I'll go back out and see if anything happens in the afternoon or evening.* So, I go down to the area near the Washington Monument. You could see these gigantic jumbotron monitors and the loudspeakers echoing over the crowd.

RON HAVIV, *freelance photojournalist on assignment for the* New Republic: It was certainly calm, but a little bit tense. Proud Boys would walk by, and then there were couples and families. So it was a real mix.

ALAN CHIN: There were two kinds of people, at least in that crowd. There were, for lack of a better word, the kind of middle-American MAGA. And these are people that drove 12, 14, 24, 26 hours all the way from Minnesota or all the way from Nebraska or wherever to come see Trump speak. They were the true believers, but they had gigantic teddy bears. By and large, it was mostly white. There was a fairly high percentage of older people, people over sixty-five.

But then, it was clear there were elements in that crowd that were not tourists, okay? They were wearing body armor, they were wearing military type fatigues. They had walkie talkies. I was like, *Okay, so we have the militants.*

STEPHEN VOSS, *freelance photojournalist on assignment for* Politico: There was a guy with a noose that he was just sort of wearing around his neck [like a scarf]. I took his picture and then I asked his name and he gave me his name. But it was weird. I've been to so many protests and so many events in DC that are sort of high-intensity, high-energy events, but I'd never seen someone bring a noose to something.

EVY MAGES, Washingtonian *photojournalist*: But then it got more crowded.

JASON ANDREW: It felt uneasy. A lot of guys in fatigues, very nervous. Everybody felt unnerving. You could tell everybody was waiting for something, but you weren't sure what.

RON HAVIV: The speeches were going on and gradually getting more angry.

BORIS SANCHEZ, CNN BROADCAST, 10:15 a.m.: A lot of them not only peddling falsehoods but also ratcheting up the idea that these folks have to fight, fight in their eyes to keep President Donald Trump in the White House to save the Republic.[16]

DAVID BUTOW, *freelance photojournalist*: It was already so packed. I was a little annoyed with myself for not having gotten there earlier. There was something ominous about that crowd, that it wasn't just going to be some sort of an ordinary protest. And I've worked a lot overseas, and I mean, I've been around mobs and I have a sense of the mob mentality, and I know how quickly things can go badly when you get that group psychology going.

EVY MAGES: It became very hostile quite quickly to photographers, at least it's how I felt. You had to move around the crowd, stay really low, and then you can pop up and take some pictures, and as soon as somebody would point you out or recognize you, you have to disappear again. You were the enemy.

JASON ANDREW: I find for myself, it's really easy for me to work around those people. I find that I can ebb and flow with them and get in and out without an issue. I don't know why. I mean, it's probably because I am a middle-aged white male, but I've always found it pretty easy to work in those circles.

RON HAVIV: I've gotten to the stage where gray hair can give you the sort of look of, *He's harmless, let the old guy go,* kind of thing, which I think probably did help me to some degree.

DAVID BUTOW: And also I thought about this, *How am I going to dress for this?* So I wore the same thing that I wore to the other Trump rallies. I have a khaki Levi's jacket. I could be a guy with a Ford F-150 working on a ranch. If you just see me, you have no idea what side I'm on. And that was all very deliberate.

10:30 A.M.

The British documentary filmmaker Nick Quested followed along with the Proud Boys that day but says he didn't know what they were planning. He was at the Ellipse with a group of two to three hundred Proud Boys.

NICK QUESTED, *documentary filmmaker:* So we get there [to the Ellipse], the Proud Boys have just started walking down the mall [away from the speech]. I was like, *Why are we walking away?*

The Proud Boys started marching down the National Mall, toward the Capitol building, not even waiting for Trump to arrive.

NICK QUESTED: Then I'm making jokes because one of the guys has got a baseball bat and I make jokes about, "I don't understand baseball very much, but don't you need a ball to play that?" And he sort of looks at me.

| Quested followed after them, filming.

THE ELLIPSE

10:47 A.M.

| Rudy Giuliani started his speech, an unhinged monologue.

CROWD: Rudy! Rudy! Rudy!

RUDY GIULIANI, ATTORNEY FOR DONALD TRUMP: It seems to me, we don't want to find out three weeks from now even more proof that this election was stolen, do we?

CROWD: No![17]

RUDY GIULIANI: Let's have trial by combat!

BORIS SANCHEZ: And that kind of got the crowd simmering and simmering.

CAPITOL VISITOR CENTER

10:50 A.M.

Capitol Police sergeant Gonell and his officers were staged and waiting to respond to any disturbances. While they waited, they watched a news livestream of the rally on a cell phone.[18]

SERGEANT GONELL: They saw—I think Giuliani calling for trial by combat and all the nonsense. So I told [my officers] at that time, "Look, just start getting ready." It looked like it shouldn't be long before Trump starts speaking and all those people are going to start heading this way. "Go ahead and start getting dressed at least the bottom part of your equipment, steel toe boots, the shin protectors, the thigh protectors, the groin protectors, and then we'll go from there."[19]

Gonell was one of the first responders who anticipated what was to come.

11:25 A.M.

Meanwhile, blocks away, vice president–elect Kamala Harris's motor-cade arrived at the DNC. Unbeknownst to them, they drove within twenty feet of the hidden pipe bomb. [20]

12:03 P.M.

EVY MAGES: And then, yeah, so then Trump spoke.

ANNOUNCER: Ladies and gentlemen, please welcome the forty-fifth president of the United States of America—President Donald J. Trump! [21]

JON FARINA, *freelance journalist on assignment for* Status Coup News: I'm still by the Washington Monument trying to live stream, and I was just having so much trouble because of the [lack of] service. And because we had this WhatsApp group chat [among freelance journalists], I knew everybody was like, "Oh, we're going to the Capitol." So I said, "Fuck it, I'm going to leave here and go to the Capitol." As I'm walking away down the Washington Mall, I hear Trump get on and he starts speaking.

DONALD TRUMP: Well, thank you very much. This is incredible. Media will not show the magnitude of this crowd.

MARK PETERSON, *freelance photojournalist on assignment for the* New York Times: I photographed him for about ten minutes and then started to try and make my way through the crowd to the Capitol. As I'm walking through the crowd, people would kind of elbow me or were very surly. There's already people leaving. So in the street there's groups of ten to twenty or fifty people walking towards the Capitol, even before he finished. This is probably twenty minutes into his speech.

NICK QUESTED: [The Proud Boys and I] walked back to Constitution [Avenue NW], where the food trucks were. And we have lunch! We had tacos. Tech-nically, they weren't tacos, they were quesadillas. So I had a joke with one of them at that point, and I go, "If you kick all the immigrants out and you don't let any Mexicans back into America, you're not going to—there's be way less tacos, dude." And he takes a big bite, and he goes [eyes wide], "But I love tacos!"

MARK PETERSON: So I get to these food trucks at Fourth Street before the Capitol, and I see a camera crew and the Proud Boys are there getting lunch! [*laughs*] I don't mean to laugh but it was so surreal at this moment. I just said something to the photographer and to the crew, just like, "What's going on?" And I think they just said, "Oh, it's a lunch break." Something like that.

THE ELLIPSE

ABOUT 12:16 P.M.

THE NEW YORK TIMES: With Congress poised to spend the day brushing aside the protests he had nurtured about the Electoral College outcome, Mr. Trump urged his supporters to take another step.[22]

PRESIDENT DONALD TRUMP: I know that everyone here will soon be marching over to the Capitol building to peacefully and patriotically make your voices heard.[23]

JANET BUHLER, *rioter*: There became a sense of urgency, like, we need to go to the Capitol.[24] I just remember standing there watching it. And then [my son-in-law] said, "Come on, let's go." I was just, like, "Well, okay."[25]

CRAIG BAKER, *assistant fire chief of operations, DC FEMS*: That's when we realized that there were large groups moving towards the Capitol.

JASON ANDREW: I had wrote a text [in the *New York Times* WhatsApp thread] at 12:18. I'm like, "Groups are headed to the Capitol." [At] 12:20, someone asked if anyone was seeing armaments, and I had wrote, "Yeah, there's knives, bats, and bear spray." [At] 12:30, I said, "Huge crowds walking down Constitution to the Capitol." [And at] 12:38, "Proud Boys were on Constitution." Somebody had asked if I had seen a lot of Kevlar and helmets, and I said, "Yeah, everything was out near the Washington Monument for the guys in fatigues. You'll see it."

I mean, my focus [was] the guys in fatigues. I was hyper focused with guys that had bear spray on the corners, were carrying batons and bats, had radios, all the militia groups that were there. They were my focus.

They were the same type of guys that created Charlottesville. And so these are the same type of guys that I was looking for. These were the guys that I figured if something was going to start, they were the ones that were going to start. It wasn't the people holding crosses. It wasn't the people with Trump signs that looked to be in their sixties and seventies. It wasn't the families with children—it was these guys.[25]

ABOUT 12:40 P.M.

Capitol Hill resident Karlin Younger was doing laundry in her apartment complex, which was next door to the RNC building. The laundry room was only accessible through a door in the back alley, so after she transferred a load to the dryer, she headed outside.

KARLIN YOUNGER, *DC resident*: That's when something caught my eye. I just saw something kind of metallic, and all I thought is someone must have missed the recycling bin. So I'm like, *Oh, is that a can or something?* And I was going to recycle it, because I'm about that life. I just looked, and it was so completely unbelievable. The first thing I saw was wires, and the next thing I saw was six inches of pipe capped on both ends. I leaned a little bit closer, that's when I see this dial. It has a hand on twenty.[26]

You're just staring at it, and you're like, *OK, it's definitely metal, but there's, like, wires attached to it, and there's a timer attached to it. What am I looking at?* It's not immediately obvious, because you're just really, really not expecting anything. You're not on high alert. You don't think you're under attack. I'm not in Iraq. This is Capitol Hill.[27]

I'm holding a wet sweater and I'm thinking, *What do I do?*[28] You don't want to go down as the person who evacuates a city block for a hoax. But at the same time, I have to have somebody check this out.[29]

I go sprinting back down the alley and go to this little guard stand that's right at the RNC. I was like, "Hey, hey, hey, please come take a look. I think I see something." Out comes a guard from the building. And he's plainclothes, but he's got his radio and, like, quite the macho man, you can tell. It's like, "All right, little lady, what do you think you saw?" He walks over. He leans over and just goes, "Holy shit, that's a bomb!" And I was like, "I knew it, I knew it. I knew this didn't look right."[30]

OFFICER HODGES: We could hear over the radio that they had found a "viable device" as they termed it, which I knew meant most likely a bomb.

So we don't know how big it is. Is it a thermonuclear warhead or is it a pipe bomb? We don't know how many more there are. We don't know what their detonation mechanism is—if they're on timers or if they're remote controlled.

KARLIN YOUNGER: They evacuated the block.[31]

FRANK LOCKWOOD, Arkansas Democrat-Gazette *reporter*: I took the subway up to Capitol Hill South, and when I got off, it's about 12:50 and there were all these police cars and they had kind of shut down the intersection there.

FRANK LOCKWOOD VIA TWITTER, 12:54 P.M.: They're hurrying everyone away from the area around Capitol South Metro & RNC headquarters.[32]

Metropolitan Police swept the area and found an unoccupied car nearby with weapons inside: an assault rifle and homemade Molotov cocktails with homemade napalm. The driver eventually returned. The police determined that he was not the bomber, though they did arrest him on weapons charges. Meanwhile, the bomb at the DNC remained hidden.

On the other side of the Capitol building, the Proud Boys finished lunch.

NICK QUESTED: We walk over [to the Capitol], it's all pretty normal. "Fuck Antifa, we love Trump"—that type of stuff.

ADAM GRAY, *Freelance photojournalist on assignment for the* Daily Mail: I'm wondering where the [Proud Boys] are. I'm speaking to my friends, somebody said they're walking up that way towards the Capitol. So I walk all the way up the Mall and get to the fountains. When I get there, there's not many people here.

But soon, the Proud Boys appeared at what is known as "Peace Circle," the traffic circle around the Peace Monument just outside the Capitol building.

ADAM GRAY: I see them coming down the street and I know things are going to change pretty quick.

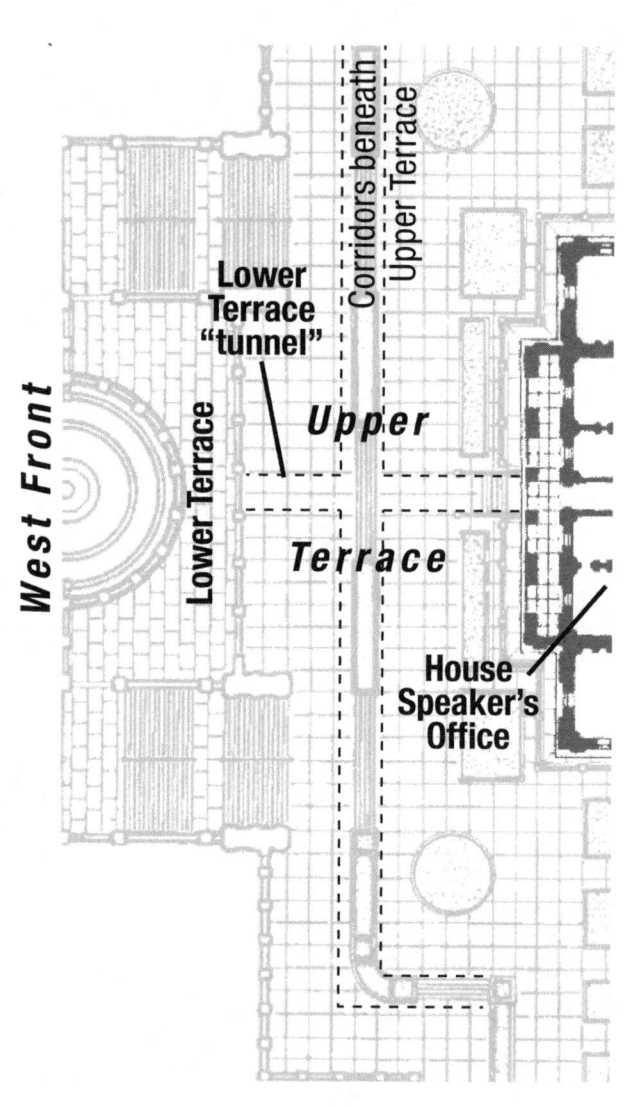

West Front

Lower Terrace "tunnel"

Lower Terrace

Corridors beneath Upper Terrace

Upper

Terrace

House Speaker's Office

CHAPTER 5

"THINGS STARTED TO GET REALLY VIOLENT"

WEST FRONT

ABOUT 12:45 P.M.

ADAM GRAY, *freelance photojournalist on assignment for the* Daily Mail: So I saw [the Proud Boys] coming down the street and I wanted to make sure I got a picture of them from behind [with] the Capitol in the background. And I think as soon as I'd gone to take that picture, I heard them shaking the barriers on the other side of the crowd.

NICK QUESTED, *documentary filmmaker:* They're pushing on the barriers and I'm like, *Oh, this is about to go crazy.* And then they've only got maybe half a dozen Capitol Police there. And of them, I'd say there were probably more women than men. And these are not big. They were not.

RIOTERS, YELLING AT CAPITOL POLICE OFFICERS: You're Nancy Pelosi's dogs. Bark for us![1]

CAROLINE EDWARDS, *US Capitol Police officer, watching from an inner police line:* I turned and was like, "Sergeant, I think we're going to need a couple more people down here." And, you know, that's the understatement of the century. But that's when I knew that something wasn't right.[2]

RIOTERS: This is our house! This is the people's house![3]

| The Proud Boys were at the front.

ADAM GRAY: As soon as I saw 'em shaking the barriers, I was like, *Well, they're going to go over.*

STEVEN SUND, *chief of the US Capitol Police, watching live feeds from the command center*: The confrontation grows more violent as the protesters become increasingly agitated. The enraged group begins shoving the barricades harder, pinning one officer to the ground and punching the others with their fists. I'm shocked. I have never seen a group turn so violent so quickly. I turn and yell, "Where the hell is our CDU?* Get them down there now!"[4]

NICK QUESTED: They were immediately overwhelmed.

JON FARINA, *freelance journalist on assignment for* Status Coup News: You could actually hear me [in the footage]. I have a microphone in my hand. I'm like, "Oh shit, guys, this is not good. Oh shit. Oh shit." So I'm running to the front. I see cops, but they don't know what to do. And I see people hopping over the [barricades]. So I'm like, *Fuck it, I'm going to hop over too.*

I got to the front, and that's where all the Proud Boys were. I'm just thinking, *All right, this is getting out of hand. This is getting out of control.* I've never seen anything like this. And in my mind I'm like, *Where the fuck are the police? Where's the barricades?* So I knew right there and then I knew it was going to be bad because the police were nowhere to be found, and I didn't know how far they were going to take it, but I had a feeling that this wasn't good.

SGT. AQUILINO GONELL, *US Capitol Police officer, inside the building*: And then I think within a few more minutes the radio call went out.[5]

RADIO TRANSMISSION: All CDU officers to the West Front! Send all you have!"[6]

SERGEANT GONELL: It sounded like an emergency.[7] It took us about three or four minutes to put on the rest of the gear.[8]

The mob reached an inner set of barriers: single-layer metal crowd-control barriers often seen along parade routes. They're often referred to as bike racks.

OFFICER EDWARDS: I went over to the link of the two bike racks because there was only four of us [guarding the barricades]. So I had two of the bike

---

* Civil Defense Unit

racks myself, and I just put my arms through, and I took like this stance of, you know, like a leaning-forward stance.

CROWD, YELLING AT OFFICERS: Traitors! Traitors!

The rioters started pushing on the bike rack in front of Edwards.

OFFICER EDWARDS: It wasn't going anywhere, so they actually—it was all males—they lifted the bike rack. I was holding onto it. And they started using the bike rack to kind of push me backwards, and the last thing I remember is going down and my chin hitting the handrail, and then that's where I fell backwards and the back of my head hit concrete.[9]

ADAM GRAY: I think the cops hold them back for twelve seconds and they're straight past them and they keep going.

When Edwards came to, her police line was broken. Rioters were streaming past.

MEMBER OF THE CROWD: Let's storm that shit!

NICK QUESTED: Everyone's just pouring forward. It's like water. It's just everyone's coming.

The west side of the Capitol building has a series of tiered terraces, like layers of a wedding cake. The base, just off the National Mall, is the West Lawn, which is primarily grass. Next is a marble apron called the Lower West Terrace, which leads to the Upper West Terrace, and then the building itself.

OFFICER EDWARDS: There's a concrete wall where the grass ends and Lower West Terrace of the West Front begins, and we rushed there. I was just screaming like, "Get back!" you know. "Don't take one more step!" Like, "Get back, get back!" And they were saying stuff like, "Make us! This is our house."[10]

NICK QUESTED: They are charging right now. And there's nothing to stop them. And they stop for twenty seconds at the low fence. Then they start kicking it and pulling it and kicking it. And then that breaks down and then they're off.

In a matter of minutes, the rioters had made it up to the Lower West Terrace, a supposedly secure area.

12:58 P.M.

ADAM GRAY: Then there's a line of police. So this is the first line of police where police have the batons out and they're going to stop them. This line of the police holds people here for quite a while.

Some of these officers had shields.

NICK QUESTED: The atmosphere had changed very much: "Push forward!" "Fight for Trump!" "Choose a side!" "Respect your oath!" The language had changed to be really aggressive at this point. They were really challenging them.

SERGEANT GONELL, *from inside the Capitol Building*: We neared the Lower West Terrace entrance. I was already sweaty and uncomfortable, but as we came closer, my heartbeat raced.[11] When we opened those double doors, I saw the crowd already flanking the two squads that were in the West Front.[12] The minute I opened those doors, you could hear the crowd. Roaring. And some of the officers screaming in pain.[13] Walking down those seven or eight steps to the platform where the [temporary inauguration] stage was, gave me a sense of this is going to be a fucking long day.[14]

ADAM GRAY: It was just complete pandemonium. A lot of pepper spray, a lot of bear spray. I'm wearing an N95 mask and I'm wearing goggles.

OFFICER EDWARDS: What I saw was just a war scene. It was something like I had seen out of the movies. I couldn't believe my eyes. There were officers on the ground. They were bleeding. They were throwing up. I saw friends with blood all over their faces. I was slipping in people's blood. I was catching people as they fell. It was carnage. It was chaos.[15]

JON FARINA: The adrenaline is running through me. I'm drenched in pepper spray and bear mace and all this shit, and it was brutal at times. There was times where I couldn't see, times where I couldn't breathe. So those times I just held my head down and just kept the camera up.

ADAM GRAY: The police have pepper ball guns.

NICK QUESTED: Which I think was actually completely justified. You've got a fucking mob of 400 to 500 people at this point, pushing the police and standing in their face and screaming at them. But one guy [a rioter] got shot through his cheek. I filmed him. He's got a hole in his cheek, and you can see they stuffed it with something or it is something yellow, maybe it's his teeth. I dunno.

RIOTER: They shot him in the face![16]

SERGEANT GONELL: Once we realized that he was bleeding, that he needed attention, we stopped [and] we tried to help him. The rioters or his conspirators, they saw us. Instead of helping him, they thought we were going to arrest him and that enraged everybody there to the point that there was a melee.[17]

NICK QUESTED: And then they started coming with the beanbags.

The Capitol Police used weapons often called "beanbag guns," which are essentially modified shotguns loaded with small cloth bags full of shot. They are usually intended to be used as a less lethal method of crowd dispersal.

NICK QUESTED: One cop, he was gray, a little portly, red face, little goatee. And he looks at me, I remember it distinctly, I got my press pass hanging out and I've got two cameras in my hand. And he looks at me, he just levels the thing, just goes *ping*. And *bang*! And it hits me and I go, "Oh, that really fucking hurt." And then just went back to work.

ADAM GRAY: It's just a battle between the police and the protesters. But the protesters . . . there's just more and more bodies on their side. And as you know, the police—there wasn't that many reinforcements.

ALAN CHIN, *freelance photojournalist on assignment for* Business Insider: The crowd was not dissipating at all. They were not even stepping back ten feet. They were literally just pushing. And in fact, you had people turning their backs so they could dig in their heels and use their backs to push against a police shield. You have more leverage that way, more body strength to push the police shields. And I have never seen anything like this. It was already extraordinary.

DC FEMS responders began to arrive on the West Front of the Capitol building.

ANGELO WESTFIELD, *battalion fire chief, DC FEMS*: The situation was developing to be more than a normal protest.[18]

DANNY MCCOY, DC FEMS *Area Commander, off-site*: Things just started happening. We started getting phone calls.[19]

THE *NEW YORK TIMES*: Kevin D. Greeson, 55, of Athens, Alabama, collapsed as he stood among a sea of Trump supporters on the West Side of the U.S. Capitol. Mr. Greeson had been talking to his wife on his phone when he fell to the sidewalk.[20]

911 CALL FROM SOMEONE IN THE MOB: There's someone down and he's having a hard time breathing. In front of the United States Capitol. The police have a man up here trying to do CPR and I don't think they're having much luck.[21]

GARY DZIEKAN, *firefighter, DC FEMS*: We were originally dispatched for an injured knee. We got to the West Lawn and just saw the mass of people and we still thought we were going for an injured knee, but there was a lot of Capitol Police officers running up to our ambulance along with the captain of Engine 13, who was already on scene. [He] said, "It's a cardiac arrest. They're bringing them out now."

I look into the mass of people on the West Lawn and there's about twenty civilians carrying a backboard, with the patient on the backboard, and a woman on top of him doing compressions. They run up next to the ambulance and set the patient down. And then we started to render aid in the back of the ambulance to the patient.[22]

DC FEMS RADIO TRANSMISSION: We got a CPR in progress inside the Ambulance 18 right now.

KEVIN COLE, *firefighter paramedic, DC FEMS*: During that time we started hearing explosions, which later turned out to be flash bangs or smoke grenades, but they didn't affect us because our scene was safe because we had US Capitol Police around our unit.[23]

1:02 P.M.

Vice President Pence and all members of Congress were expected to gather in the Capitol for a joint session at 1 p.m. to certify the election results. Pence announced via Twitter that he wouldn't support any attempts to overturn the election.

LETTER FROM VICE PRESIDENT PENCE VIA TWITTER: Some believe that as Vice President, I should be able to accept or reject electoral votes unilaterally. Others believe that electoral votes should never be challenged in a Joint Session of Congress. After a careful study of our Constitution, our laws, and our history, I believe neither view is correct.[24]

Most of the lawmakers and staff members inside the Capitol building did not know the extent of the fight outside. They were focused on preparing for the joint session of Congress.

REP. ERIC SWALWELL: [It's] largely ceremonial. Congress convenes in what's called a joint session, meaning the House and the Senate are in the Congress. The vice president of the United States, the president of the Senate, presides over the count.

And each state alphabetically has their votes called. If there's an objection, you need somebody to meet your objection from the other chamber. So, for example, if a House member objects, a Senator would also have to object. And then both bodies would go back to their chambers and debate the objection, and then come back for resuming the count.[25]

As the president of the Senate, the vice president, you know, presides over the count. There are tellers who are seated just below the vice president from both chambers, both parties. They tally the counts that are sent from the states, and the vice president literally—you know, kind of like in an award show—opens up the count and reads how the state went for each individual candidate.[26]

At least, that's how they were expecting the day to go.

Elsewhere in the building, Speaker of the House Nancy Pelosi's daughter Alexandra was with her teen son, Paul Vos, whom she had brought to witness the historic moment.

ALEXANDRA PELOSI, *Speaker Nancy Pelosi's daughter:* We started seeing the mob coming.

Alexandra, a journalist and documentary filmmaker, pulled out her camera to record through the window.

ALEXANDRA PELOSI: I bring my camera with me everywhere. It's like a part of my body. I mean, I have it at every birthday party, every family activity. I mean, I have thousands of hours of footage of things that nobody would ever want to watch.

ALEXANDRA PELOSI, LOOKING OUT THE WINDOW WITH PAUL: They're marching up. You can see them marching up.[27]

PAUL VOS, SPEAKER NANCY PELOSI'S GRANDSON: What if they try and run the Capitol? They're going to run the Capitol. They're just going to like, charge in.[28]

ALEXANDRA PELOSI: He saw it before anybody did. That morning, he saw it. He kept saying, "They're going to break in." Everyone kind of giggled like, "Oh yeah, kid, come on." It was like childish musings. Paul kept saying, "What if they break in?" And everyone looked at him like, "Kid, this is not a reality television show. This is democracy. No one's going to break the windows of the Capitol."

THE DEMOCRATIC NATIONAL COMMITTEE OFFICES

1:05 P.M.

Kamala Harris was watching coverage of the joint session on TV with her aides when the police and her Secret Service detail rushed in. Another pipe bomb had been found—this one right outside the DNC building. It took seven minutes to evacuate Harris.

THE ELLIPSE

1:10 P.M.

Trump finished his speech, but not without a final call to action.

PRESIDENT DONALD TRUMP: We fight. We fight like hell and if you don't fight like hell, you're not going to have a country anymore. . . . So let's walk down Pennsylvania Avenue.[29]

As he climbed off the stage, Trump was pleased at his rousing speech and ready to head to the Capitol with his supporters. He climbed into the Beast—the blast-proof presidential SUV—and it pulled smoothly out of the Ellipse. But soon his mood turned when the Secret Service told him he could not safely go to the Capitol. According to a staffer who was told about the incident, he became "irate" and lunged for the steering wheel.

PRESIDENT DONALD TRUMP: I am the fucking president, take me up to the Capitol now![30]

They drove the angry president back to the White House. He stormed into the private dining room off the Oval Office, where he immediately turned on FOX News to watch the coverage of the march he'd ordered.[31] He would stay in this dining room for the next few hours.

THE NATIONAL MALL, BETWEEN THE ELLIPSE AND THE CAPITOL
ABOUT 1:10 P.M.

JANUARY 6 REPORT: President Trump had summoned a mob, including armed extremists and conspiracy theorists, to Washington, DC on the day the joint session of Congress was to meet. He then told that same mob to march on the US Capitol and "fight." They clearly got the message.

ADAM GRAY: When Trump stopped speaking, that's when a lot of people came.

BORIS SANCHEZ, *CNN correspondent*: That big crowd started to gravitate toward the Capitol.

BOBBY SCHORNAK, *rioter*: As we were walking, it was really just kind of a sea of people.

DANIEL HERENDEEN, *rioter*: There was people chanting, people with flags, people with banners. The phones kind of stopped working. You know, like being at a big sporting event or something, they just didn't work.[32]

ERIC BARBER, *rioter*: It's hard for me pinpoint exactly when the mood changed, but it was on the march. . . . It was like you could cut it with a knife. It was drastic.[33]

BOBBY SCHORNAK: People were saying all kinds of stupid stuff. I did hear people say, "Hang Mike Pence." I wasn't going to get involved in that one. You know, they were saying other stuff like, "Drag him out," and it was kind of humorous, to be honest, but, you know, it was really just people chanting and saying different stuff.

As the marchers got closer to the already-embattled Capitol build-ing, they passed an ominous sight: a homemade wooden gallows. Around 1 p.m., a baseball hat–wearing rioter had added the final touch: a noose of bright orange rope.[34]

1:12 P.M.

Inside the Capitol building, the joint session began the certification process, calling each state in alphabetical order. As with every session of Congress, Capitol Police were stationed on the Floor.

When Arizona was called—one of the states Trump falsely claimed to have won—Republican lawmakers objected to the certification of the vote. Each body went back to their respective chambers to deliberate the objection. Some of the press hung out in the hallways.

MARK PETERSON, *freelance photojournalist on assignment for the* New York Times: So then I'm sitting there and it's like, it's going to be a waiting game.

LOUIE PALU, *freelance photojournalist on assignment for* National Geographic: I think, well, I'm going to go eat my prosciutto arugula panino now with my San Pellegrino in Dirksen [Senate Office Building].

Meanwhile, inside the chambers, the lawmakers were cut off from the outside world: there are no windows, no TVs, and no radios, and photography is prohibited. Only remotely operated cameras from C-SPAN are allowed to record.

REP. RUBEN GALLEGO (D-AZ): At that point I did not fully grasp what was happening outside. And I don't think any of us really did.[35]

SHANE SMITH, *aide to Speaker Nancy Pelosi*: You're inside the chamber, there are no TVs, there are no radios. I mean, you're not really supposed to be on your phone. We were kind of oblivious to it.[36]

While the lawmakers were unaware of the threat outside their building, people around the country were watching livestreaming videos of the rioters on social media and TV.

MARY MCCORD, *executive director of the Institute for Constitutional Advocacy and Protection at Georgetown University*: As I'm watching it [at home], I'm thinking, *Okay, I'm sure law enforcement has a plan. They've got their own intelligence. We've shared intelligence. I'm sure we're just one of many who shared it.* Even I thought the Capitol would be secure because there'd been enough information that should have triggered enhanced security at the Capitol.

SANDEEP PRASANNA, *congressional staffer*: I was at home and at some point we had a conference call set up with all of the senior staff from the Homeland Security Committee, and we were all just kind of talking and for various periods just sitting all in silence as we were all watching our own TVs at home.

JACOB WARE, *Council on Foreign Relations research fellow*: I was working from home. It was COVID, of course. So working from home and intending to watch the certification of the election and to do so in a way that allowed me to keep an eye on the kind of online forums that I was hiding in—Telegram, 8chan.

CIERRA STEWART, *aide to Sen. Sherrod Brown, working remotely from Dayton, Ohio*: We had just seen a whole summer of Black Lives Matter protests that were peaceful but were met with so much more police presence and pushback and tear gas and rubber bullets. My first thought was, *Where's the police? Who's stopping them? What's going on? Why is there no tear gas?*

CHERYL BOYLAND, *Rosanne Boyland's mother*: [My husband] Bret and I were home [in Georgia] all day. He called [Roseanne] and couldn't get through, and he texted her and said, "Things are getting kind of crazy. Make sure you stay away," or something like that. And she sent back, "We're walking to the Capitol," and sent a picture.

LONNA CAVE, *Rosanne Boyland's older sister:* My boss always watches FOX News, and so I was working, and then I heard [Trump] start amping up the rhetoric and getting people all riled up, and I was like, *Oh, Lord.* And then it got to the point where I was like, *I got to go. I'm not working. This is stressing me out. My sister's up there. I'm bailing.*

WEST FRONT

ABOUT 1:15 P.M.

GARY DZIEKAN: The tension of the crowd was getting higher and higher. The flash-bang grenades were going off around us. Capitol Police had no idea what was going on. A few minutes into that, a civilian runs up to us and goes, "There's a man down in the crowd and they're doing CPR." We say, "No, we've got him in the back." He says, "No, I just came from there. They're doing CPR on them."[37]

DC FEMS RADIO TRANSMISSION: Be advised. We're getting a second call for Independence Avenue SE at US Capitol. And a call taker is supposedly giving CPR instructions.[38]

KEVIN COLE: We were notified that there was a second patient and we had to scramble half of our personnel to go to that cardiac arrest while some of us stayed here with the cardiac arrest that we were working on.[39]

GARY DZIEKAN: So the captain has me and another crew member grab a cot, an AED,* oxygen and just go assess what was going on. So we run with this gentleman through hundreds and hundreds of people.[40]

Sure enough there's another individual down with Capitol Police and a couple other civilians around administering CPR. So we get the AED hooked up. Within a couple minutes of that, [more colleagues] showed up with all their ALS supplies and took over.

---

* Automated external defibrillator

ROCCO GABRIELE, *firefighter paramedic, DC FEMS*: Just getting help to the patient or the patient out to help from their location was extremely challenging.[41]

GLENN HANNA, *firefighter paramedic, DC FEMS*: For the first time in my life, I got to see what a true mob mentality was. It was definitely an experience. I've never seen a group of people that were that worked up and agitated.[42]

RADIO TRANSMISSION: We have another CPR in progress.[43]

ROCCO GABRIELE: We were able to provide some good medicine on scene at which point the police officer started to disperse concussion grenades over top of our heads to kind of push the crowd back. The scene kind of got out of control, became pretty unsafe from that point.[44]

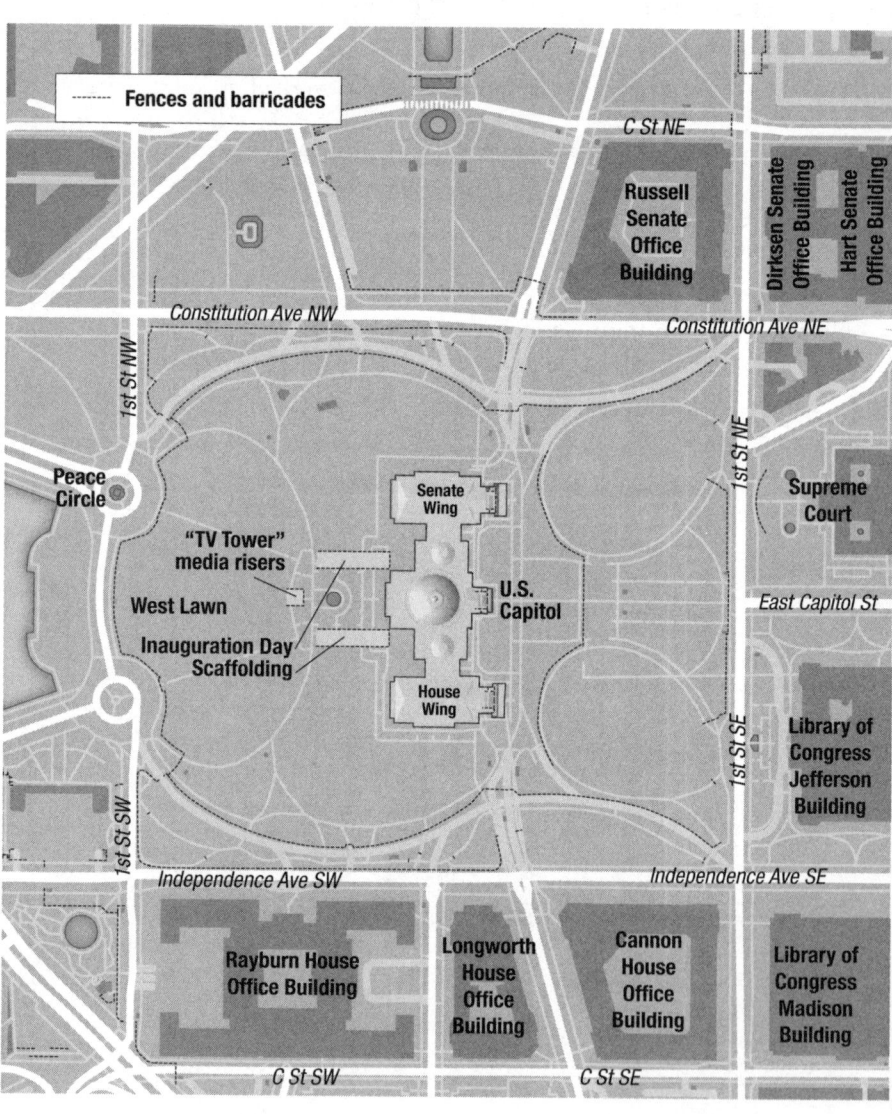

CHAPTER 6

"HAND-TO-HAND BATTLE"

NICK QUESTED, *documentary filmmaker:* What happens next is then [the police] create another line and they try to push everyone back. And then more and more people are coming, more and more people are coming.

JANE, *staff photojournalist for a major mainstream outlet:* It was very much like a classically very old-school battle, two lines coming up against each other with the flags.

ALAN CHIN, *freelance photojournalist on assignment for* Business Insider: I probably was watching this for ten minutes when I spotted a big tower, temporary tower that they had erected for the inauguration that was going to happen in a couple of weeks. And the tower was where they were going to put lights and remote cameras and things like that. And there were a lot of these rioters that climbed onto that tower. But also I could see there were other photographers and journalists up there, and I thought, *You know what? That's a good spot. I'll climb up to that tower.* And I did. I climbed up to the tower. I had a bird's-eye view now of the West Front.

ADAM GRAY, *freelance photojournalist on assignment for the* Daily Mail: I chose to climb up that just to get more of an overview and be able to really see from above what's happening, and also to get out of the spray for a minute because there's just so much. I mean, I was definitely thinking when I was on it, looking at how many people were on the structure, *Is this going to hold?*

And again, I expect them to use tear gas. So thinking if we're up here, we could be above the gas, which might be okay, but also we might be trapped in the gas if it comes up. And I didn't have a gas mask. None of us that day [did] because the violence had always been at night. Every single time it was the same pattern. Daytime: peaceful, big protest. Go back to your hotel, put on your vest, take your gas mask, take your helmet for the night. And yeah, this kind of spiraled so fast.

RON HAVIV, *freelance photojournalist on assignment for the* New Republic: I had brought a gas mask and I brilliantly left it in the car. I said, "Oh, I'll get this later." I was like, "I'm just going to go check out what's going on right now and then I'll go get this stuff later." And I never got back to the car.

NICK QUESTED: I was still like, this is not lethal force. I was like, *Where's the dogs? Where's the water cannons? Where's the CS gas?** There was really an underwhelming response at this point. And this was the point it really needed to happen because there's more and more people coming, more and more people.

At 1:49 p.m., the DC Metropolitan Police Department declared a riot.[1]

Metropolitan Police Department (MPD) officer Michael Fanone had been with the force for almost twenty years. He wasn't scheduled to work until the afternoon, but when he heard on his police radio how dire the situation had become, he headed to the Capitol.

MICHAEL FANONE, *DC Metropolitan Police officer:* Some have asked why we ran to help when we didn't have to. I did that because I simply could not ignore what was happening. Like many other officers, I could not ignore the numerous calls for help coming from the Capitol.[2]

WEST LAWN

Inside the Capitol building, while Congress debated the challenge to the Arizona votes, a group of photojournalists who were covering the joint session started seeing tweets and receiving texts about what was happening outside. They ran to investigate.

---

* One of the most common types of tear gas

LOUIE PALU, *freelance photojournalist on assignment for* National Geographic: You could hear the crowd. It got louder and louder, and you could see chaotic anarchy kind of happening from a distance. And as we got closer, you could see it more and more. So we kept walking up, and it kind of dawned on me like, *Wow, it is kind of an emergency going on here.* And you kind of crest a hill getting over there. And as we crested the hill and I saw down into the West Front, I got goosebumps.

I just felt like, I've been a war photographer for ten years—it hit me like, *Oh my God, I have to do my job. I have to do that thing I do.* And I just knew I had to go down in the crowd where the attack was kind of really unfolding in the middle.

And I thought, *Oh, I know these guys.* Kevlar vests, Kevlar helmets, baseball bats, two-by-fours, flagpoles that are really masking a club or a weapon of some kind. And gas masks—big, big organized guys. A lot of the gloves— you'd see 'em in Afghanistan—gloves with these fiberglass knuckles. Just people who came prepared to fight, not to just protest but prepared to attack.

DAVID BUTOW, *freelance photojournalist:* I have been in many dangerous situations before in my job—not as much as a lot of other people, but some. So it's not an unfamiliar feeling to me, where you're going into something that's going to be kind of hairy, but that you have a job to do. And so I did basically steel myself, sort of where you just crunch your stomach in.

So I just felt that sort of focus and motivation as I was making my way up to the steps, and immediately I'm in the middle of everything.

WEST FRONT

1:50 P.M.

ADAM GRAY: The crowd's just getting bigger and bigger behind them.

The last marchers—those who had stayed at the Ellipse till the end of Trump's speech—were now arriving at the Capitol.

RIOTERS: Whose Capitol? Our Capitol!

STEPHEN VOSS, *freelance photojournalist on assignment for* Politico: I just basically ran the last mile from where I was on the Mall to the Capitol. I was like, *I got to be there for this.* I immediately ran into a friend of mine, David Butow, who's an exceptionally great photographer. And I just looked at him and I was like, "What the hell is this?"

DAVID BUTOW: This sounds a bit hyperbolic, but it is true. Right away, within the first five or ten minutes, I did get a sense that my primary function was photographing this for history—not for a magazine that was going to come out the next week, but it was something much more lasting. I have not had that feeling before for a single event. I never had that feeling like I did.

LOUIE PALU: I put my back up against a tree and I just held the camera. People were putting on gas masks, flash-bangs were going off. There were few police spread out on the front line and they just started retreating.

I've covered probably a hundred protests, very violent protests, even in Europe with hundreds of neo-Nazis and water cannons. I'd never seen police get knocked out like this. I'd never in my life—and I've covered Iraq, war protests, everything. Never, never seen this. And as I was filming, I thought, *Hold the shot and think of the edit. Hold the shot. Don't move it around. Don't start fricking running all over the place.*

I was thinking very technically. I was thinking, *I'm against a tree. No one's paying attention to me. I'm safe. I've been in this before. Make sure you don't hit the mic.* I'm just thinking, *Don't make any mistakes. This is so important.*

And as I moved in, I took my big camera out and this woman pointed at me in such an active way, like, "Antifa photographer, Antifa photographer." And while she's yelling it, there's the screams of eight thousand people around me. And I usually just don't fight or argue with people. I just turn around and I'd go somewhere else. I thought I'd walk away, but she kept pointing at me screaming and people started running toward me, like attackers.

And this really large man who had no shirt on with a beard. And [someone had] a piece of wood with a nail out of it. I remember distinctly the nail. He ran up and kind of blocked me. And then I tried turning, and before I knew it, there were four guys around me and I was encircled. And I put my hands in the air and I thought I said, "I have to deescalate this."

I explained it slowly. I said, "I work for *National Geographic,*" and the guy with the beard screams, shrieking, angry, "Prove it!" And they're all pretty serious. Next thing is going to be they hit me. And I said, "I have a press pass in my pocket. Is it okay if I take it out of my pocket?" And I apologized.

I thought, *Okay, make them feel like they're in power. Deescalate the situation.* I said, "I'm just taking photos, I apologize." So whenever I'm in a riot, I never wear [my press pass] on my neck so I don't get choked. I had it kind of tied up between my belt loop and I take it out and they lean in to make sure they read it clearly. And they're like, "Oh, zebras and giraffes, *National Geographic?*" I said, "Yeah." And they're like, "Oh, okay." And they kind of relaxed their stance. They said, "Okay." I said, "I'm really sorry." I said, "I'm going to leave now. Is it okay if I leave?" And they're like, "Yes." So I kind of backed out.

That lower area was too hot. It was too hot for me. And so I moved back up the West Front grass.

NICK QUESTED: Now the police are being pushed back. We got right to the corner where you can go up the stairs to the Upper West Terrace, and that's where they just dropped a whole bunch of tear gas on us. And I got mashed up then because I didn't know which way to go out. So I went the wrong way. And I'm just sucking tear gas, so I get out. I'm all sick. So they're pouring water in my eyes to get the tear gas out. And I'm being a little sick and I lost all temporal sense and spatial sense for ten or fifteen minutes, because when you get tear-gassed, you're trying to open your eyes and you can't, they burn. You're trying to open them and you can't and you're just you, you're a sitting duck, literally.

And then we climbed up onto the right-hand scaffolding.

To assist workers building the temporary inauguration stage, scaffolding had been erected around the construction site. It was closed to the public, but that didn't stop the insurrectionists.

DAVID BUTOW: And so because of the inauguration, you had all that scaffolding that was being erected basically on either side of the steps. So just the volume of people then making their way up the steps wasn't enough room for everybody to walk up the steps. So there were people who were climbing over the scaffolding. There were people who were making their way along the—I mean, I guess you'd call it the railing. Just the volume of people scrambling up in every possible inch that you could get up.

STEPHEN VOSS: Any other day, you get anywhere near those, and the Capitol Police is going to be on you in a second. But there were hundreds of people climbing up them. And it was just wild. I mean, people were twenty, thirty feet in the air just holding on. If they had fallen, they would've been in a lot of trouble.

RON HAVIV: And then they started to climb up the scaffolding. Instead of trying to go up the wall, which they did on other parts of the Capitol, they used the scaffolding to climb up so they could get to the main platform on that side, which I did as well.

So I was climbing up the scaffolding, photographing, and at this point, again, conscious of the several things are now in play in terms of danger. One is just a simple sort of anti-media feeling that exists for these people. Second is, I have no idea if this whole thing is going to collapse and we're all going to die. I don't think it was built for three hundred people to climb on it simultaneously, swinging back and forth. So I think that was definitely an unknown. And then third, which was prevailing throughout the thing, was COVID.

As rioters climbed the scaffolding on the sides of the terraces, the police were still trying to hold another line on the Upper West Terrace. They called for reinforcements.

EVY MAGES, Washingtonian *photojournalist*: It just was amazing to just see a couple of officers facing all these people. And they were negotiating with them! I didn't understand why they were negotiating. In my experience in all the previous protests, especially during Black Lives Matter, protests were met with great force, and that was a clear contrast.

Daniel Hodges was one of the reinforcements called toward the building.

DANIEL HODGES, *DC Metropolitan Police officer*: We formed up into two lines and started making our way toward the West Terrace on sort of a stone pathway that leads up to the building, which meant getting through the crowd. The crowd was initially less dense, the further out from the Capitol, they were more content to just shout insults at us, calling us traitors, oath breakers, telling us to remember our oaths, telling us to be on the right side of history.

RIOTER, SARCASTICALLY: Here come the boys in blue! So brave![3]

RIOTERS: Traitors![4]

2 P.M.

OFFICER HODGES: And then as we got closer, they became more dense and more aggressive until eventually they physically attacked us. And since we were moving in two columns, they sort of cut us off in the middle. So the people that were at the head of the column [including police leadership] kept moving forward to the West Terrace, and the people at the rear couldn't go forward. I was at the rear.

It's the usual punching, kicking, trying to steal equipment. We repelled them and then they surrounded us. I tried to push through the crowd to forge a path for the rest of my platoon to follow, and I looked back and I saw that they were still being assaulted by these members of the mob. So I start pulling 'em off my colleagues by their backpacks until eventually then someone tried to steal my baton.

RIOTER, TO HODGES: You're on the wrong team![5]

RIOTER: You will die on your knees![6]

OFFICER HODGES: We wrestled for control over it. We went to the ground. He kicked me in the chest where I was able to retain my weapon, but I fell to the ground on all fours. The medical mask I was wearing at the time got pulled up over my eyes, so I was on all fours surrounded by a mob, and I couldn't see. So I thought at that point I was just going to get torn apart. Thankfully, my colleagues got themselves free and had my back, and I was able to stand up.[7]

One of the reasons why I didn't want to start using lethal force [was] because I thought that that might've been a signal to whoever was in control of those bombs to set them off.[8] I was wondering, *How many more bombs are there? What's the trigger? Is it going to be a cell phone? Is it on a timer? How many guns are there in this crowd? If we start firing, is that the signal to them to set off the explosives, however many there are in the city? Is that the signal for them to break out their firearms and shoot back?* So, that's the reason why I didn't shoot anyone. [9]

I got back up. Everyone else was free, so I again tried to forge a path through the crowd to get to the West Terrace. This time I was successful and we made our way to the West Terrace.[10]

DAVID BUTOW: I found there was a metal railing along one of these steps, and I sort of positioned myself next to it. So I felt like at least I'm blocked just from one side. So the railing was to my right. I thought, *If there's a stampede down this thing, shit tons of people are going to get knocked over and stampeded on, and I don't want to be one of those people, so I'm just going to position myself using that railing as kind of a barrier.* Then, yeah, so I was sort of working in and out there. I was also working for a period right next to the photographer, Jane.

JANE: I was utilizing the railings that were still attached to the ground to try and protect myself from getting crushed. This is the battle, right? They're just full-on fighting with each other, falling down the stairs. Spraying back and forth. I've just never seen this before between police and protesters. Just the fact that it just kept going and going. And all that was happening is [the police] were pepper spraying them and then backing up. Pepper spraying and backing up. Pushing, pushing. Just trying to hold this line and it just wasn't working.

DAVID BUTOW: There was a point when I was on the west steps that I just sort of put my camera down for a few seconds or however long it was, and I just looked at the whole thing. I just want to take this in just as a human being, actually just see this. I cannot fucking believe it. And I remember at one point looking over at Jane, and she was just wide-eyed looking at this, and I'm sure I looked exactly the same way, just sort of slack-jawed.

I felt like I was standing there watching a scene that would have been painted in some kind of American history painting that I would've seen when I was a kid, something from the Civil War. Or you go to museums in Europe and you see these enormous paintings of battle scenes, hand-to-hand battle, which is very different from the kind of battles in modern warfare where often people don't even see the enemy. But in this case, it felt medieval. It really did.

JANE: There's moments at events, at protests and stuff where the energy is shifting and you can feel things like kind of getting out of control. And that's kind of the feeling here is that this is clearly, *The police are not handling this. They're going to get through.*

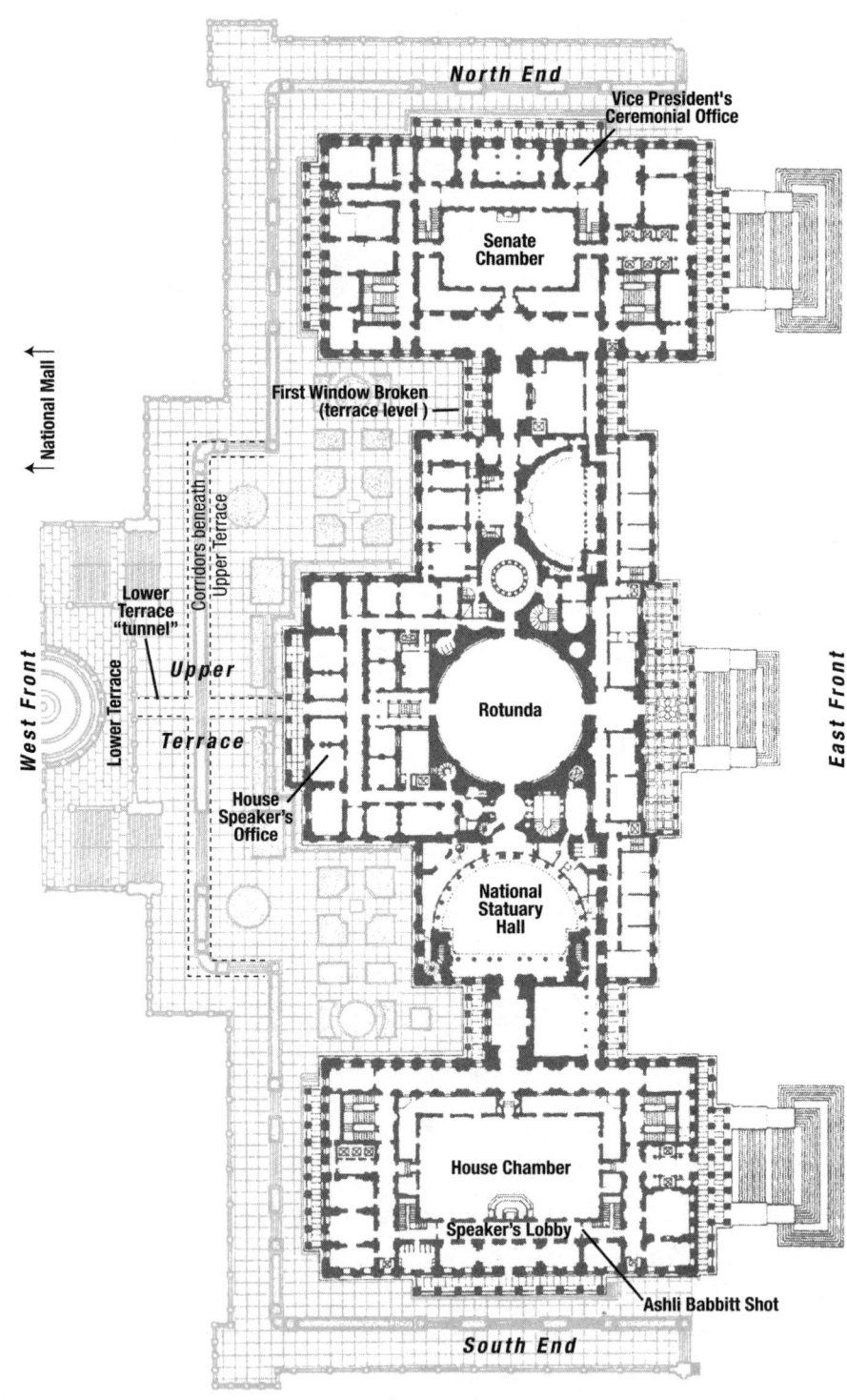

North End

Vice President's
Ceremonial Office

Senate
Chamber

National Mall

First Window Broken
(terrace level)

Corridors beneath
Upper Terrace

Lower
Terrace
"tunnel"

Upper

Lower Terrace

Terrace

West Front

East Front

Rotunda

House
Speaker's
Office

National
Statuary
Hall

House Chamber

Speaker's Lobby

Ashli Babbitt Shot

South End

CHAPTER 7

"THEN ALL OF A SUDDEN WE WERE INSIDE"

2:10 P.M.

DANIEL HODGES, *DC Metropolitan Police officer*: Terrorists were scaling the scaffolding on both our sides, the tower that was in front of us, and attempting to breach the waist-high metal fencing that was the only barrier we had, aside from ourselves. To my perpetual confusion, I saw the Thin Blue Line flag, a symbol of support for law enforcement, more than once being carried by the terrorists as they ignored our commands and continued to assault us. The terrorists alternated between attempting to break our defenses and shouting at or attempting to convert us.[1]

RIOTERS: We outnumber you, join us.[2]

RIOTER: Do not attack us! We are not Black Lives Matter![3]

RIOTER: This is the time to choose what side of history to be on![4]

RIOTER: Show solidarity with "we the people" or we're going to run over you! Do you think your little pea-shooter guns are going to stop this crowd? No! We're going in that building![5]

The Proud Boys were still at the front of the mob. Having broken through the barriers and the police line, they now finally reached the Capitol building. Only wooden doors and glass windows stood between them and the interior.

DOMINIC PEZZOLA, PROUD BOY, TO CAPITOL POLICE OFFICERS AT THE TOP OF THE OUTSIDE STAIRWAY: We ain't stopping! We ain't fucking stopping! Fuck you![6]

2:11 P.M.

The Proud Boys heaved a stolen police riot shield against a window leading into the Senate side of the building.

PROUD BOYS: One! Two! Three!

The glass broke. The rioters punched a big hole through the window, allowing the first rioter to climb inside. More followed, including Pezzola.

RIOTER: This is our fucking house!

DOMINIC PEZZOLA: Go, go, go![7]

The Capitol was officially breached. Photojournalists Ron Haviv and Louie Palu followed the rioters inside.

LOUIE PALU, *freelance photojournalist on assignment for* National Geographic: People are jumping through the window. Because of the architecture, it looked like a medieval siege of a castle. It was really strange. People were going in and people were yelling all kinds of stuff like "fight for Trump" or just all those kinds of lines.

RON HAVIV, *freelance photojournalist on assignment for the* New Republic: The question was, Do I want to follow them in and take that risk or not? To be honest with you, I had been in Moscow in 1993 when there was a coup against [Boris] Yeltsin by the Communist Party and they did something similar and they broke into their White House and I didn't go inside—I stayed outside with the army and basically photographed the assault on the Capitol. And I said to myself, *This time, I'm going to go in. I want to see what it's like on the inside.* I was also thinking, *Where are the police? What are their orders? Are they afraid? What's going to happen? Are they going to open fire?* It would make perfect sense to defend the building: you barricade yourself inside and they get close, [then] you just open fire.

My end conclusion was that I think that they're going to just kind of pull back and let them in and not start killing people, especially unarmed people on the steps of the Capitol.

So a few guys went through the window and they came around and opened another door, and then I went into the crowd through that door. Then all of a sudden we were inside.

INSIDE THE CAPITOL BUILDING

2:13 P.M.

Most of the lawmakers and staff were still in the chambers, focused on certifying the election. They were unaware that the building had been breached. For many, the first indication of a serious threat was when the Secret Service whisked Vice President Pence off the Senate Floor.

THE *WASHINGTON POST*: At 2:13 p.m., Pence was hastily removed by his Secret Service detail and rushed through a side door to his ceremonial office nearby, along with his family members. The Pences came harrowingly close to danger, as rioters chanting his name charged up the stairs to that precise landing about a minute later.[8]

IGOR BOBIC, HuffPost *reporter, at his desk in the Press Gallery*: I was kind of engrossed and watching C-SPAN, and all of a sudden I hear a colleague of mine, Paul Kane, who works at the *Washington Post*, veteran reporter, comes running behind me, screaming, "Pence just left the chair! Pence just left the chair!" And in congressional parlance, anytime the vice president is taken out abruptly either by somebody or it's some kind of an unforeseen event, that means there's a security reason.

So as soon as I heard that and I heard my colleague Paul Kane, who has been there for much longer than I have, kind of freaking out, I was like, *Oh shit, something's going down.* So I immediately left my desk and followed him.

In a nearby hallway, officer Eugene Goodman, a fifteen-year veteran of the Capitol Police force, was trying to make sense of his radio traffic. He'd already been fighting outside, gotten tear-gassed, and thrown up multiple times, at which point he moved inside.

EUGENE GOODMAN, *US Capitol Police officer:* The radio was haywire. I could just hear officers trying to come across and I guess give their positions or individual battles that they happened to be dealing with around the Capitol. Not too many people could get across the radio. It was just haywire.[9]

But at 2:13 p.m., he was able to make out one radio call in particular.

OFFICER GOODMAN: Somebody said something to the effect of, "The Senate [side wing] has been breached," or "breach to the Senate [side wing]," over the radio.[10]

Goodman sprinted toward the Senate side hallway. As he ran, he passed Senator Mitt Romney, who happened to have just left the Senate Floor to go to his office.

THE *WASHINGTON POST*: Goodman motioned for Romney to turn around to avoid rioters. "There are people not far. You'll be safer inside," Goodman told Romney.[11]

Romney turned around and ran back to the Senate Floor, where there was more protection. As the Senate gaveled into recess because of the threat, Goodman kept running toward the sound of the rioters, who he could hear just downstairs.

OFFICER GOODMAN: And I round the corner. I passed another leadership office and I see an officer and a few staffers and doorkeepers.[12] I said, "I think you guys might need to get inside. I think they're in here." And then I go downstairs. This would be the East Grand Staircase.[13]

OFFICER GOODMAN: So when I went down there and I get confronted by people, I'm like, *Oh hell, they're actually in the building.* I honestly didn't know that they were that far in the building. And then they lock eyes on me right away and then just like that, I was in it.[14]

Reporter Igor Bobic also heard the commotion and followed the noise.

IGOR BOBIC: I'm running down the stairs, I know something's going on. I don't know who it is or what happened. When I got down to the first floor, it was Goodman facing off against the mob.

Although Bobic didn't know Goodman personally, he recognized him from their years working the same halls.

One floor up, Mark Peterson, freelance photojournalist on assignment for the *New York Times*, also followed the noise.

MARK PETERSON: I suddenly hear this banging, this huge banging, the floor below me, and I go down one floor and there's Officer Goodman trying to hold the first breach back. There's dozens of 'em at this point. And at that point, I see two photographers I know very well. Ron Haviv is one of them. And so I just said, "Hey." It's almost surreal. Just, "Hey, nice to see you," kind of thing.

OFFICE GOODMAN: I approach [a rioter] and I tell him: "You need to get out. You need to leave."[15]

KEVIN SEEFRIED, RIOTER, ANGRILY SCREAMING: Fuck you. I'm not leaving. Where are the members at? Where are they counting the votes at?[16]

OFFICER GOODMAN: The mass is slowly starting to advance on me.[17]

KEVIN SEEFRIED: We're taking back our country. We're thousands. You're just one. You're by yourself.[18]

OFFICER GOODMAN: The guy that's directly in front of me, he's advancing the most. I'm telling him to back up. "You need to leave." I even pushed him a few times. And he sort of is being sly, like he's inching closer. That was aggressive to me.[19]

He couldn't hold them back any longer. The rioters were chasing him up the stairs.

RON HAVIV: Goodman takes out a baton and tries to hit the guy, and we're basically all kind of moving up the stairs until we get to this hallway.

| **Bobic filmed the scene on his phone.**

IGOR BOBIC: I was backing up, backwards up the steps, trying to keep [Goodman] in frame and making sure that he somehow didn't bump into me.

At the top of the stairs were two hallways. The hall to Goodman's left led to the packed Senate chamber. To Goodman's right, around the corner, unbeknownst to the rioters, were police reinforcements— more of his fellow officers.

Goodman made a split-second decision. He leaned forward, pushed the lead rioter, and ran to the right. The lead rioter and the mob chased after him.

RON HAVIV: We encounter other Capitol Police, and then we also encounter the photographers who were there documenting the vote. The hallway is filled with paintings of various politicians from the 1800s, and it was a very kind of congressional hallway kind of thing.

OFFICER GOODMAN: The group began to come in, and they're still shouting stuff at us: "This is our America." "We're here to stop the steal." "You guys need to be on our side." "Where are they counting the votes at?" The same rhetoric that I confronted when I was down at the base of the stairs. They're saying the same things.[20]

RIOTER: What's the point of stopping us at this point?

CAPITOL POLICE OFFICER: This is as far as it's going to go.

RIOTER: Go arrest, go arrest the vice president.[21]

RIOTER, YELLING: We're ready for war. We're ready to take down this place. We're ready to take down this building. We're ready to take over. We're ready for war.[22]

OFFICER GOODMAN: They filled up the [hallway], but they don't come any further than the line we established.[23]

MARK PETERSON: They had no idea that they were right at the Senate door and that they could have probably overpowered that group of police officers and gone into the Senate chambers. Or else it would have been a pretty equal fight.

RON HAVIV: And then eventually, I think the police get word that everybody's been evacuated [from the Senate]. So I think that they basically just say, "Okay, you guys just should leave because there's nobody here to talk to."

And at that point everybody kind of disperses into different directions. I went off trying to find other situations.

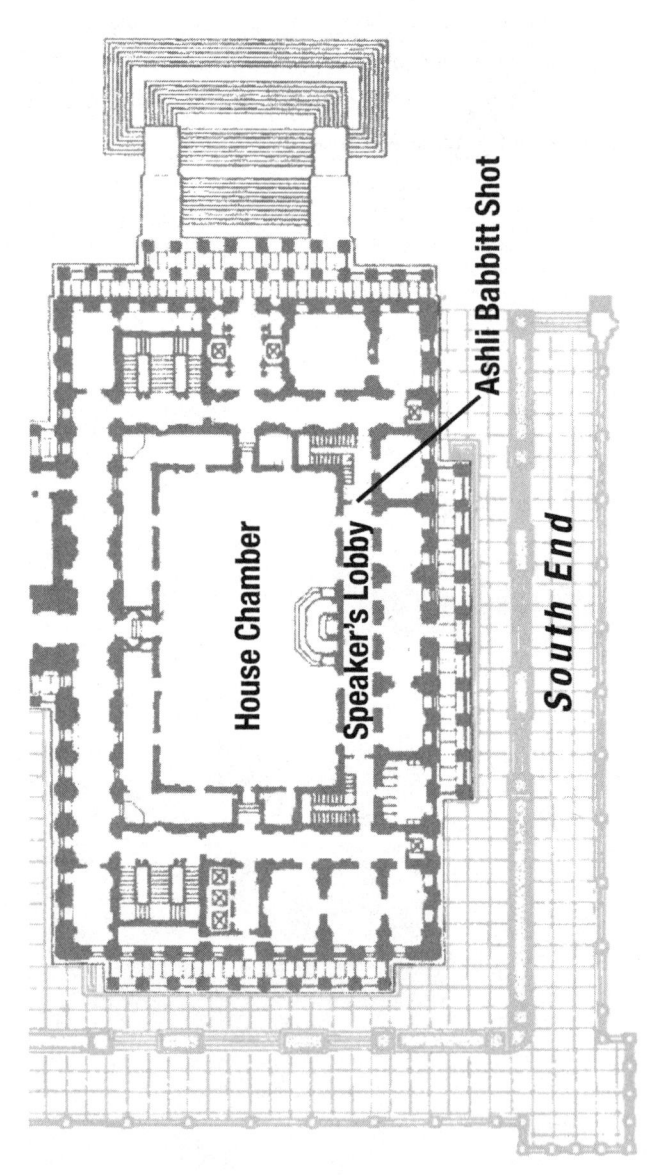

House Chamber

Speaker's Lobby

Ashli Babbitt Shot

South End

"IF THEY STOP THE PROCEEDINGS, THEY WILL HAVE SUCCEEDED IN STOPPING THE VALIDATION OF THE PRESIDENT OF THE UNITED STATES"

FLOOR OF THE HOUSE OF REPRESENTATIVES

2:15 P.M.

On the other side of the Capitol building, the lawmakers in the House chamber didn't know that rioters were roaming the halls. They were still debating the electoral challenge to the Arizona vote. Speaker Nancy Pelosi recognized Republican Rep. Paul Gosar to speak. He pulled his American flag mask down below his nose and mouth.

FRANK LOCKWOOD, Arkansas Democrat-Gazette *reporter*: He was saying we had thirty thousand illegal immigrants vote in Arizona. And of course there's zero credible evidence for that, but he's making these claims and I'm thinking, *We got a mob in the hallway and he clearly has no idea what's going on outside those doors.*[1]

He seemed completely unaware that the perimeter had been breached and that people were streaming in.

REP. ERIC SWALWELL: I think we just had kind of a false sense of security. You keep getting all these texts from friends all over the country who you'd not heard from in a long time saying, *Be safe.* And you're like, *No, no, we're fine. We're going to be fine.* And then it shifted from, *We're going to be fine* to, *All of the barriers and security that you thought was going to protect you was being breached.* And so it was just kind of this escalating sense of disbelief. How is this happening?

MICHELLE, *congressional staffer:* At this point there started to be more just kind of background noise in the chamber, like more security on the Floor than is normal, and the Speaker was still presiding. Her security detail kind of moved in a little bit more than they normally would.[2]

ALEXANDRA PELOSI, *Speaker Nancy Pelosi's daughter:* We were in the Speaker's office, we were watching the proceedings on television, and the security came and got us and said, "We have to go." Then we heard the mob. We heard them.

AIDE: We're in lockdown.[3]

Speaker Pelosi's security detail rushed her daughter and grandson into the Speaker's Lobby, a long, narrow room off the House Floor.

ALEXANDRA PELOSI: They told us to stand there while they got her.

Alexandra texted her husband.

TEXT FROM ALEXANDRA PELOSI TO HER HUSBAND, MICHIEL VOS, 2:16 P.M.: It's getting weird. We're being evacuated.

Inside the chamber, Speaker Pelosi's security team whisked her away while Representative Gosar was still speaking.

ALEXANDRA PELOSI: My mother was up at the podium and they grabbed her and they didn't even let her take her cell phone. She thought that they were just taking her to tell her something. She did not know that they'd broken into the building. So she was not happy that they were making her leave the ship. They were taking her out against her will, and she was saying, "I have to go get my stuff." She left everything behind. She didn't even get to take her cell phone with her.

Of course, the documentary filmmaker in me, when they were evacuating us, I asked if I could stay and the security said, "No, you have to come with us." And I was bummed. I wanted to stay behind and film because that was an opportunity of a lifetime, but I don't know how that would've gone over if they figured out my last name.

The second- and third-highest-ranked House members after Pelosi, Majority Rep. Steny Hoyer and Majority Whip Rep. Jim Clyburn, were also evacuated. The rest of the members were left in the chamber.

REP. ERIC SWALWELL: There was also a lot of gallows humor. A lot of us were just kind of joking like, "Well, now we know where we are in the pecking order of continuity of government. Now we know where we stand. We're going to stay here and die in this chamber." So there's a lot of that.

Representative Gosar looked up from his speech, seemingly annoyed by the commotion around him.

REP. PAUL GOSAR (R-AZ): Madam Spea—.

He seemed to notice for the first time that Pelosi was gone. Rep. Jim McGovern had taken her place on the dais.

REP. PAUL GOSAR: Can I have order in the chamber?

Representative McGovern pounded the gavel twice.

REP. JIM MCGOVERN (D-MA): The House will be in order. The House will be in order. Okay—

REP. DEAN PHILLIPS (D-MN), YELLING AT REP. PAUL GOSAR: This is because of YOU!

REP. JIM MCGOVERN: The House will be in order. The House will be in order. [Commotion.] Members will take their seats. The House will be in order. [Commotion.] Okay, if we can get order, we can resume.

Someone handed McGovern a piece of paper. He reads, then speaks into the mic.

REP. JIM MCGOVERN: Without objection, the chair declares the House in recess.

He gaveled. The C-SPAN feed cut out. The representatives began to hear the shouts of rioters. They were getting closer and closer.

THE *WASHINGTON POST*: Some members of Congress rapidly lost faith about their security when they saw Capitol Police officers stationed with them anxiously trying to determine who had the keys to lock the doors from the inside.[4]

The doors are usually never locked from the inside. It took a moment to find the key.

SHANE SMITH, *aide to Speaker Nancy Pelosi*: It's a sound that will stick with me. The clicking of those doors locking.[5]

MICHELLE: I've never seen the doors be locked before.

2:19 P.M.

Capitol Police sent an alert email to everyone working on the Capitol campus.

US CAPITOL POLICE ALERTS: Capitol staff: Due to a security threat inside the building, immediately move inside your office or the nearest office . . . close, lock and stay away from external doors and windows . . . find a place to hide or seek cover . . . remain quiet.

OLIVIA BEAVERS, *Politico congressional reporter*: Because of COVID, members [of Congress] were in the gallery as well as reporters and some staff who had gone to go watch.

ANDREW HARNIK, *Associated Press photojournalist*: The scene below us on the House Floor was tense.[6]

OLIVIA BEAVERS: Members were first being told to take cover, because their seats would be bulletproof, and so they could hold up their seats.

REP. ERIC SWALWELL: At two o'clock, my wife texted me and said, "Are you on the Floor?" Because she's watching the coverage. And I said, "Yes, they apparently have bombs," because one of the cops [stationed on the Floor] said that, at the podium, that they may have explosive devices. And then I said, "I love you and the babies. Please hug them for me." And then she lost it. She's like, "Don't say that." And I don't know—what do you say? We just didn't know what was on the other side of the doors. You could just hear it. I regret that I didn't even pick up the phone and call her, but it was just so—she would have heard the announcements and people scrambling to put gas masks on. And she's like, "You don't have to tell me you love me. I know. You don't have to do that." But other members were doing that. One member called her husband and told him where the will is.[7]

EAST FRONT

2:15 P.M.

The rioters who were still outside were overflowing from the West Front to the East Front.

ADAM GRAY, *freelance photojournalist on assignment for the* Daily Mail: They're all on the steps on the east side, all the way up to the door. They haven't breached the door.

Photojournalist Jason Andrew followed the flow of rioters as they went around the north end of the building.

JASON ANDREW, *freelance photojournalist on assignment for the* New York Times: There was a family [of Trump supporters] and there was a little girl that looked like my daughter's age, four. And she's just sitting there shaking and she's drinking bottles. And I just went up and I was like, "You need to get the fuck out of here. You have no business being here." I'm screaming at these people because at this point I'm pissed as a parent—I'm like, how do you bring your children into this? And I remember the [older] kid going, "But they've overtaken the Capitol. They're climbing the walls." I look and everybody is up on the walls and everybody starts climbing and they're all climbing this wall.

ALEX MARQUARDT, *CNN correspondent:* You've got these large stones [on the facade] that have pretty deep indents so people could climb it like a ladder. And I think there were around a dozen—if not more—people climbing up onto that outside area, the promenade around the Capitol and I'm thinking, *Oh my God, people are actually scaling the walls to get inside.*

STEPHEN VOSS, *freelance photojournalist on assignment for* Politico: If you know the Capitol complex at all, it's kind of absurd because if you walk another fifty feet, there's stairs that get you to the same place. But it's just this wild scene where people are like, "We're going to scale the Capitol!"

JASON ANDREW: They start climbing, and I remember making pictures and I'm kind of trying to give this overview. I just keep thinking, I'm like, *How big is this going to be?* Everybody's climbing. I just kept thinking about my daughter and my wife and what the fuck am I doing here and why am I standing here?

And sometime between, I don't know, sometime between 2:14 and 2:15, I remember standing there and I'm just shaking and I'm kind of watching everything happen. I'm shaking. And Michael [Chavez Robinson, of the *Washington Post*] comes up and he puts his hand on my shoulder and he is like, "Are you okay?" And I just said, "Yeah, yeah, I'm good. I'm good." No, I was fucked. Are you kidding me? Not at all. I was just fucking scared. I was just absolutely scared. I've never been on a shoot where I was literally shaking and could not get my shit together.

I think it was a moment where I'm like, I have a kid. I have a kid on the way.

And if this was the BLM protests that I had been covering, I'm looking to see where I'm going to hide because everybody would be shooting right now. In my view, at that time, if this was the BLM protest and all of these young people of color were climbing the Capitol walls, they would've shot them all. And that's all I kept thinking. So I kept looking up going, *Why are the police not shooting these people? Why are they letting them climb these walls?* I just could not understand it.

And so I was like, *We have to get closer.* And I just kept moving closer and closer and closer. Fuck man, I was so close.

ADAM GRAY: Then I get my way to the door and it's evident they're trying to get in this door, like the east entrance. They're right up against the door. And the door, it's been smashed. They're trying to get it open. They keep trying to open it and the police are trying to pull it shut.

These are the first people that would be going in on the east side. They've now got the door open. People are getting inside.

I just walked through the door. We go in with them. I've never been in the US Capitol before. I've got absolutely zero idea what's inside. So I'm following, I'm going to see what's going to happen.

And then they go into Statutory Hall and the red ropes, gold stands and people actually kind of walked through them. It was really surreal. It kind of felt like people were almost on a field trip.

WEST SIDE OF THE CAPITOL

2:23 P.M.

Even as some rioters were entering the Capitol at the East Front, others at the west side were still outside, trying to fight their way through the police barricade line. With cell phone signals still mostly down due to the size of the crowd, rioters were largely unaware that other areas had already been breached.

BOBBY SCHORNAK, *rioter:* And then it just kind of devolved into a chaos, really. You know, there was one point where there was a line of people walking out that were all sick, basically, from the pepper spray and tear gas or whatever else was going on.[8]

CAROLINE EDWARDS, *US Capitol Police officer, on the police barricade line:* At one point, I ended up on the south side of the West Front where I was on the line with Officer Sicknick, and we—we were holding that line for a while. There were—you know, there were people who—the chants were the same, like, "Bark for me, Nancy Pelosi's dogs." One guy tried to kiss me, which is really gross.[9]

One rioter pulled out some kind of chemical spray and unleashed it in the face of one officer at point-blank range. It was Officer Brian Sicknick.

OFFICER EDWARDS: I saw movement out of the corner of my eye, and I turned, and I saw Officer Sicknick, and his face—I could tell he had been sprayed with something, and his face was like white. It was pale. And, you know, if any of us here gets sprayed with something, our faces turn beet red. Like, that's usually the reaction. So I can remember alarm bells going off. I was like, *What's wrong with Sicknick?* Because if you looked around, everybody was red faced, but he was pale. And I didn't like that, so I turned towards the crowd to see who sprayed him, what he had gotten sprayed with, and that's when I got a direct hit in the eyes with chemical spray.

And it turns out it was the same chemical spray that he got hit with. It was just pain unimaginable. I couldn't even begin to open my eyes. And so I was stumbling around a bit. Some officers got me to the middle of the West Front, like they got me off of that section.[10]

| **Officer Sicknick had his eyes washed out.**

OFFICER EDWARDS: They had begun to kind of get it out of my eyes a little bit, but that's when I got hit with tear gas. So the combination of the chemicals made my throat immediately close. I couldn't take a breath at all. That was one of a few times that day where I was like, *Yeah, this is probably like where I'm not going to make it.*

But thankfully, there was an officer who was up there with oxygen. They took off my vest and my gun belt, started giving me oxygen, and I started breathing normally.[11]

| **Meanwhile, at the other breach points, more rioters entered the building.**

DANIEL HERENDEEN, *rioter:* Me and Bobby [Schornak] got separated. I looked for Bobby basically at the foot of the steps for a while and then walked up the steps. I mean, he had a red hat on, I kept thinking I'd see him, so I walked this way, walked that way. And then I was at the door of the Capitol. The windows were broke, but the doors were wide open. People were just walking right in. There wasn't anyone stopping them, telling them not to come in or anything. I seen the glass broken, took video, looked in, and then I walked in. That was my mistake right there is walking in. It was kind of like a car crash, you want to see it but you don't want to get in it. And I got in it.[12]

| **Nearby, Schornak also entered the building.**

BOBBY SCHORNAK: Somebody was, like, "Hey, they're going in the Capitol," and for some reason, I decided that was a good idea. I'd never been to the actual Capitol building before.[13]

| **Meanwhile, security was still hustling Speaker Pelosi and her family away from the House Floor. They soon determined a need to**

leave the building and the area altogether. But they could not just leave through the Capitol building; every door led toward the mob. Instead, they headed underground to escape through the network of tunnels connecting the Capitol building to the other congressional office buildings nearby. Pelosi's daughter, Alexandra, the documentarian, recorded their escape.

ALEXANDRA PELOSI, *Speaker Nancy Pelosi's daughter*: When we were evacuating, we were going through the tunnels of the Capitol and then through the House office buildings. Over and under and through the tunnels. And they were saying to us, "They may be coming." Security were worried that they were going to come at us from the other way. They were afraid they could have gassed the hallways too.

As Alexandra recorded, her mother was still upset about being evacuated.

SPEAKER NANCY PELOSI (D-CA): If they stop the proceedings, they will have succeeded in stopping the validation of the president of the United States.[14] If they stop the proceedings, we will have totally failed.[15]

ALEXANDRA PELOSI: So she kept saying she was mad at her own security for removing her from the building. She was not happy.

Meanwhile, the rest of Pelosi's staff was hiding under a conference table in a locked meeting room within their suite of offices.

LEAH HAN, *aide to Speaker Nancy Pelosi*: Everyone just held their breath. It was just silent.[16]

They could hear rioters entering the outer office, shouting and turning over tables.

RIOTERS, TAUNTING: Nancy! Nancy![17]

RIOTER: Do you see Nancy Pelosi? Where the fuck is Nancy?[18]

RIOTER: Where the fuck are the traitors? Drag them out by their fucking hair.[19]

| **A rioter picked up a random phone and held it to his ear.**[20]

RIOTER: Can I speak to Pelosi? Yeah, we're coming, bitch. Oh, Mike Pence? We're coming for you too, fucking traitor.[21]

LEAH HAN: I was thinking, *If they find us, are they going to keep us hostage? Are they going to torture us? Am I going to get raped?*[22]

| **Then, they got closer. The rioters started banging on the locked door of the conference room. A staffer recorded a cell-phone video of the moment.** [23]

VOICE OF PELOSI STAFFER, WHISPERING ON THE VIDEO RECORDING: We need Capitol Police. . . . They're pounding on doors trying to find her.[24]

LEAH HAN: I thought I was going to die. I didn't think I was going to go home that day.[25]

| **But the lock held, and the rioters moved on.**

| **Meanwhile, Vice President Pence and his team were sheltering in a ceremonial office. They were still extremely close to the rioters.**

WHITE HOUSE SECURITY OFFICIAL, *listening to their radio from the White House*: The members of the VP detail at this time were starting to fear for their own lives. There were a lot of—there was a lot of yelling, a lot of very personal calls over the radio, so it was disturbing. I don't like talking about it. But there were calls to say goodbye to family members.[26]

MESSAGE SENT IN THE NATIONAL SECURITY COUNCIL CHAT: [Secret] Service at the Capitol does not sound good right now[27]

WHITE HOUSE SECURITY OFFICIAL: They're running out of options, and they're getting nervous. It sounds like that we came very close to either Service having to use lethal options or worse. At that point, I don't know. Is the VP compromised? Is the detail—like, I don't know.[28]

| **In the midst of this panic, President Trump was taunting Pence via Twitter.**

DONALD TRUMP VIA TWITTER, 2:24 P.M.: Mike Pence didn't have the
courage to do what should have been done to protect our Country
and our Constitution, giving States a chance to certify a
corrected set of facts, not the fraudulent or inaccurate ones
which they were asked to previously certify. USA demands the
truth![29]

2:25 P.M.

Secret Service agents hustled the vice president down a back stairwell. Just feet away but out of view, rioters were chanting.

JANUARY 6 REPORT: At 2:25 p.m., the Secret Service rushed the
Vice President, his family, and his senior staff down a flight
of stairs, through a series of hallways and tunnels to a secure
location . . . The angry mob had come within 40 feet of the Vice
President as he was evacuated.

THE *WASHINGTON POST*: The vice president and his family and
aides were led on a safe path down a staircase to a secured
subterranean area that rioters couldn't reach. Pence's armored
limousine was parked there.[30]

JANUARY 6 REPORT: Staff hurried into the waiting vehicles.

THE *WASHINGTON POST*: [Tim] Giebels [head of Pence's protection
detail] asked him to get inside.[31]

JANUARY 6 REPORT: But the Vice President refused to get in
the car.

VICE PRESIDENT PENCE: I'm not getting in the car, Tim. I trust you,
Tim, but you're not driving the car. If I get in that vehicle, you
guys are taking off. I'm not getting in the car.[32]

GREG JACOB, *counsel to the vice president*: He was determined that unless there
was imminent danger to bodily safety that he was not going to abandon the
Capitol and let the rioters have a victory of having made the vice president
flee or made it difficult to restart the process later that day.[33]

JANUARY 6 REPORT: President Trump never called to check on Vice President Pence's safety, so Marc Short called [Trump's chief of staff] Mark Meadows to tell him they were safe and secure. It was an unprecedented scene in American history. The President of the United States had riled up a mob that hunted his own Vice President.

2:27 P.M.

JAKE TAPPER, CNN ANCHOR, LIVE ON CNN: President Trump could stop this with one tweet, but instead he's on Twitter attacking Vice President Pence for refusing to go along with his attempt at a coup, at a bloodless coup—we hope it stays bloodless. . . . I've been in Washington for decades now, I've never seen anything like this.[34]

JANUARY 6 REPORT: Although no one could convince President Trump to call for the violent rioters to leave the Capitol, Ivanka persuaded President Trump that a tweet could be issued to discourage violence against the police.

DONALD TRUMP VIA TWITTER, 2:38 P.M.: Please support our Capitol Police and Law Enforcement. They are truly on the side of our Country. Stay peaceful![35]

| **But it was too late. The police on the West Front lost the line.**

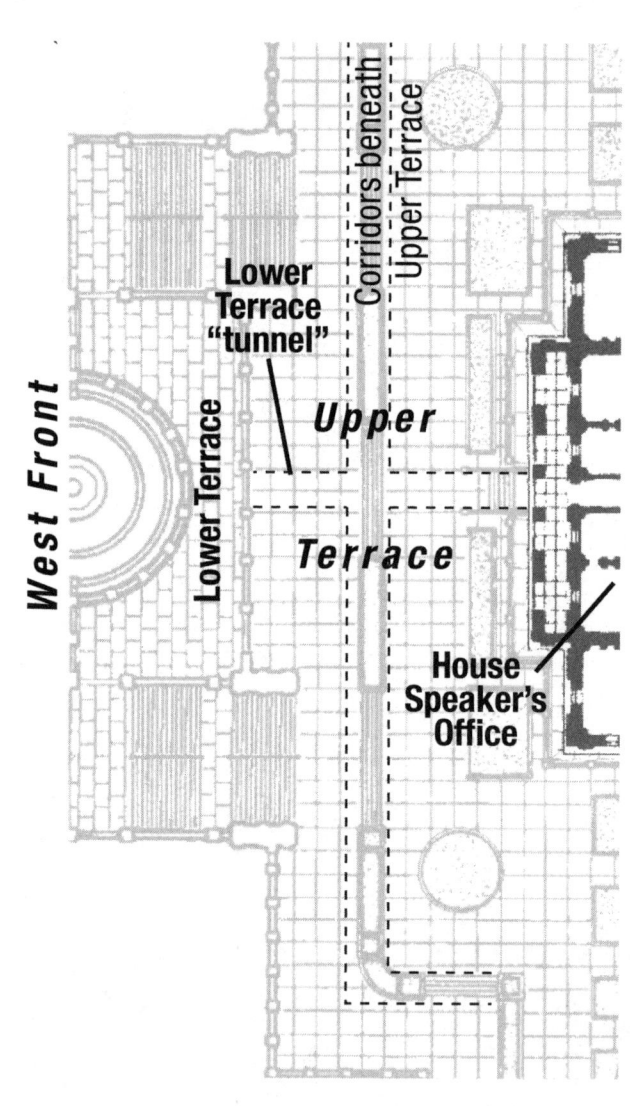

West Front

Lower
Terrace
"tunnel"

Lower Terrace

Corridors beneath
Upper Terrace

Upper

Terrace

House
Speaker's
Office

CHAPTER 9

"YOU CAN SEE THE LINE OF LOSS. THE TERRITORY IS THEIRS"

WEST TERRACE

2:28 P.M.

DANIEL HODGES, *DC Metropolitan Police officer*: We were holding the West Terrace for as long as possible until eventually they broke through.

RADIO TRANSMISSION FROM DC POLICE COMMANDER ROBERT GLOVER: We've lost the line. We've lost the line![1]

ALAN CHIN, *freelance photojournalist on assignment for* Business Insider: Instead of the police clearing the crowd, the crowd cleared the police. The police line broke. I couldn't believe it. In my whole thirty years as a working journalist, I've never seen a police line break like that.

OFFICER HODGES: The West Terrace devolves into a series of individual pitched battles. No way to re-form [the line] after that. There's just too many of them flowing through and surrounding us.

SGT. AQUILINO GONELL, *US Capitol Police officer*: Backtracking my steps or retreating, but yeah, facing the crowd, I was able to pull some of the officers that were getting left behind and separated from that group. I even occasionally went forward just to grab some of them because I didn't want them to get left behind. That's one thing that we are trained for in terms of don't leave people behind, because you don't want to be that person [that] got left behind.[2]

OFFICER HODGES: There was four or five people who started pushing me back until I was pushed back against a waist-high concrete wall, and I was held there while one of the insurrectionists sort of wrapped his—I think it was his left arm around my head and neck while he reached underneath my visor to try and gouge out my eye with his thumb. And we struggled there for a bit until I was eventually able to shake him off before any permanent damage was done.

If it was a couple more millimeters, and I might not have a right eye right now, but thankfully I was able to get 'em off. And you look up and you can see the line of loss. The territory is theirs.

ANGELO WESTFIELD, *battalion fire chief, DC FEMS*: I ended up turning to my sergeant and telling them, "Hey, we need to start prepping for a mass casualty incident."[3]

ALAN CHIN: The crowd at that point controlled the entire outdoor area of the Capitol. Let's look at this tactically as someone who has had to navigate situations like this. And if the government is not in charge of its outdoor area, what do you think is going to happen? Well, as a journalist, as a student of history, as someone who's actually seen some of this happen in other countries, you very much fear on a human level. You very much fear that the next thing that's going to happen is that the security forces are going to start shooting people because that's what you do when your presidential palace or your legislature or your other seats of authority are overrun by hostile forces. This is when you expect the shooting to start in earnest. Okay? This is . . . At some point someone's going to decide we've had enough, and we're going to start. We have to just kill these people.

TEXT FROM DC METROPOLITAN POLICE OFFICER JEFFREY SMITH TO HIS WIFE: London has fallen.[4]

JANE, *staff photojournalist for a major mainstream outlet*: They're chanting and they're waving these flags and they're literally fucking climbing the scaffolding around me. I remember just looking around and being in shock. It felt like an old-timey battle.

DAVID BUTOW, *freelance photojournalist*: You kind of had to make a deliberate attempt if you wanted to go up further. So eventually that's what I did, and

I remember turning to Jane and I was like, "How do you feel? You okay? I think I'm going to leave." And she's like, "Yeah, I'm okay." And then, I mean, she stayed in that spot, and then I moved north along the steps and sort of made my way up.

Suddenly, the sound of a rousing bagpipe floated above the concussive blasts of the police who were firing crowd-control munitions. A rioter was playing a recording of Scotland the Brave, the traditional march usually played at patriotic parades in the US.

The crowd of rioters pushed the police back to the wall.

SERGEANT GONELL: We were still fighting. They're still assaulting us. They're still spraying us. The only way to go was up through the [temporary inauguration] stage stairs.[5]

OFFICER HODGES: And so we fell back further to a temporary stairway that connected the Lower West Terrace and the landing where the presidential inauguration ceremony would be held.

SERGEANT GONELL: I started making hand signals to go back up, but the process to getting up the steps was very slow because with all that Civil Disturbance Unit gear on, instead of two or three people fitting at the same time through the steps, you only fit one person. The officer[s] themselves, we started pushing one another, trying to get out of harm's way, so that was very claustrophobic, on top of having a mask on in the inaugural staircase. There was smoke that prevented us from seeing. I think some of the officers were like, "I don't know what that is, so I ain't going up there." But I had my gas mask on, so I continued to go through.[6]

| Next to the base of that temporary staircase was journalist Jon Farina.

JON FARINA, *freelance journalist on assignment for* Status Coup News: I'm filming some guy who I thought he had died, maybe he had a heart attack, whatever. He wasn't moving. There were people that were trying to resuscitate him.

RIOTERS: Is there a doctor?

Medic!

Back up, back up.

Just a few feet away, the other rioters didn't seem to notice the fallen man. They were able to open the scaffolding staircase door that the police had just retreated through, and they climbed upward.

RIOTERS, CHANTING: Whose house? Our house!

But the crowd around the fallen man was frantic.

RIOTER, YELLING OVER THE CROWD: Medic! Medic!

It'd been at least five minutes since he'd lost consciousness. He was still unresponsive.

RIOTERS: We need a medic.

RIOTERS: Medic coming, get out of the way. Make way!

RIOTERS: We got a medic. He's a medic.

A man wearing full camouflage, seemingly a fellow rioter, bent over the patient.

RIOTERS: Is he breathing?

RIOTERS: Yes. He's got a pulse.

Some rioters yelled at the growing crowd to make a path to allow the patient out.

RIOTERS: Medical! Medical! Clear a path! We need an ambulance!

REST OF THE CROWD: USA! USA! USA!

RIOTERS: Make way, make way, make way, make way.

JON FARINA: What they ended up doing was carrying him out. I don't know if he was alive or not, but they carried him out. And then I see a text that people are inside, and I'm like, *Shit, where's everybody going?* So I see them walking up the stairs and I'm like, *All right, maybe that's the way in.* So I walk up the stairs.

OFFICER HODGES: So we went inside the building itself where I took a moment to get myself together. I think I had been in the Capitol as a child. But other than that, I'd never been in the Capitol before. So I didn't know where I was or where anyone else was. My radio had been stolen at that point, so I didn't have any communications.

SERGEANT GONELL: I'm one of the last three people who goes in after we lost even the stage itself. Then once we go inside through those double doors, and they broke the glass, and they opened the doors. They forced them open. Somebody yelled, "Shields to the front," and I immediately went to the front—to the front of that entrance. We did that for several minutes. We were able to hold them off. Then they became more aggressive, started pushing us further inside. Then we got reinforcement[s]. We push them all the way out.[7]

FLOOR OF THE HOUSE CHAMBER

ABOUT 2:30 P.M.

OLIVIA BEAVERS, Politico *congressional reporter:* There was so much visceral reaction starting to happen. And I think the fear made my body feel really heavy, my legs felt super heavy, my thumbs felt super heavy and were shaking. My phone was blowing up in a way that I've never experienced. And so I think I just silenced notifications in a way of trying to concentrate. I wasn't even really responding to my mom.

FRANK LOCKWOOD, *ARKANSAS DEMOCRAT-GAZETTE REPORTER*, VIA TWITTER, 2:36 P.M.: Someone just stood up in the visitors' gallery and urged Republicans to get Trump to intervene. "Call your friend and tell him to do something," he shouted.[8]

FRANK LOCKWOOD: There was an immediate sense that if President Trump called the mob off, that the violence would cease. I mean, that was from the very beginning.

REP. ERIC SWALWELL: And what I thought was remarkable was, in the moment, both sides of the aisle turned around and screamed back, "Shut up! We will do this and there will be a reckoning over who caused this. But right now we're just trying to get directives that get us to safety. We're not hashing this out right now." And that, I think, just really describes the fear and the intensity that was in the room. And it was largely just because of the unknown. I mean, thankfully we had Twitter and our news streams that we were watching to see what was going on outside the building, but when you're in the chamber, there's no windows, you can't see. . . . So you can just hear the chanting and the pounding and the disbursement of the tear gas, but you can't see anything. So it's just that unknown of, What do they have? Are they armed? Do they have explosives? What is their intent?

A police officer took the podium and told the terrified members to retrieve the emergency gas masks stored under their seats.

REP. ERIC SWALWELL: Until that moment, I did not know that there were gas masks under our seats. And we had also never rehearsed any type of scenario like this. So first, I think people were surprised that they were even there. We sit on top of them every day; we just didn't know.[9]

RICHARD, *congressional staffer*: We've drilled on those before, but even with that preparation, there was mass confusion amongst probably a hundred people on the Floor at that point, how to get these things open.[10]

REP. ERIC SWALWELL: Ruben [Gallego] had served a combat mission as a marine in the Iraq War. And so as we were pulling out the gas masks, he saw immediately that I had no idea how to use or even open the gas mask. And so he started having women first throw him or toss him their gas masks, and he was ripping them open, sometimes using his teeth to rip them open, and was just handing out the gas masks and telling people to not breathe too quickly because that could lead you to pass out. [11]

MICHELLE, *congressional staffer*: I had mine in my hand and I was kind of fumbling with it. And Ruben Gallego, I think he could just tell that I was not doing great and I could feel like my breathing getting labored. And he was like, "You're going to be okay. It's going to be okay. You're going to be fine. Open your gas mask." And he was showing me how to do it.[12]

OLIVIA BEAVERS: I tried to put it on, and you don't have good visual to your peripheral vision. And I remember thinking I'd rather have the gas in my lungs and have my vision at this point.

RICHARD: And when those things [gas masks] open up, they have that homing transponder, that beep that you hear. So if you can imagine almost all at once, probably a hundred of those things all beeping at the same time.[13]

FRANK LOCKWOOD: It sounded almost like an alarm. I mean, it was just this buzzing coming from all directions.

BRUCE, *congressional staffer*: I kind of describe it like a constant kazoo, just kind of like a whirring noise. And you probably had about, I don't know, 400 of those or so, 300 of 'em going off at once, both on the Floor and in the gallery.[14]

FRANK LOCKWOOD: And one moment that was really scary in the midst of the bedlam, a woman stepped to the microphone and began to pray. And the prayer was absolutely terrifying. Because typically in Washington, public prayer is this unemotional, rote, pro forma kind of deal. The prayers read like they were written by a committee and that they were vetted, make sure no one would be offended, and nothing surprising would be said.

But this woman stepped to the microphone and began to pray. And this was not a written-out prayer. This was a prayer delivered from the heart. This was a prayer delivered off the top of her head, and it was fervent, and it was genuine, and it was scary as all get out. She was a new chaplain, so I'd never seen her before, never heard her before. I just assumed things had gotten desperate enough that a house employee had stepped to the microphone and started praying. I mean, it was really something.

FRANK LOCKWOOD VIA TWITTER, 2:36 P.M.: Someone at the dais is praying. Reverently. Fervently.[15]

FRANK LOCKWOOD VIA TWITTER, 2:40 P.M.: It's honest-to-God prayer[16]

FRANK LOCKWOOD: My sense of it was, "Dear Lord Jesus, we are in tremendous difficulties and we call for your help and we call for your protection. We call for your guidance." And it was so sincere and so heartfelt and so genuine. That scared the living daylights out of me. I mean, I was listening along and I was thinking to myself, *Amen. Amen.* Yeah, I hope He's hearing and I hope He's granting those requests.[17]

OLIVIA BEAVERS: I remember typing out [a tweet describing the prayer], and then I deleted it. I was like, *No, this can't be happening.* And so I deleted the tweet. That happened multiple times where I would see something that did actually happen, but I'd be like, *No, I don't want to be putting misinformation out there.* This is so chaotic. And I'm like, *Did that really happen?*

REP. ERIC SWALWELL: [Ruben Gallego's] wife had reached out to me. She was worried that Ruben would probably not follow orders of the Capitol Police and that he would want to fight the mob or the protesters.[18]

REP. RUBEN GALLEGO: I didn't find any weapons. The best thing I found was a pen and that was going to have to be it. It looked bad. I was teaching [my colleagues] how to stab [the rioters] in the neck and stab them in the eye. . . . I don't give a fuck. Like, I would have killed all those motherfuckers to save this democracy. Fuck those guys.[19]

REP. ERIC SWALWELL: She asked me if I could just look out for Ruben. And so I went over and sat—sat with Ruben Gallego.[20] I have a lot of guilt over this. I was seated next to Barbara Lee and Cheri Bustos, and when I started communicating with [Ruben's wife] Sydney, I got up and went over to where Ruben was seated, which was closer to one of the tables that has a podium. So I left and went over to Ruben to make sure that he was going to be okay. Bustos and Lee have good-naturedly joked with me that I left them. And I still just feel awful about that. I didn't even think that they would view it that way that I left them and they were on their own.

| **Elsewhere in the Capitol, it was also chaos.**

LARRY, *US Capitol Police officer*: Everything echoes in the Capitol building. Not to mention all the alarms that were going off on all those doors because they were all breached. And again, thousands of people inside of a small hallway all screaming at the same time. It's deafening. So your radio is non-existent at that time.

2:33 P.M.

POLICE RADIO COMMUNICATIONS: Please be advised that the US Capitol [garbled] . . . all military and sworn officers to come to . . . [garbled] Team 2 copy.[21]

OFFICER LARRY: Essentially every door, every facet of the Capitol building I responded to, I got OC sprayed,* I got bear-sprayed, I got CS-gassed, I got hit by flags, batons, fists, you name it. But I do want to make it very

---

* Also known as pepper spray

clear: it wasn't everybody in that building that was doing that. It was a small percent of that happening. Again, there was a lot of followers that followed those people in those buildings. I mean, there were some people dressed in full fatigues and there was women hitting us. I don't know, it was just all different people. But again, it wasn't all of them. It was a small percentage that were attacking us, but it was kind of like the mob mentality, right? When they see one person strike, more people are going to start striking. And when you have ten of us versus hundreds of them, it is a losing battle for us. We didn't see an official in that building all day long. It was the frontline officers doing the work.

Mayor Bowser ordered a 6 p.m. curfew for the entire city. Meanwhile, rioter Daniel Herendeen was still looking for his friend Bobby Schornak inside the Capitol building.

DANIEL HERENDEEN, *rioter*: It was a right-handed search. I was a firefighter, so I stayed along the walls with my right hand. I got to the end of it. I didn't find Bobby. I turned around, followed the wall back with my left hand and out. And I wasn't going any deeper. Didn't want to—there was too many people. [22]

BOBBY SCHORNAK, *rioter, inside the Capitol building*: I think I tried to talk to some police, and they were just basically ignoring me. The police seeming to be gathering for something, you know, I definitely knew and realized that, *Hey, I'm definitely not supposed to be in here. I gotta go.* So as I was walking out, or walking towards where I had come in, the police had the door shut and then that's when they were actually telling us to leave. That was the first time an officer told me to leave, when I was leaving, and he said, "Go through the window," and I just said, "Yes, sir," and I left. [23]

DANIEL HERENDEEN: And I didn't find Bobby, and I wasn't going to go through the whole place looking for him. So I turn around, I left on my own accords. And the police, they made me climb out through a window, because I think they were trying to get the doors shut so no more people would come in.[24]

TEXT FROM BOBBY SCHORNAK TO HIS BROTHER: We stormed that bitch!! Shit was crazy as fuck!! This is what a revolution looks like.[25]

TEXT FROM BOBBY SCHORNAK TO SOMEONE ELSE: We stormed the
Capital!! . . . They were scared today, and I'm damn proud of it.
The capital has never been breached before, we did it.[26]

EAST SIDE OF THE CAPITOL

2:30 P.M.

One group of Oath Keepers rode in golf carts toward the Capitol
and live-streamed it on Facebook.[27]

ROBERTO MINUTA, OATH KEEPER: Patriots are storming the Capitol
building; there's violence against patriots by the D.C. Police;
so we're en route in a grand theft auto golf cart to the Capitol
building right now. . . . It's going down, guys; it's literally
going down right now Patriots storming the Capitol building . . .
fucking war in the streets right now. . . . Word is they got in
the building. . . . Let's go.[28]

Once they got to the building, they continued on foot.

COURT DOCUMENTS: [The Oath Keepers] maneuvered in an organized
fashion up the steps to the east side Rotunda Doors—each member
keeping at least one hand on the shoulder of the other in front
of them.[29]

Photographer Mark Peterson had just exited the Capitol through the
east side Rotunda Doors. He saw the stack of Oath Keepers coming
toward him.

MARK PETERSON, *freelance photojournalist on assignment for the* New York
Times: And so then I saw this militia group starting to go up the stairs back
up to the door that I came out of. So I followed, they were way up a hundred,
two hundred yards in front of me, but I said, "Okay, I got to go back into the
Capitol." So I forced my way back up the stairs, and when I got to the top
of the stairs, there was another one of these tactical police units, all with the
total body armor on from head to foot. Yeah, head to foot. And they were
up there, and the militia group is kind of staged at the top of the stairs, and

they're talking to each other. So when I'm looking at the militia and they're whispering in their ear, I photographed this and stuff. I see their insignias and all that, and one of the police officers said, "If you really want to help out, you can help us secure this door." And they just started whispering to each other. And of course, they didn't do anything. And this is the group that supposedly had the guns across the river.

MESSAGE FROM OATH KEEPER, 2:38 P.M.: QRF standing by at hotel. Just say the word.[30]

The Oath Keepers got past the group of law enforcement and into the building. A few minutes later, they joined a mob already inside that was pushing against a line of police officers guarding the hallway that connected the Rotunda to the Senate chamber.[31]

OATH KEEPERS: Push, push, push! Get in there, get in there. They can't hold us![32]

At the same time on the other side of the Capitol building, an eerily similar scene played out outside the House chamber, like mirror images of each other.

ADAM GRAY, *freelance photojournalist on assignment for the* Daily Mail, *in a hallway outside the House chamber*: [The rioters] go into this corridor. And again there's a line of police, but there's less than ten police there. They're not riot police, they don't have shields, they don't have helmets, they don't have pepper spray.

They argue with these police for a while and they just walk through them. The police can't do anything. They get to these doors.

RIOTER: Well, we came this far, what do you say?

RIOTER: Drag 'em out!

RIOTER: Hang 'em out![33]

RICHARD, INSIDE THE CHAMBER: You could hear them. There was yelling, there was screaming, there's noise that can get through those doors and onto the chamber.[34]

2:39 P.M.

ADAM GRAY: They're still not through the door. It's like a very solid door. You can see them trying to go through it and it's just not moving.

REP. ERIC SWALWELL, INSIDE THE CHAMBER: I noticed that Capitol Police officers, along with some of my Republican colleagues, were pushing furniture against the back door. We could hear the pounding on those doors and the shouting of the rioters outside.[35]

RICHARD: All of a sudden, I looked up and I saw people start leaving and everybody moved quickly. Everybody kind of understood that it was time to leave.[36]

REP. ERIC SWALWELL: I immediately started to follow the police officers as we were asked to leave. But I did see Ruben Gallego, who is not a rule follower, did not follow the orders of the police. And I saw that he was standing on the House chairs, yelling at the members in the gallery, that they were going to be okay and just reminding them about their gas masks. Many of them were lying under the chairs of the gallery. Some of them had their gas masks on. Some of them looked like they were in kind of like a prayer group, praying together. The Capitol Police had not yet secured the exit for the third-floor doors. And so I went back and started yelling, "Ruben, Ruben, time to go. We've got to go." And was ultimately able to get Ruben to walk out of the chamber with me.[37]

ANDREW HARNIK, *Associated Press photojournalist*: Suddenly, we heard glass breaking.[38]

RICHARD: I heard glass break and I could see the window panes on the House main door start to pop.

FRANK LOCKWOOD: They were right outside. The mob is trying to smash the doors down.

MICHELLE: So [the police] swung the doors open to the Speaker's Lobby, and they were like, "We're moving, everybody get off the Floor." We go out through the Speaker's Lobby.[39]

ANDREW HARNIK: By now, the Floor was almost completely evacuated. The police, most of them dressed in a suit and tie, pulled out their handguns and pointed them at the people on the other side of the door.[40]

FRANK LOCKWOOD: Law enforcement has weapons drawn, and they're pointing them at the door, and they're ordering people to get away. And that may have been the scariest moment, really for me. I felt like it switched from being a congressional proceeding to being a crime scene, I really felt like we're smack dab in the middle of a major crime, and it's unfolding all around us.[41]

My sense was that if they got through the doors, we could be in danger. Legitimate, real, genuine danger. President Trump had referred to the media as the enemy of the people, and he had demonized the press for years. And so there was not a lot of warm feeling among that crowd for media of any stripe. I said, *Okay, I'm taking off all my press passes, tucking those away.* I took off my tie, took off my jacket at some point, so that if I had to drop it, I could just drop it. And my plan was, I'll drop the computer if necessary. I don't want to look like a reporter. I don't want to look like media, and if they get through, I'll just do my best to get through it.[42]

Outside the House chamber, Adam Gray was watching the rioters struggle to break down the doors.

ADAM GRAY: I noticed some people have peeled off and gone up this corridor. So I decide they're not going to get through this door. I'm going to see where else they're going. So I take the left and walk along this corridor. You get to the end of this corridor and there's another right and you end up in the Speaker's Lobby. There's a staircase to my right with a big drop-off that side and the stairs going down. There's a lobby and then people are shouting, and I can see them pushing and banging on these doors and windows at the front.

This is the exact spot where Alexandra Pelosi, thirty minutes earlier, had waited for her mother to be whisked off the podium. Through the glass doors on the far side of the Speaker's Lobby, the rioters could now see the lawmakers hurrying past, evacuating. Officers barricaded the door.

REP. ERIC SWALWELL: As we were leaving, I looked down the long hallway of the Speaker's Lobby at the—where they had stacked the chairs and saw the mob, you know, pressed up against the—the glass doors that lead into the lobby.[43]

Between the lawmakers and the rioters were just a few officers and the glass doors. The lawmakers escaped through a back door. That left the officers defending the glass doors from the rioters.

MICHAEL BYRD, *US Capitol Police officer*: Once we barricaded the doors, we were essentially trapped where we were. There was no way to retreat. No other way to get out.[44]

Rioters punched through the glass door, leaving a gaping hole. Standing behind them was a young female rioter, Ashli Babbitt, wearing a flag around her waist.

ADAM GRAY: There's a window smashed out there. I remember holding my camera up above my head, behind the crowd, taking pictures. This is 2:43. And then I put my camera down.

Inside the Speaker's Lobby, Capitol Police Lt. Michael Byrd pulled out his service weapon.

RIOTER: He's got a gun!

LIEUTENANT BYRD: If they get through that door, they're into the House chamber and upon the members of Congress. I tried to wait as long as I could. I hoped and prayed no one tried to enter through those doors.[45]

Ashli Babbitt hoisted herself up to get through the hole in the door's window.

2:44 P.M.

ADAM GRAY: There was a bang and I heard a gunshot.

Ashli seemed to freeze in space, then fell backward.

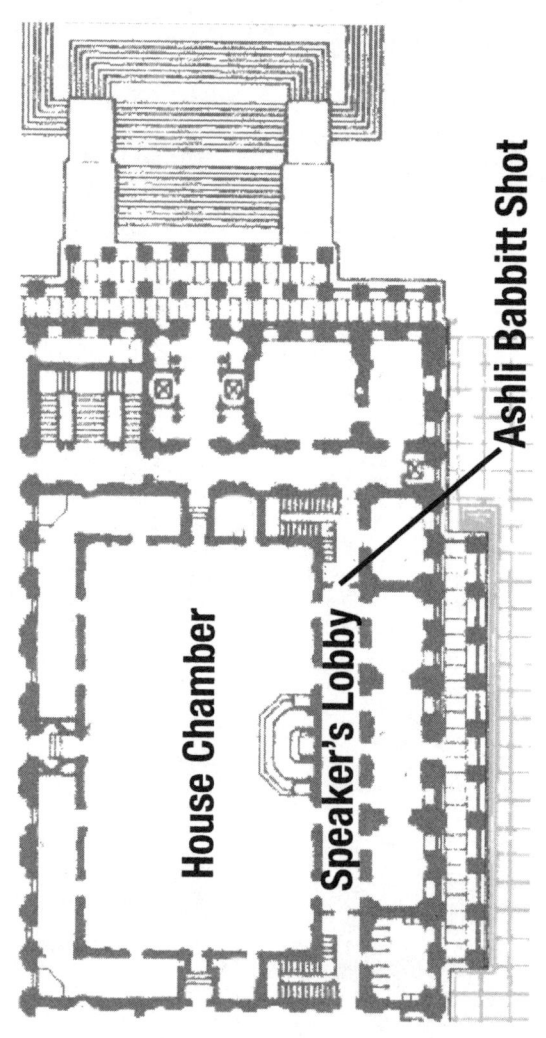

House Chamber

Speaker's Lobby

Ashli Babbitt Shot

CHAPTER 10

"THEY JUST KILLED A GIRL"

ADAM GRAY, *freelance photojournalist on assignment for the* Daily Mail: Then people started screaming, "They've shot her! You've shot her!"

RIOTER: They just killed a girl!

ADAM GRAY: My instinct's to go to the front of the room. I kind of forced my way through this crowd. I see this woman lying on the floor, the flag's underneath her, and there's blood coming out of her, just below her head, like her neck. It's hard to tell. There's a lot of blood and she looks in a very bad way. It's just a horrific scene. It's horrible. You can see she's in a very, very bad way. She's barely alive.

It's just a really chaotic scene. There's rioters behind me and to my right. There's police on the staircase. People are shouting at the police. The police . . . stood there, guns drawn. This [cop]'s holding a rifle, one of those SWAT-looking guys, stood above her. I mean, this guy's got his finger almost on the trigger. And it's just complete chaos. And they're surrounded. They're screaming at the crowd; the crowd is screaming at them.

This is the first time I've seen somebody shot and dying in front of me. I mean, in the moment, I didn't really think about that. You're just working, you're just very focused on documenting what's happening and your own safety. Police are trying to stop the bleeding. The rioters are constantly shouting and then a few minutes have passed and I'm thinking, *How are they going to get this woman out?* I remember taking a step back and going back along the corridor and I think everybody was kind of pitching in. It was like, *Right, everyone make space. Let's make space so we can carry her through.* They carried her down the stairs rather than through the crowd.

[Then] riot police showed up. Yellow jackets, helmets, batons out, and they're telling everyone to get out and they're forcing them out. And, again, it gets really rough. Kind of felt like being in a washing machine, to be honest. The batons are hitting everybody and, yeah, it's just rough. So, yeah, you're trying to shoot, trying to stay on your feet, and then also do what they say.

The gunshot was audible from the House Floor.

REP. ERIC SWALWELL: You just heard a pop as we were leaving and going to the right. Because we had heard the disbursement of tear gas, I don't even think we are registering what that was. And there was so much banging. I wasn't distinguishing what was a gunshot.

The police evacuated Swalwell along with the other lawmakers on the Floor. However, those in the galleries—journalists, observers, staffers, and even some lawmakers—were left behind.

FRANK LOCKWOOD, *ARKANSAS DEMOCRAT-GAZETTE* REPORTER, VIA TWITTER, 2:46 p.m.: Sounded like a gunshot a few moments ago[1]

FRANK LOCKWOOD: I said, "Was that a gunshot? Because it sure sounded like one." So you don't know who has the gun, who's doing the firing, how many more guns are out there, how many shots, more shots are going to ring out, and it's close enough that you can hear it.

OLIVIA BEAVERS, Politico *congressional reporter*: I remember asking [Rep.] Markwayne Mullin and some of the others like, "Hey, was there a bullet fired?" And they were like, "No, they broke the door. There wasn't a bullet." And so other people were like, "No, there was a bullet fired." So I was like, "Really? Because they're saying it was the door." So there was just sort of this broad confusion.

RADIO TRANSMISSION, DC FEMS: Report of one shot in the Capitol.[2]

RADIO TRANSMISSION: Capitol Command to Recon. Is this going to be an active shooter event or is this just one shot? I need more information.[3]

MITCHELL KANNRY, *fire marshal, DC FEMS*: I'm trying to figure out what exactly was going on, if it was an active shooter situation, how to get units to the best location, how to extricate that victim.[4]

RADIO TRANSMISSION: Not an active shooting. Just one shot.[5]

RADIO TRANSMISSION: Recon Priority. We do have one shot in the chest. I need the resources up here now, immediately.[6]

CHRISTOPHER HOLMES, *battalion fire chief, DC FEMS*: I was inside the Capitol building, was actually assisting with an injured officer at the time and we were notified by Capitol Police that there was a gunshot wound victim at the south entrance—immediately went there, found that there was a victim there.[7]

LA'KISHA LACEY, *EMS captain, DC FEMS*: We quickly extradited the patient out of the area where we found her into a transport unit where we continued ALS measures.[8]

RADIO TRANSMISSION: Ready. Patient's coming out. South-side Capitol. CPR in progress.[9]

TIMOTHY BENNETT, *sergeant paramedic, DC FEMS*: The only time I ever felt a little bit, you know, cautious, was when we brought her to the ambulance. The crowd was quite angry and upset.[10]

CAPTAIN LACEY: The scene was very, very, very chaotic but I must say that in the height of all of it, even with the protesters being surrounded, they, too, were very much concerned about the patient that we had. When we came out with her on the stretcher to move her to the transport unit they made way for us.[11]

JANUARY 6 REPORT: President Trump's Chief of Staff—and President Trump himself—were informed that someone had been shot. There is no indication that this affected the President's state of mind that day.

At this point, police officers were leading the evacuated members of Congress to a safe room.

REP. JAMIE RASKIN (D-MD): Our downward flight into the darkened basement of the Capitol was chaos. We did not know where we were going. Masked and frantic, our staccato steps bouncing off of walls, we kept bumping into one another, especially with so many phones pressed to ears to call spouses, children, parents, staff. Someone told us, *Shh, keep it down, keep it down.*

Down the hallways and exit ramps, I glimpsed in my peripheral vision the "rioters." They lunged forward in clustered groups, looking to me like zombies in a horror movie, but whenever they came into view, our group broke into a healthy trot pretty impressive for middle-aged politicians.[12]

REP. ERIC SWALWELL: And again, the gallows humor was like, no one wanted to be near me or [Rep. Adam] Schiff. They figured we would be two of the most recognizable people. And people were joking, "Well, I don't want to catch a stray from one of you. If they're intending to hit you, I don't want to catch a stray."

The weirdest part of it was you would go fast and then you would bottleneck you would stop and there'd be twenty to thirty seconds where we just kind of bunched up in traffic almost. And you're like, the officers just yelling, "Move, move, move. Just don't stop. Everyone keep moving." And that would be impossible sometimes.

And so it just so happened that you would sometimes bump into colleagues who spoke at the rally with Trump and you would just be like, "Are you fucking kidding me? How is it that both of us are running for our lives now?"

So at one point we're going up a ramp and Madison Cawthorn looks back at me and asks for help because he can't wheel up the ramp. And again, I was like, *Are you fucking kidding? You were there. This is your fault, pal.* And of course I was not going to *not* push him, but it was just absurd that he was part of what caused this and now he needs help to evacuate or to go on the route. And as I said, of course I'll push him, but I wasn't happy to.

HOUSE CHAMBER, GALLERIES

OLIVIA BEAVERS: I remember the moment where they had basically gotten everyone out. And I look and [Rep.] Jason Crow shouts down—he's in the gallery, and Jason Crow works out with Markwayne Mullin, they have a bipartisan workout group—and he goes, "What about us?" And I remember Markwayne Mullin looking up and like, *Oh sh*—he didn't say it, but it was like an *oh shit* response. I think he had completely forgotten that there were members, there were staffers in the gallery.

SHANE SMITH, *aide to Speaker Nancy Pelosi*: So for us in the gallery, we watched the members down there and the staff down there being evacuated off the Floor kind of left wondering, *What about us?* There was this sense that we might've been trapped up there.[13] I was directly behind Congressman Jason Crow from Colorado and was just kind of following his lead as he was telling members to do certain things. I knew his background as a former Army Ranger, so I was like, this guy knows what we need do in a time of crisis like this. So I kind of just blocked everything out and was like, this is what we need to do.[14]

OLIVIA BEAVERS: Crow, I believe, if I remember correctly, was the one who told us to get out anything that we could use as self-defense. So he had told members to pull out pens or anything that could be sharp that we could use if we were in a hand-to-hand combat sort of situation. And so I remember they were trying to figure out if it was safe for us to go, and we were basically told, "Not yet. Not yet. We think there's activity outside."

They were right. Rioters had made it to the upper floor where the entrances to the galleries were located. PBS reporter Lisa Desjardins was in the hallway watching. She stood behind a desk so as to have at least some barrier between her and the rioters. Many yelled at her, demanding to know who she was.[15]

LISA DESJARDINS, *PBS NEWSHOUR* CORRESPONDENT, TO RIOTERS: PBS. Sesame Street! Big Bird![16]

She video-called into *PBS NewsHour's* **live broadcast.**

LISA DESJARDINS, LIVE ON PBS: On the other side of me, Judy, is the House Chamber . . . A short time ago, witnessed some house members being escorted out of the area.

[*Rumblings off camera*] I'll give you just a second, sir. I'll speak to you in just a second, sir.

[*Turns back to camera*] So I've also seen protesters access police security areas where police equipment is. I can hear that they're in Statuary Hall below me as well. This seems to be the farthest they've come inside the Capitol right now, but you can see there's no security and it's unclear to me how this situation resolves or ends all across the Capitol.

There was a bang and some yelling. Desjardins's video feed cut off.

JUDY WOODRUFF, *PBS NEWSHOUR* ANCHOR, LIVE ON PBS: It looks like we've lost the signal from Lisa, at least for the moment and we're hearing some sort of alarm go off. Lisa, if you're there, we'll stay with you. We do want you to stay safe—

Desjardins's feed came back online. She was crouched behind a desk.

CAPITOL POLICE OFFICER, SHOUTING IN THE BACKGROUND: On the ground! On the ground!

LISA DESJARDINS: Yeah, Capitol Police are now on this floor. They are now working to secure this floor. They're asking protesters to go on the ground.

She began to stand up to show the scene to the camera, but an officer yelled at her.

OFFICER: Get down, stay down!

She quickly crouched back down.[17]

LISA DESJARDINS: The police do seem—the police have gained control for the moment of this corridor of the Capitol.

SHANE SMITH, *inside the gallery*: I remember a US Capitol Police officer standing kind of just right over my shoulder saying, "Is it clear in the hallway? Is it clear in the hallway?" Again, we had no idea what was out in the hallway.[18]

Once that officer got confirmation that the hallway was clear, they began to evacuate the gallery.

CAPITOL POLICE: Move, move, come on, let's go. Come on, everybody get out. Come on, let's go. Down the steps. Hurry.[19]

FRANK LOCKWOOD: And so out the door we went. I believe we were the very last group evacuated. When we went out the door, we could see people [rioters] that had made it to [that hallway] and they were laying spread-eagle on the ground, and law enforcement had them in their scopes.[20]

SHANE SMITH: And we just evacuated right on by these people laying on the ground. And that's an image that will stick with me for sure.[21]

OFFICER: Down the stairs!

As the evacuees went past the detained rioters, Desjardins joined the crowd being hustled away, all while continuing to live stream on PBS. Behind Desjardins was Olivia Beavers.[22]

OLIVIA BEAVERS: We got near a stairwell. I looked to my left and there were about three rioters who were spread eagle on the ground with a Capitol Police officer with an automatic rifle standing over them pointing, trying to get them to stay down. And that I remember gasping, thinking I should take a photo, but I was being rushed along.

OLIVIA BEAVERS VIA TWITTER, 2:52 P.M.: Passing cops who have guns drawn.[23]

OLIVIA BEAVERS: You're having weird thoughts also at this time: *I'm glad I wore flats.* Some people were like, *I'm glad I wore pants.* Just sort of dumb stuff that kind of came to your mind. You're like, *Huh, glad I can move quickly.* Stuff like that. I remember that being sort of a thought in my head: *Wow, I'm having these dumb thoughts.*

FRANK LOCKWOOD: People were just talking as they were going down the stairs. One woman said, "Oh, I wish I'd worn more comfortable shoes." And people were saying, "Was that a gunshot?" And someone said, "No, I don't think it was a gunshot."[24]

OLIVIA BEAVERS: So then we're running down these spiral staircases. We definitely took a weird route. We're going through the tunnels and stuff. Capitol Police officers are ushering us through, but at one point they were leading us, and then me and [my colleague] were ahead of the Capitol Police officer turning back and being like, "So where are we going? We're confused." And they're like, "Keep going." We're like, "We don't know where we're going."

So we get out to the safe room and we're kind of waiting in this line to go in. And I'm now with a few other reporters. They're all mid-twenties to just early thirties-something women, probably five [of us]. And we know each other, but we don't know each other that well. And we're walking in and the police officer goes, "Press is not allowed." And we're like, "What?" And they go, "You have to go down the hallway and talk to the police officers and figure out where you're supposed to go."

And we had no idea where the rioters were, so we're just looking down this long hallway and we're like, *Wait a minute.* But then [Rep.] Abigail Spanberger came and sort of planted herself on the floor between the police officers and us, and she goes, "They were evacuated with us. We know them. They're with us. Let them in." And they went back and forth, and then he just sort of pushed her in and she went in. And so then we're standing in this circle outside of the safe room being like, well, *What are we going to do?*

So we're standing there, freaking out, and a member we knew walked by and he said, "What's happening?" And [my colleague] knew him better than I did, but she was like, "They're not letting us into the safe room." And Congressman Gallego of Arizona was like, "Oh, you can come to my office, I'm nearby." And I think it was a floor up from the safe room. And so we were like, "Oh my God, thank you." And so all five reporters went with him.

Meanwhile, Nancy Pelosi, her family, and other congressional leaders were evacuated off Capitol Hill entirely. They were taken by motorcade to the nearby US Army base Fort Lesley J. McNair in southwest DC. In the safe room at the base, Nancy Pelosi was getting belated updates about what was happening on the Floor.

FORT LESLEY J. MCNAIR

2:44 P.M.

CONGRESSIONAL STAFFER TO NANCY PELOSI: Now apparently everybody on the Floor is putting on tear gas masks to prepare for a breach. I'm trying to get more information.

SPEAKER NANCY PELOSI, CONFUSED: They're putting on their . . . ?

STAFFER: Tear gas masks.

SPEAKER NANCY PELOSI, SHOCKED: Do you believe this? Do you believe this?[25]

LOWER WEST TERRACE TUNNEL

ABOUT 2:45 P.M.

Outside, the rioters on the West Front converged on a tunnel leading to a door. Journalist Jon Farina followed them.

JON FARINA, *freelance journalist on assignment for* Status Coup News: I get to this tunnel, and you can't see the fight in the front line, but you could see [rioters] directing, saying, "Hey, we got to fill this in." They're just trying to get people in to fill in the front line.

Inside, police officers were engaging with rioters who had made their way to the door, attempting to force them away and back out of the tunnel.

DANIEL HODGES, *DC Metropolitan Police officer:* I followed the noise to the tunnel where it was just, you know, wall-to-wall people, packed, fighting with everything they had.[26] It was a battle of inches, with one side pushing the other a few and then the other side regaining their ground. At the time I (and I suspect many others in the hallway) did not know that the terrorists had gained entry to the building by breaking in doors and windows elsewhere, so we believed ours to be the last line of defense before the terrorists had true access to the building, and potentially our elected representatives.[27]

We just had to hold on. We couldn't let anyone through, and they always had essentially an infinite number of replacements. They'd say, you know, "We need fresh patriots up here," and there would be more.[28]

JON FARINA: People were coming out [of the tunnel] pepper sprayed. It looked like a dangerous situation because I didn't know if a gun was going to get shot off or people were going to trample each other.

RIOTERS: We need fresh people! We need fresh people!

JON FARINA: So I kind of just eased my way into [the tunnel and behind a] section of the doorframe—I was crushed in there. I had my hands up, holding the tripod with the camera above everybody's head. So it left my core open. So when they pushed in and they started doing, "Heave-ho, heave-ho," trying to break through the police line, that's when I felt my ribs being crushed.

That was the weirdest feeling I've ever felt was having my ribs crushed. And I had a bulletproof vest on. I had a jacket on. I had a book bag on, but I was still crushed. And so I dropped my elbows down and I kind of pushed the guy in front of me. I pushed him into whoever was in front of him, just to kind of give my ribs some room. And at that point, I kept my elbows tucked in to kind of prevent that from happening again.

There was a time where I almost collapsed because I was so dehydrated and so out of it that I fell into the person who was in front of me. Luckily, I didn't fall to the ground and hit my head and then get knocked out and nobody would know I was down there. But yeah, I almost collapsed. I was so dehydrated and so out of it, but I just hung in there. I stayed in there and I knew I had to stay as long as I can.

OFFICER HODGES: Officers were stacked deep, but every so often one would fall back from the front line, nursing an injury or struggling to breathe, and those who remained would take a step forward.[29]

Hodges was able to move forward step by step. The tunnel was chaos—alarms were blaring on top of the screaming. Within about ten minutes, he was at the front of the line in the doorway. Sgt. Aquilino Gonell had also moved toward the front and was about two rows behind Hodges.

2:56 P.M.

OFFICER HODGES: Once I got out to the front, I didn't want any more pressure on the officers behind me, so I tried to insert myself to where I could use the door frame, brace myself, and push forward so I could take back more territory. Unfortunately, that backfired. I was crushed up against the door frame.[30]

On my left was a man with a clear riot shield stolen during the assault. He slammed it against me and, with the weight of all the bodies pushing behind him, trapped me. My arms were pinned and effectively useless, trapped against either the shield on my left or the door frame on my right. With my posture granting me no functional strength or freedom of movement, I was effectively defenseless and gradually sustaining injury from the increasing pressure of the mob.

Directly in front of me a man seized the opportunity of my vulnerability. He grabbed the front of my gas mask and used it to beat my head against the door. He switched to pulling it off my head, the straps stretching against my skull and straining my neck. He never uttered any words I recognized but opted instead for guttural screams.

Eventually he succeeded in stripping away my gas mask. And a new rush of exposure to CS gas and OC spray hit me. The mob of terrorists were coordinating their efforts now.[31]

NICK QUESTED, *documentary filmmaker, watching from outside the tunnel*: You literally have people going "heave-ho," and they're trying to push their way past the thing and it's like, it feels medieval at this point. I did not know anyone was inside at this point. I really didn't. My phone wasn't working. I just wasn't getting connection. I think there was too many [people trying to use their phones], but I thought that [the government had] gone into sort of a siege mentality and eliminated communications for people.

RIOTERS: Heave-ho![32]

OFFICER HODGES: They synchronized pushing their weight forward, crushing me further against the metal door frame. The man in front of me grabbed my baton that I still held in my hands and in my current state I was unable to retain my weapon. He bashed me in the head and face with it, rupturing my lip and adding additional injury to my skull.[33]

Crushed behind the door, Jon Farina—and his camera—had a clear view of the assault on Hodges.

JON FARINA: I heard him screaming. And in that moment, I wanted to help him, but I'm like, *Oh, I can't step in and get involved.* I wanted to [say] to the person in front of me, "Hey, hey, hey. He's hurt. He's hurt," but I figured somebody would step in and stop it. I felt bad.

At that point, I didn't know what to expect. I thought after this guy was screaming, I thought they were going to stop, I admit. Because these are all people that claim they backed the blue and support the police, and they're like, "Oh, we support our police," and all this bullshit. And then to see them do this. . . .

SERGEANT GONELL: I hear Hodges in front of me screaming in agony and there was nothing I could have done. My hands are crisscrossed. I couldn't move even if I want to.[34] I could feel myself losing oxygen and recall thinking to myself, *This is how I'm going to die: trampled defending this entrance.*[35]

OFFICER HODGES: At this point I knew that I couldn't sustain much more damage and remain upright. At best I would collapse and be a liability to my colleagues, at worst be dragged out into the crowd and lynched. Unable to move or otherwise signal the officers behind me that I needed to fall back, I did the only thing I could still do and screamed for help.[36]

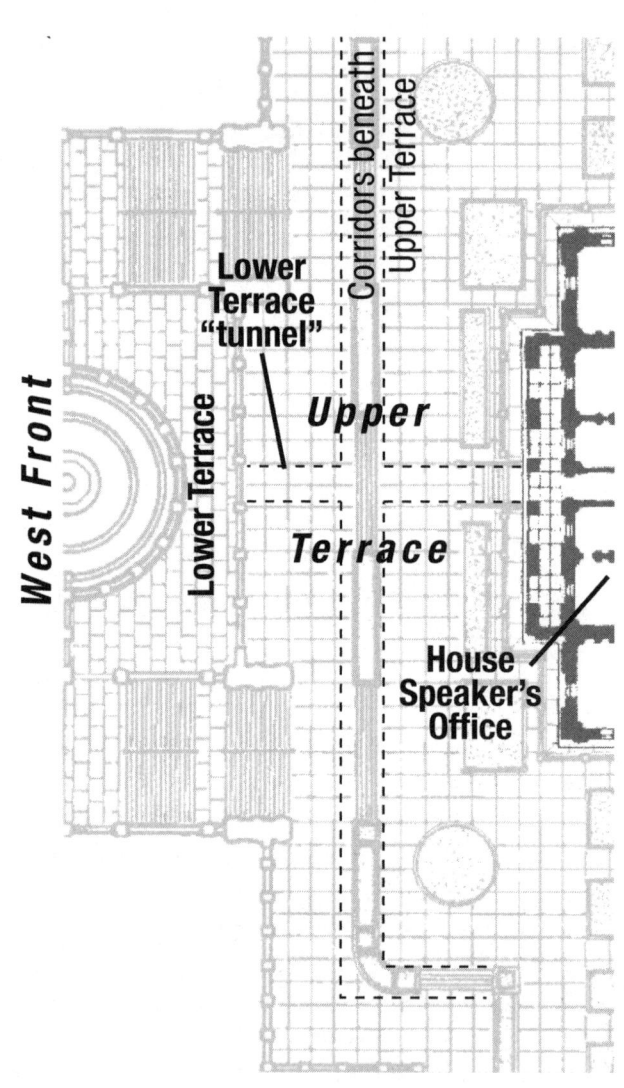

West Front

Lower Terrace

Lower Terrace "tunnel"

Corridors beneath Upper Terrace

Upper Terrace

House Speaker's Office

CHAPTER 11

"KILL HIM WITH HIS OWN GUN"

LOWER WEST TERRACE TUNNEL

ABOUT 3 P.M.

DANIEL HODGES, *DC Metropolitan Police officer:* Thankfully, my voice was heard over the cacophony of yells and the blaring alarm. The officer closest to me was able to extricate me from my position and another helped me fall back to the building again.[1]

JON FARINA, *freelance journalist on assignment for* Status Coup News: He got pulled to the back and off the front line.

OFFICER HODGES: I fell back and someone gave me a water bottle and put it in my hand and dumped it on my face. And then I went back and just sort of sat down, tried to get myself together again. I knew that the fight wasn't over and that we were sorely outnumbered and we needed everybody we had.

I remember going in a bathroom and just taking a minute and photographing my injuries, and I went into a stall and closed the door, and then on the side that was facing me, it said, "F Nancy Pelosi," or something. And it was just very jarring to see that. Yeah, okay. So they had been here, too, where I'm standing.

| The rioters and the police continued to clash in the tunnel.

JON FARINA: There were moments where they would stop and the mob people would be like, "Hey, we love you guys. We're not here for you. We're here for them inside," talking about the politicians.

RIOTER, TO THE COPS: We don't want to hurt you guys! Are you okay?[2]

JON FARINA: They would have these moments where they would just stop and rest, and then next thing you know, it would start back up again. They would sandwich each other and try and break through each other's lines. It was just a wild thing to see.

SGT. AQUILINO GONELL, *US Capitol Police officer*: I had to relieve myself badly, so I didn't hesitate when a tall white officer with a mask covering his face offered to take my spot.

It was Michael Fanone, the Metropolitan Police Department officer who had self-deployed to the Capitol. They switched places. Fanone was now on the front line by the door.

OFFICER FANONE: Push 'em back! Push 'em back!³

3:13 P.M.

At about the same time, President Trump finally tweeted a call for peace at the Capitol.

DONALD TRUMP VIA TWITTER, 3:13 P.M.: I am asking for everyone at the US Capitol to remain peaceful. No violence! Remember, WE are the Party of Law & Order—respect the Law and our great men and women in Blue. Thank you!⁴

OFFICER FANONE: Of course, no one on the front lines saw the tweet at the time. The police were too busy defending the Capitol. The rioters were too busy rioting.⁵

At some point during the fighting, I was dragged from the line of officers into the crowd. I heard someone scream, "I got one!" as I was swarmed by a violent mob.⁶

A rioter wrapped his arm around Fanone's neck and pulled him into the crowd.

OFFICER FANONE: They ripped off my badge. They grabbed my radio. They seized the ammunition that was secured to my body. They began to beat me, with their fists and with what felt like hard metal objects.⁷

NICK QUESTED, *documentary filmmaker*: They beat him a bit with an American flag. I thought that was kind of ironic.

OFFICER FANONE: At one point I came face to face with an attacker who repeatedly lunged for me and attempted to remove my firearm. I heard chanting from some in the crowd, "Get his gun," and, "Kill him with his own gun." I was aware enough to recognize I was at risk of being stripped of, and killed with, my own firearm. I was electrocuted, again and again and again with a taser. I'm sure I was screaming, but I don't think I could even hear my own voice.[8]

During the assault, I thought about using my firearm on my attackers. But I knew that if I did that, I would quickly be overwhelmed. And that, in their minds, it would provide them with the justification for killing me. So instead, I decided to appeal to any humanity they might have.[9]

OFFICER FANONE: I've got kids!

OFFICER FANONE: Thankfully, some in the crowd stepped in and assisted me. Those few individuals protected me from the crowd and inched me toward the Capitol until my fellow officers could rescue me.[10]

Meanwhile, Sergeant Gonell had made his way to a bathroom.

SERGEANT GONELL: After Fanone relieved me, I went to the back [of the crowd in the tunnel] and then used the bathroom because I almost pissed myself after fighting those people for more than two hours.[11]

I forgot to rinse the chemicals off my hands before using the urinal. A searing pain burned through my groin. When it passed, I washed my hands with soap and rushed back to my colleagues.[12]

By the time I got back, Fanone was already pulled in. I struggle sometimes because he got pulled after he relieved me. There's no doubt in my mind that if I had stayed there a couple more minutes, I would've been the one that had gone through whatever he went through that day.[13]

By approximately 3:21 p.m., Officer Fanone was back inside the Capitol building, unconscious. A number of officers rushed to administer first aid, including his partner, Jimmy Albright.[14]

JIMMY ALBRIGHT, DC METROPOLITAN POLICE OFFICER: I got it! It's
my partner. Mike, stay in there, buddy. Mike, it's Jimmy. I'm
here.[15]

OFFICER FANONE: I stirred. I was on my back, looking straight into a harsh
ceiling light in one of the Capitol's labyrinth passageways. Officers in helmets
and gas masks hovered, studying my face. They looked like aliens in some
kind of sci-fi movie. Hazy smoke lingered. My eyes stung. Jimmy returned
into view, maskless.[16]

OFFICER ALBRIGHT: C'mon, Mike. C'mon, buddy. We're going duck
hunting soon.

OFFICER FANONE: Did we take that door back?

OFFICER ALBRIGHT: Yes, we did. We took that fucking door back.
They're all outside.[17]

The door was closed, but back in the tunnel, rioters and police
continued to clash. The rioters assaulted at least three other police
officers, wielding crutches, pepper spray, and even a hockey stick.
Most in the tunnel were unaware that other rioters had already
breached the building on both the west and east sides.

CHAPTER 12

"IT JUST WAS ANOTHER LEVEL INTO DANTE'S INFERNO"

Lawmakers sheltered in their respective safe rooms, one for the
Senate and one for the House.

SEN. BEN SASSE (R-NE), IN THE SENATE SAFE ROOM: Nobody announce your
location to your staff!

SOMEONE ELSE: Or your family![1]

REP. ERIC SWALWELL, IN THE HOUSE SAFE ROOM: Some people chose to
go to their office, but I'm the son of a cop and so I'm a rule follower. When
police officers give orders, I'm like, *Okay. So you were not really supposed to leave
the safe room.* And I think for good reason, because they couldn't guarantee
that they could protect you. But there was still a fear that the safe room was
not safe. Who knew if the mob would get there?

There was an open mic at the safe room, which I thought was funny. So
there was a microphone that at first I think [Rep. Liz] Cheney spoke from,
and then Rep. Hakeem [Jeffries] spoke from, and then people would just
kind of go up there like open-mic style and some people would pray, people
would offer their hot takes.

And the sergeant at arms* would mostly just give an update about every
hour about what's going on. And they would keep saying, "The building's not

---

* An officer for a legislative body who maintains order and security.

secure. We're waiting for the building to be secure." And it felt like an airline captain telling you that it's going to be another hour before we leave the gate.

I remember so many of us were pissed off because we thought these COVID deniers were going to fuck up our COVID shot and we're like, "Goddamn it, we just got this shot and these maskless idiots are going to make it irrelevant." I just remember that was the vibe in the room was: *I cannot believe that we all—we finally get a vaccine, we get it, and now these morons aren't putting their masks on and we're all going to get it in this room.*

We were very protective of our senior colleagues, and many of them were very worried about getting it, and we had to keep asking Republicans to put their masks on, and many of us were like, "If you don't like me, that's fine, but please do it for them."

Meanwhile, journalist Olivia Beavers was sheltering in Representative Gallego's office.

OLIVIA BEAVERS, Politico *congressional reporter:* One girl in the room had tweeted, "We're safely in Congressman Gallego's office." And I guess Gallego found it, and he ran into the room and he's like, "Who tweeted this? You need to delete that right now." And we're looking out the window. We think we see buses to take members out of the complex altogether, but he's lowering the blinds. He's former military.

I think I was dealing with blood sugar issues. I was very thirsty and hungry at that point, and some staffers I knew tried to pull out these chocolates and we're eating them.

FRANK LOCKWOOD, Arkansas Democrat-Gazette *reporter, sheltering elsewhere in the Capitol:* I think somehow somewhere we managed to locate some chocolate. There was a soda machine that had Diet Cokes, so I'm sure there were a few Diet Cokes and whatever chocolate we could forage from staffers' desks and whatnot. But I think that was pretty much—it was chocolate and Diet Coke and not much else.

Honestly, I was worried about my dog who was expecting a walk at some point that evening, and I felt bad that she wasn't going to be going anywhere anytime soon.

FORT MCNAIR

3:22 P.M.

ALEXANDRA PELOSI, *Speaker Nancy Pelosi's daughter*: There were a flurry of calls. My mother didn't have her cell phone, so she was using other people's phones. There's a whole sort of like, "Can I use your phone? Can I use that phone?"

Alexandra Pelosi filmed Senator Schumer and Speaker Pelosi as they spoke on the phone with Jeffrey Rosen, acting attorney general.

SPEAKER NANCY PELOSI: They're breaking windows and going in, obviously ransacking our offices and all the rest of that. That's nothing. The concern we have about personal harm—

SEN. CHUCK SCHUMER (D-NY), CUTTING IN: Safety.

SPEAKER NANCY PELOSI: Personal safety is—it just transcends everything. But the fact is, on any given day, they're breaking the law in many different ways. And quite frankly, much of it at the instigation of the president of the United States. And now, if he could at least—somebody—

SEN. CHUCK SCHUMER, CUTTING IN: Yeah, why don't you get the president to tell them to leave the Capitol, Mr. Attorney General, in your law enforcement responsibility? A public statement they should all leave.

JEFFREY ROSEN, ACTING ATTORNEY GENERAL, OVER THE PHONE: We're treating this with the greatest—

SEN. CHUCK SCHUMER: Will you ask the president to make a statement to ask them to leave the Capitol?

JEFFREY ROSEN: So, uh, as you might guess, we're coordinating this quickly—

SEN. CHUCK SCHUMER: No, no, no. Please answer my question. Answer my question![2]

ALEXANDRA PELOSI: [Rep.] Jim Clyburn had his feet up in the air. He was on a couch and his feet up in the air, and he just about every ten minutes he would chime in. "If they were Black, they'd all be shot by now! I'll tell you something, if they were Black, they'd all be dead by now!" Almost like in a chorus if you were watching this play out in a Broadway show. And that was amusing. My son, he goes like, "Cue the chorus."

. . . There was a lot of that, which was funny.

Alexandra Pelosi kept recording as Senator Schumer, Senator Mc-Connell (R-KY), and Speaker Pelosi spoke on the phone with acting secretary of defense Christopher C. Miller.

SEN. MITCH MCCONNELL: We're in one helluva hurry, you understand?

CHRISTOPHER C. MILLER: Gotcha loud and clear, Leader.

SEN. CHUCK SCHUMER: We cannot be, "We're just waiting for so-and-so." We need them there now. Whoever you got.

SPEAKER NANCY PELOSI: Just pretend for a moment it was the Pentagon or the White House, or some other entity that was under siege. You can logistically get people there as you make the plan and you have some leadership of the National Guard there—they have not been given the authority to activate.[3]

ALEXANDRA PELOSI: At some point it got too crowded because they had to mark off all these spots because of social distancing. They made a decision to put the Republicans in one room and the Democrats in another room. I don't know who made the decision and I don't know why, but at some point they said, "We have too many people in this room. How can we separate them?" And so somebody came in and announced we're going to move the Democrats into their own room. And my mother was like, "Why are you separating us? That doesn't make sense." But they did. And so the Democrats were in one room and the Republicans were in their own room, and they kept coming back and forth.

The conversation that they were having was: Do we bring the whole Congress here? We have buses. We can take all of Congress and the Senate—the House and the Senate—put them on buses and bring them here and do it in a big auditorium here at Fort McNair and certify the election results here. Let's do it here. And there was a whole conversation that people wanted to do that.

But there was this whole conversation: If it happens at Fort McNair, there are no cameras. So the conspiracy theories will abound. We really need to get back to the Capitol. How can we get back to the Capitol?

My mother said from the very beginning, "We have to go back because if we do it here, it will open up a can of worms. Just think of the conspiracy theories. We have to get back into that building. We have to be able to secure the building." There was some disagreement. Other people were saying, "We should just bring 'em here and get it over with, so it's done." And there was a whole back and forth about that. But they did have the buses lined up.

So she was just dialing a million people to try and get us back to the Capitol. How can we get back to the Capitol? That was her big thing: getting us back to the Capitol. Because she knew that if we didn't certify the election that day that they will have succeeded.

Now, very important to point out: everybody was getting along, everybody was working together. Everybody was in crisis mode. Nobody thought this was okay. Everybody was properly panicked. Nobody enjoyed seeing people sitting in the Senate chair or whatever.

Mitch McConnell came in the room. He said, "I'm going to make sure Donald Trump is not invited to this inauguration. I don't want him at this inauguration after what he's done to this country. This is a shame that he let this happen. How dare he." And he was not happy with the president at that moment.

HOUSE SAFE ROOM IN THE CAPITOL

REP. ERIC SWALWELL: There were rumors and talks that there were going to be busses sent. And I remember Schiff and I and Gallego kind of huddled together and saying, "Absolutely not. We are not leaving." We were like, "First, safety-wise, you're a sitting duck on a public street. We are not getting in a bus. But also rule number one of a coup is don't leave the seat of power. If you leave, then they could hold it." So that was also in our mind.

The Virginia and Maryland National Guards were finally activated and mobilized toward the Capitol, along with other local and state police departments.

UPPER WEST TERRACE

3:30 P.M.

DANIEL HODGES, *DC Metropolitan Police officer:* So eventually I made myself get back up and get back out there. I had lost my gas mask at that point, obviously, because someone had ripped it off, so I didn't go back in the tunnel because I was afraid that I would be overwhelmed by all the chemicals in there. So I found a staircase and went back out to the Upper West Terrace, joined a line out there, stood on the line until eventually reinforcements started to arrive. I believe the first ones I saw were from Montgomery County, Maryland. Their police showed up and I started clapping. [*Laughs.*]

ALEX MARQUARDT, *CNN correspondent:* We saw some police showing up from Montgomery County, and I remember thinking, well, the cavalry's finally gotten here and they're going to sort of quash this and put an end to the riot.

ALEX MARQUARDT, LIVE ON CNN: Jake, we are seeing a number of local police officers from Montgomery County, Maryland, who have arrived in the past twenty minutes en masse. . . . It feels like the cavalry has arrived, more than a dozen vehicles with all sorts of officers piling out of those vehicles, and suiting up in riot gear.

ALEX MARQUARDT: But they seemed to go into the melee and then just disappear.

INSIDE THE CAPITOL BUILDING

3:41 P.M.

RIOTERS, CHANTING: U-S-A! U-S-A! U-S-A! U-S-A!

LOUIE PALU, *freelance photojournalist on assignment for* National Geographic, *inside the Capitol:* I went down the hall and there was a broken group of police somewhere in riot gear somewhere, and there's pepper spray dripping off of some of them. They looked terrified, exhausted, and at the bottom of their morale, and they're trying to just hold the crowd. People were screaming profanity at the police. And I was trying to take photographs, and I just felt terrified at this point. I thought, *I am just in this by myself here. There's no other photographers.*

And I just felt like it was kind of one of those back-in-time moments. My mother was a child in the Second World War in Italy and [she had] relatives who were partisan. So the Nazi secret police used to come looking for the resistance. And I remember my mother used to teach me to hide under the stairs, as a kid. And I never understood until I was an adult, like, oh, okay, that's what she did in the war. And she'd always be afraid of the government or the state sort of security apparat like, Can you report on that? Are you allowed to? Because she was afraid. I said, "The war is over."

It was in that moment [when I saw the police that] I actually felt embarrassed. My mom warned me that this was going to come one day. And there I was, and in that hallway I felt embarrassed. My mother was right. You know how you don't want to admit to your parents? Wow, you're totally right. And I just thought, *Fuck, I got to hide, man.*

| **But before he could, the police reinforcements arrived.**

LOUIE PALU: They're like, "Everybody get out." And I could hear that sound I remembered from the summer—the rubber bullets being fired, those little round pellets, those stinger balls, they're called. I could hear it. And I was just turning my back and people are pulling their Carhartts up and it was like rubber bullets being fired down the hallway of the first floor of the Senate.

And it's like, *What the hell?* It just was another level into Dante's Inferno. I'm getting shot up by rubber bullets. I can't get out. I'm in the crowd. I kind of turned and I saw the police wall. There's a group of them and the rioters are struggling with them, and I thought it was some Greek mythology scene where they're fighting the creatures. And I just thought, *I have to photograph this. This is so important.* So I squeezed myself over into the corner beside the door and I just held my camera up the air and I turned my face in. I just took photos from up in the air.

OUTSIDE THE LOWER WEST TERRACE TUNNEL

3:45 P.M.

JANE, *staff photojournalist for a major mainstream outlet*: So I realize that there's still a battle going on. And at that point, I heard them chanting, "Heave-ho." And I was like, *Oh my God, they're trying to break into that door.* So I'm like, *How can I get a perspective that will show that door?* So that's why I decided to climb the [TV tower] scaffolding.

I remember saying to myself something like, *Well, fuck it. Here we fucking go. You're going to do this, aren't you?* Just kind of talking to myself. And I slung my cameras behind me. I'm also in a gas mask and a helmet, you're not moving as well. So I'm like, I need to be careful. It was January—people forget this. It was January. So it was cold. I start climbing this metal ladder, which doesn't have a cage around it or anything. And I just remember really distinctly how cold the metal was and how my hands were absolutely burning because they were covered in chemicals. They were covered in pepper spray, mace, whatever other chemicals were flying around there that are skin irritants.

And I just remember that weird, intense physical dichotomy between the cold of the metal and the burning sensation of the top of my hands from all of the chemicals that were on them as I was climbing.

There's definitely some Trump supporters up there. So I was being careful. I was aware of who I was around, and definitely didn't feel safe, but I felt like, *Okay, I have a perspective of what's going on here.* So I stood up there and I stayed there for a while, and I just photographed this battle that was going on at the door.

4 P.M.

RADIO TRANSMISSION, DC FEMS: We're evaluating an officer that was dragged down the steps, kicked in the head three times, had a vomiting episode. He's going to need to be transported for evaluation. We need a transport unit for him.[4]

Injured officers were taken to dedicated law enforcement triage zones around the Capitol campus.

GUS PAPATHANASIOU, *US Capitol Police officer:* I was assigned to the south-side triage area, and that's where I was the entire day. So we tended to a lot of the injured officers from MPD and Capitol Police. It was the loading dock in the Rayburn [building]. They were just bringing officers in with wounds. There was one officer from Metropolitan, he just had a blank stare on his face. He didn't really talk to anybody. He had a patch over his eye and he didn't want to talk to anybody. I tried to go up to him and talk to him, but he just had this . . . stare and just didn't want to deal with anybody.

I remember another short Metropolitan officer who got popped in the mouth with some kind of a pipe. He got punched in the mouth and he said he just got up and kept fighting. There was another officer from our department that was covered in one of those warm blankets, those bright silver warm blankets. And he ended up leaving the department. All he was worried about was his CDU gear. He goes, "I don't know where my CDU gear is." I go, "Who cares?" I mean, he was injured. A lot of these guys were.

THE WHITE HOUSE

4:03 P.M.

President Trump finally agreed to read a statement that staffers had prepared, calling for the rioters to stand down. Preparations were made to film him reading the statement in the Rose Garden, but when they began to shoot, Trump refused to read the script. Instead, he ad-libbed, claiming again that the election was stolen and fraudulent.

PRESIDENT DONALD TRUMP: I know your pain. I know you're hurt. We had an election that was stolen from us. It was a landslide election, and everyone knows it, especially the other side, but you have to go home now. . . . We love you, you're very special.

Trump's video was posted to Twitter at 4:17 p.m. Almost immediately, rioters saw the video and began to disperse.

GROUP CHAT MESSAGE FROM OATH KEEPER: Gentleman [*sic*], Our Commander-in-Chief has just ordered us to go home. Comments?[5]

STEPHAN AYRES, *rioter:* That's basically your president, you know, asking you, you know—that's how I look at it, like, "Hey, chill out." Because he said, "All right, guys, let's cool it out." I wish he would have done it, you know, ten minutes after he seen what started and what was going on. But kind of following that as like, you know, let's get out of here, which I wish it would have been done a little earlier, honestly.

For people that were like me that were there—we weren't there to cause trouble; we were there to basically be a peaceful protester—I think that would have really swayed people like me.[6]

4:21 P.M.

JAKE TAPPER, CNN ANCHOR, LIVE ON CNN: Now, we brought that to you because President Trump on the tape says to his supporters who are right now conducting an armed insurrection at the US Capitol, he tells them to go home.

But I also want to note that, in that video, he lies about the election being stolen and pours more fuel on the fire. He continues his shameful behavior of lying to his supporters about what happened.

It is absolutely disgraceful. I hope they listen to the part in which he said for them to go home. But, to be completely frank, there were mixed messages in that video.

And I feel ambivalent about the fact that we even aired it, to be honest, although I certainly understand and support the idea that we did.

REP. RUBEN GALLEGO'S OFFICE

ABOUT 4:25 P.M.

OLIVIA BEAVERS: I still didn't have the mind at that point to discern what was happening besides realizing [Trump is] not giving a hard message of pulling back to his messengers. And Gallego just screams like, "Fuck you!" so loud that the entire room is just sort of stuck. And I think that everyone was just in shock looking at him. And that was the first real anger expression that

I'd seen, where I was sort of—another moment where you understood the gravitas of what had happened.

OUTSIDE THE CAPITOL, NORTH SIDE

ABOUT 4:30 P.M.

DAVID BUTOW, *freelance photojournalist*: So it seemed like things were dying down.

ADAM GRAY, *freelance photojournalist on assignment for the* Daily Mail: We can see a load of riot police coming. There's some kind of green-suited ones who look way more serious. This is state patrol, this is the SWAT teams, and they start forcing them back. So it's very obvious. This is the beginning of the end.

CHAPTER 13

"THE MOB KEPT ATTACKING EVEN WHILE WE TENDED TO THEIR WOUNDED"

FORT MCNAIR

4:22 P.M.

Speaker Pelosi got Vice President Pence on the phone. Alexandra Pelosi filmed her mother's side of the conversation.

SPEAKER NANCY PELOSI: Hi. Mr. Vice President? . . . Hi. Yeah. We're okay. We're with Mr. Schumer, Mr. McConnell, the leadership—House and Senate, and how are you? [*Pause*] Oh my goodness. Where are you? [*Pause*] God bless you. [*Pause*]

We're being told it could take days to clear the Capitol, and that we should be moving everyone here to get the job done. We're at McNair, which has facilities for the House and the Senate to meet. We'd rather go to the Capitol and do it there, but it doesn't seem to be safe. [*Pause*]

We've gotten a very bad report about the condition of the House Floor, with defecation and all that kind of thing.

Nancy Pelosi held the phone in one hand and in the other a piece of unopened jerky that she was trying to rip open with her teeth.

ALEXANDRA PELOSI: She was devouring the Slim Jim. Yeah, no, we were starving.

SPEAKER NANCY PELOSI: Okay. Then call us back. I worry about you being in the Capitol, though. Don't let anyone know where you are.[1]

ALEXANDRA PELOSI: They had a very polite conversation. She was very worried about him and his family. She kept saying, "I'm worried sick about him and his family." I mean, he is the vice president, and we've gotten sort of hints that he was hung out to dry and he was being left behind in that building.

LOWER WEST TERRACE TUNNEL

| **The police and the rioters continued to spar at the same door.**

ALAN CHIN, *freelance photojournalist on assignment for* Business Insider: They fought at that gate for two, three hours.

JANE, *staff photojournalist for a major mainstream outlet*: This whole time you can see they're passing all these objects from different parts of the crowd—a hockey stick wrapped in a flag—and they're yelling at each other for things. They were working together to fight this battle, and they're just people in the crowd. They're shouting to people on the sides. They're trying to find objects. It's like, again, this is where it feels almost like a game in some ways. I don't want to downplay it, because again, this was an extremely scary, very dangerous day, but there's this idea of them like, "Oh yeah, find a ladder. Does anyone have a blah?" They were passing furniture out through the window, and they were using anything they could find as battering rams.

4:26 P.M.

| **Justin Winchell and Roseanne Boyland were in that crush of people.**

JUSTIN WINCHELL, *rioter*: It was crowded. I kinda lost Rosanne. She was like two people away from me.[2]

CHERYL BOYLAND, *Rosanne Boyland's mother*: He said the only reason they were up that far was because they got pushed by the crowd. They were actually on their way down, headed out because it was too much crowd, and then they got shoved into the crowd.

JUSTIN WINCHELL: Like, pushing people, pushing people, pushing people to get closer to the door, to go into the building. So they basically created a panic. And then the police in turn pushed back on them so people started falling.[3]

| A video caught Winchell realizing Boyland had collapsed.

JUSTIN WINCHEL: She's gonna die! She's dead!

| Instead of responding to his pleas, rioters sprayed some kind of chemical irritant over his head, aiming at the police behind him.

JUSTIN WINCHELL: Rosanne! Rosanne!

RIOTER, TO AN OFFICER: I'll kill you!

JUSTIN WINCHELL: Roseanne turns her head up, lips blue. I think she had been without oxygen face down and people laid on top of her. And then there's two other guys I pulled off of her. And then the last time I tried to get her up, I got my arm underneath her. And then another guy fell on top of her. And then another guy was just walking. I mean, there was people crushed. We finally got her out, myself and two patriots. One of 'em had med scissors and a med kit, and they performed CPR on her. They were goin' up and down on her chest.[4]

| Nick Quested was filming too.

NICK QUESTED, *documentary filmmaker*: They pull Roseanne Boyland out, and she's already dead. She looks like a Smurf at this point, she's so blue.

She got pulled out from exactly the spot where there'd been a huge pressure of large men. She was absolutely, completely, overmatched in that situation, people pushing. It's not like someone trying to get into a concert. This was a concerted effort to push from both sides. I can't imagine what the pressure—I used to play a lot of rugby and I can't imagine what that pressure would be like. There was real forces being exerted with a lot of people pushing. There's got to be more than a hundred people on both sides pushing each other.

I knew she was dead.

The rioters dragged Boyland toward the police at the door. The officers pulled her inside.

SGT. AQUILINO GONELL, *US Capitol Police officer*: Inside the tunnel . . . I watched several officers carrying a young protester who'd collapsed to safety. "Request medical assistance and DC Fire!" I yelled as someone checked her vitals.[5]

CHRISTOPHER HOLMES, *battalion fire chief, DC FEMS*: We immediately were notified that, hey, there's a CPR victim. This area was also almost like a battleground between protesters and the police and the individual that was experiencing the cardiac event was right there in that area.[6]

RADIO TRANSMISSION, DC FEMS: What is the best access to you?[7]

FIRE CHIEF HOLMES, OVER THE RADIO: [*Coughing*] I'll let you know. We have heavy CS in the area.[8]

FIRE CHIEF HOLMES: I remember seeing a lot of injured officers on the side of the hallway. They were gasping for air and I couldn't really understand why, from a distance. They were gasping for air and some of them were bleeding. I asked them if they were okay. They said they're just taking a breather and some of them were wounded but didn't need medical assistance, so we kept on going through, and that's when we encountered almost like a wall of tear gas. So they were gasping for air because it was so much tear gas.

When we got to the—to the victim, there was almost like a puddle of CS gas or pepper spray that the victim was laying in, that's how much that was being utilized. Also there was a lot of dry chemical extinguishers that were being utilized on the police, so that was all in the air. It was very rancid. We finally made it to where the victim was.[9]

FIRE CHIEF HOLMES: One of the medics intubated the patient right then and there. CPR was started.

SERGEANT GONELL: No pulse. A flagpole landed next to us, then a hammer. . . . The mob kept attacking even while we tended to their wounded. "Move her. It's not safe here!" I screamed over the noise.[10]

They moved her out of the tunnel and carried her up one floor.

DC FEMS PERSONNEL OVER THE RADIO: Recon to Capitol Command. We are on the scene with the CPR patient. Can we get a unit to come with a stretcher?[11]

FIRE CHIEF HOLMES: We were able to find an old army-style cot.

SERGEANT GONELL: A black military two-wheeled gurney that six of us carried up two flights, since the elevators were in evacuation mode.[12]

When I get to the top, that's when I see all the chaos that happened in the area. Fire extinguishers, the firefighters, the officers, the military, all trying to catch a breath. I was just shocked that so many people got in and all the damage and when I asked, "What happened here?" [they said,] "Well, they all came here."

I'm like, "Who?" And then that's when somebody said, "Well, the rioters, they got inside." I'm like, "Through which door? Not through where I was."

So that was very stunning to me that—I'm like, *I did everything I could to prevent these people from coming in. So where the hell did they came in at?* And then that's when I find out there were all the breaches in the Capitol. Even though I had a radio, I wasn't listening to the radio because I was a little busy.[13]

ELLEN KURLAND, *EMS captain, DC FEMS*: When we got into the Capitol, they had her on some kind of dolly or pull cart and they were pulling her down the hallway towards us. We'd worked her for thirty minutes and she had been down approximately twenty minutes before we were even able to get to her.[14]

SERGEANT GONELL: We tried for another 20, 30 minutes with new medical machines, whatnot, and there was no sign of [life].[15]

| **The paramedics decided to transport her to the hospital.**

SEAN MCGEE, *firefighter paramedic, DC FEMS*: To get out of the building, we had to figure out a way to get the stretcher down steps because all the exits with the ramps were blocked.[16]

ELLEN KURLAND: So we loaded her up on the medic unit,* which is also kind of difficult because we were nowhere near where the medic unit had

---

* An ambulance staffed with a paramedic.

initially parked and the medic unit then transported her to the hospital. This was the most hostile, angry crowd, large crowd that I've ever seen.[17]

GEORGIA

5 P.M.

CHERYL BOYLAND: Justin called, freaking out . . . saying, "I want you to know Roseanne was taken to the hospital. I don't know which hospital. I don't." And he was talking so fast about what happened. There's no way this guy was telling me a lie. Some of the patriots, he called 'em, there were trying to give her CPR. And finally the police took her in and they were supposed to put her in an ambulance and send her to the hospital. And he was, I mean, everything he told me I knew was true, and we were freaking out. I called every single solitary hospital in Washington, DC. I called every emergency room listed. I called the fire department, the police department, the Capitol Police, the Metro PD police. I called everybody.

Nobody seemed to know where her daughter was.

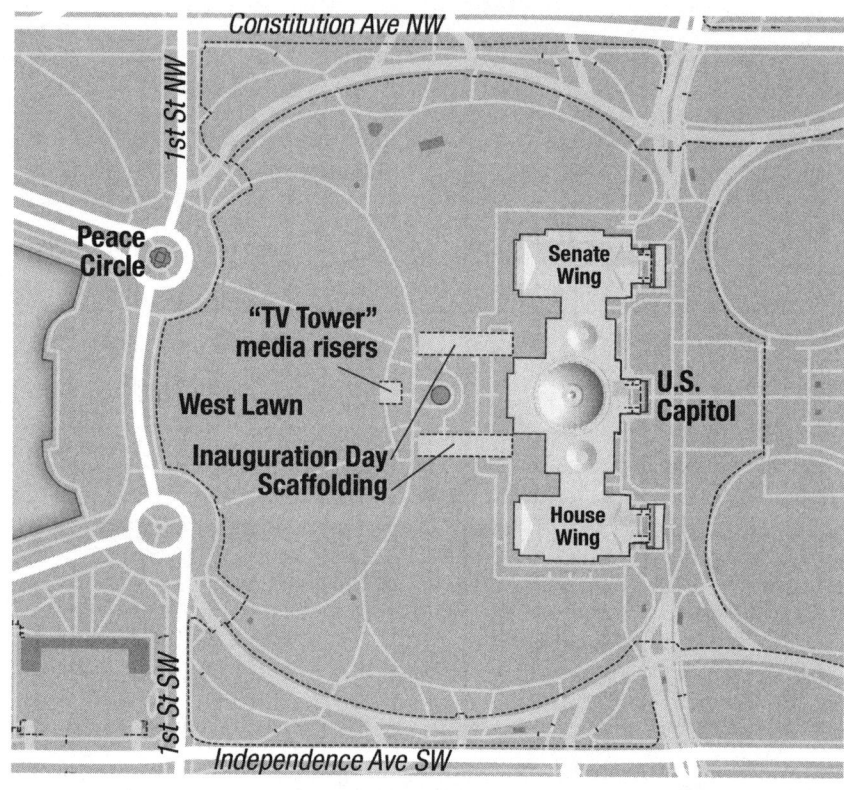

CHAPTER 14

"YOU STARTED TO SEE THE POLICE OFFICERS MAKE PROGRESS"

ABOUT 4:50 P.M.

Back outside the Capitol building, the sun was beginning to set, casting the whole scene in eerie blues and grays. Clouds of tear gas and smoke hung over the crowd. The police were still in the process of clearing the crowd, even after Trump's tweet calling for them to go home.

SAUNDRA KICZENSKI, *rioter*: It just looked so neat. We weren't there to steal things. We weren't there to do damage. We were just there to overthrow the government.[1]

RON HAVIV, *freelance photojournalist on assignment for the* New Republic: The ending was the ending because the military support came in and basically cleared it out. They had the confidence; they had the numbers, people were exhausted, also—just five, six hours of this.

And basically they were also announcing on a loudspeaker, "You're going to be arrested. You have to get off federal property." So I think that scared many, many people, like, "All right, we're out of here." And again, with no goal, nothing to achieve, they're like, "Okay, we're going to go. The day is over." And basically they were pushed to the outskirts of the [police] lines, and the lines formed and protected the Capitol.

I took some photographs on the outskirts and then I had to make my deadline, so I had to go and file.

EVY MAGES, Washingtonian *photojournalist*: As it started to get dark, the cops from the top down kind of started clearing the protesters. They just started from the very top, top steps here and pushed them down. People were saying that Trump said to go home. They just regained control over the front steps of the Capitol.

STEPHEN VOSS, *freelance photojournalist on assignment for* Politico: You started to see the police officers make progress, starting to push people out of the upper levels, out of the inauguration stage and stuff like the top risers where the VIPs, the Supreme Court justice, that they would all sit, those areas started to get cleared. You saw flash bangs being used.

JANE, *staff photojournalist for a major mainstream outlet*: So then I was also like, *Hmm, I should get some wide photos of this situation.* Just because, having worked in DC, it's drilled into your mind to give that DC context. And so it's kind of always in the back of my mind of showing the Capitol, showing whatever, to make sure that you're getting that context. So that's why I was like, *I should get a wide shot of this situation from here.* So I started taking a few of those, and that's when a flash bang [starts] going off.

In her photo, the Capitol almost looks like it's on fire. It captured a lightning strike, a moment in time.

JANE: You have to just remember the context of the moment, that I had spent the last year photographing protests. So you start to also get the rhythm of explosions and of working in a situation where things are blowing up.

LARRY, *US Capitol Police officer*: Once we saw the Virginia State Police and those six-foot-five military-style type guys come in and finally take that Lower West Terrace door back, I think that's when we knew the fight was finally over.

But tensions were still high. As CNN correspondent Alex Marquardt reported live from the scene, a man in a red hoodie waving an enormous American flag came up behind him and yelled at him loud enough to be heard through his mic on TV.

ALEX MARQUARDT, LIVE ON CNN: So, this is a faceoff between law enforcement and the rioters here. We have seen riot police showing up—

MAN: They're not rioters! You are lying. They are not rioters. They are not rioters.

ALEX MARQUARDT: Sir, I'm on TV.

MAN: They are not rioters!

ALEX MARQUARDT: It was kind of in that moment that the crowd kind of clocked onto the assembled press. They kind of turned on us. It felt like a zombie movie where one zombie sees you and then they all turn towards you and start coming at you. And I thought in that moment, *We've seen this movie before.* We pulled back immediately. And after that, all kinds of gear [got] trashed.

STEPHEN VOSS: There was camera equipment, tripod stands, lights, and there were rioters who were just destroying it, who were kicking up or picking up and throwing it down. And I just remember there was this guy who was streaming all this live, and he kept saying, "This is the end of the legacy media," or something very hyperbolic, a grandiose statement.

ADAM GRAY, *freelance photojournalist on assignment for the* Daily Mail: I mean for me, this is more one of the most sinister parts of the day, besides the shooting: they're smashing all the camera stuff, but especially thinking about your own safety because they're starting to say, "Enemies of the people." I heard someone say, "We're going to drop a list and we're going to hunt them down one by one." They're speaking about my colleagues—they could be speaking about me.

LOUIE PALU, *freelance photojournalist on assignment for* National Geographic: And I thought, *Oh, okay, now I'm scared. I'm out of gas. I have no adrenaline.* I'm like, *I just want to go hide.* And I just kind of walked. And I was just standing there and I think I was in a daze. And a friend of mine who was working for AP, came over and he said, "Louie, are you okay?" And I was like, kind of—I couldn't talk.

US Capitol Police officer Caroline Edwards arrested a rioter and took him to prisoner processing. Suddenly, she passed out.

OFFICER EDWARDS: I just slumped over, and I woke up in a cold sweat. And I went to the captain who was there and I said, "Something's wrong." I hadn't really processed that I had been hit as badly as I thought. But, you know, he started asking me what day it was, like simple questions. I couldn't really answer them, so he put me in an ambulance.

Back at the Capitol, reporters began leaving, too, ahead of the 6 p.m. citywide curfew.

ALAN CHIN, *freelance photojournalist on assignment for* Business Insider: It was almost anticlimactic. Because intellectually, you know you've just witnessed this unprecedented assault on the Capitol by this crowd, and specifically, I should say, by the very militant members of that crowd. And as you're leaving, you almost feel like, *Wow, okay, that's it.* Right?

Many other reporters, police officers, and witnesses say they felt the same thing: that the day could have gone much, much worse.

SGT. AQUILINO GONELL, *US Capitol Police officer*: We were lucky that we individually [and] collectively decided to exercise so much restraint. I knew I was justified to use lethal force. I just thought I would have made things worse. Not only for myself but for my other officers. I think it could have been a lot worse. We didn't want to get in a bloodbath.[2]

DANIEL HODGES, *DC Metropolitan Police officer*: The reason why I didn't shoot anyone, and I imagine why many others didn't, [is] there were over nine thousand of the terrorists out there with an unknown number of firearms, and a couple hundred of us maybe. So, if that turned into a firefight, we would have lost, and this was a fight we couldn't afford to lose.[3]

There was still some fighting as officers pushed rioters away from the building. MPD officer Jeffrey Smith—who had texted his wife earlier that "London has fallen"—was hit in the head with a metal pole.[4]

Some of the journalists remained on the site as well.

JANE: We stayed around for a while just to just see, because people were kind of still lingering.

I was running into colleagues, and we were checking in with each other. We were all worried about someone getting cornered or taken, so we were trying to stick together at this point.

We're waiting for the [6 p.m.] curfew because in other places, other protests I've covered, the curfew is like, go-ahead for the police to just go nuts and do whatever the fuck they want.

At that point, I was quite tired. You're basically just babysitting a situation.

And at some point, me and another person, another photographer I was with, we were able to leave. So we left together. Nobody left alone. We made sure that everybody had someone to leave with, and I'm talking about across—it doesn't matter who you work for. We looked out for each other as fellow journalists because we were just such major targets, and people had had their lives threatened and been attacked, and so there was still a very strong fear that people could get attacked again or even killed or whatever. So we just made sure that people were okay, at least safe when they were leaving.

LOUIE PALU: I went back to [the press workspace in the] Dirksen [Senate Office Building] and the door was locked. No one was going back in. I don't know what time it was at this—6, 6:30, I don't know—maybe an hour of being—staring at the ground like, *What the fuck just happened?*

I sat on the curb at one point and just thought, *What the hell happened? Like, what the fuck just happened?*

And the riot was kind of coming down by now. You could hear explosions and flash bangs, screaming, weird shrieks.

I could see photographers that were kind of in different other positions, further down with their laptops on the sidewalk filing on the concrete. It seemed like a war zone there.

STEPHEN VOSS: It was a few miles' walk to my car. So I knew it was going to take a while. There were people walking alongside me who had Trump stuff, who were clearly walking from the Capitol too. I remember this one guy walked by the Canadian embassy, which had a nice Christmas tree, and he just paused to take a picture of it. And it was just any old tourist walking through and being like, *Oh, that's really nice. This is a nice thing.* And he had just been down at the Capitol.

FORT MCNAIR

5:59 P.M.

| **Speaker Pelosi and Senator Schumer spoke on the phone with Vice President Pence again. Alexandra Pelosi recorded the conversation.**

VICE PRESIDENT PENCE, ON SPEAKERPHONE: I'm literally standing with the chief of police of the US Capitol Police. He just informed me that what you will hear through official channels: Paul Irving, your sergeant at arms, will inform you that their best information is that they believe that the House and the Senate will be able to reconvene in roughly an hour.

| **Schumer and Pelosi exchanged surprised glances.**

SEN. CHUCK SCHUMER: Good news.

VICE PRESIDENT PENCE: The sergeant at arms will be in touch about—about the process for, for getting members back into the building.

SPEAKER NANCY PELOSI: Thank you very much, Mr. Vice President. Good news.[5]

RICHARD, *congressional staffer, back at the Capitol*: I think there was a collective sigh of relief when people realized that we would be going back. On the one hand, when you go through something like that, you just want to go home and be with your loved ones. But on the other hand, there was a huge part of me that said, *I want to get back over there. I want to finish this joint session*, and I truly want the message to be that you didn't win, that we did what we were supposed to do, that we completed the task that we had to do.[6]

| **At the White House, President Trump drafted a tweet.**

PRESIDENT DONALD TRUMP VIA TWITTER, 6:01 P.M.: These are the things and events that happen when a sacred landslide election victory is so unceremoniously & viciously stripped away from great patriots who have been badly & unfairly treated for so long. Go home with love & in peace. Remember this day forever![7]

JANUARY 6 REPORT: At 6:27 p.m. President Trump retired to his residence for the night. As he did, he had one final comment to an employee who accompanied him to the residence. The one takeaway that the President expressed in that moment, following a horrific afternoon of violence and the worst attack against the US Capitol building in over two centuries, was this: "Mike Pence let me down."

LOUIE PALU: I remember the ride home on my bike. It felt like it took four hours to ride home, and it was really just like a twenty-minute ride. I was like—I couldn't even breathe. I had all that tear gas and fire extinguisher powder in my throat. I rode home, and I don't want to reveal where I live, but I have to go up a big hill. And that hill felt like I was in the fricking Tour de France, man. I had to get off my bike a couple of times and walk my bike. I was just so fried from the day.

JANE: I remember at one point—I believe I was in my car by that point. I remember sitting there and just having this moment where I thought, *You need to hold on to the clarity that you have right now about what happened today.* I felt like after that day our country's broken. I didn't know how we could come back from something like that.

And I felt like I needed to really meditate on that truth because I just knew that there would be so many narratives spun, and people would try and make their own stories about what had happened that day. It was just like this moment where I took the time to actually really think about cementing that feeling and just saying to myself, *Don't forget this feeling. This is clarity. You have clarity on where we are as a country. This is where we are.* And I knew to hold onto that.

For others, the long day was far from over. The police had to clear the Capitol building so that Congress could reconvene.

OFFICER HODGES: Eventually I went back into the building and just waited there for everybody to gather again. We all just sort of eventually found our way there and until—stayed there until, I mean, they were telling us we could have to go back out there.

OFFICER LARRY: But it wasn't over for us. We still had to go back. I still had to go back to the Senate side where most of the members were. And we had to essentially wait until the Capitol building was cleaned up to escort all 'em back to the Capitol so that they could finish their electoral votes.

6:48 P.M.

| **Speaker Pelosi finally was able to return to the Capitol.**

ALEXANDRA PELOSI: I think that was the most heartbreaking experience I've had as a human on this Earth because I felt so sorry for my mother because people literally pooped in the Capitol.

And when we walked into our office, people had—they broke everything. Yeah, that was hard because how would you feel if someone broke into your house and just trashed everything? That's how she feels about the Capitol. It's like her home. It was not just an office building to her—it was the sacred ground where her father served and where she served for thirty-some years. These places are sacred to some people. I mean, you may not have any respect for the institutions, and every day that goes by, Americans don't seem to have much respect for the institutions anymore. But my mother's an old-school relic. She really respects democracy and the institution of Congress. And so for her, this was very personal because they had shit all over this place that she holds to be sacred. And that was tough. And then they left threatening notes—they left, "We will be back," and all those stupid notes that they left behind on the tables and stuff.

I mean, the staff were crying. Remember, they'd been left behind, locked under a desk. They thought they were going to be killed. For the people that were left behind, the staffers that were hiding under a table, they had post-traumatic stress. A lot of 'em left their jobs. A lot of 'em left their jobs. I'm not sure there are any left that work in that building that were there that day, that worked for her in that capacity.

HOUSE SAFE ROOM

7 P.M.

CRAIG, *congressional staffer*: All of a sudden the Speaker and [House majority leader] Steny Hoyer appeared.[8]

SHANE SMITH, *aide to Speaker Nancy Pelosi*: The room broke out into applause.[9]

CRAIG: And that was the first moment where I thought, *Wow, they're here. They're with us. This is going to be okay. They're here. They're not in hiding.*

I just remember the look of shock on the Speaker's face and on Mr. Hoyer's face too. I've never seen their faces like that. And this is going to sound very strange, but in that moment, I didn't feel like it was the Speaker of the House and the Leader. I felt like we were all human for a moment.[10]

SHANE SMITH: Members were ready to go back to work and finish certifying an election, a mundane constitutional exercise. And then before I left, the Speaker just came over and talked to my colleagues and I and thanked us for what we do, and told us how sorry she was, that we had to go through something like this.[11]

RICARDO MITCHELL, *Labor Division of the Architect of the Capitol:*★ Once they got everything under control, we had to come back in the building and clean up the mess, because the members were going to return to finish voting. We had to go into the chambers and prepare them so they would be able to come back. It was a lot of masks and a lot of broken glass, some broken furniture. They had to barricade the doors. . . . It was a lot of debris, you know? And we had a short time to clean it up. But we just got it done. I have a hardworking team.[12]

JEFF WALTERS, *Architect of the Capitol carpenter:* There's not a whole lot that surprises us anymore, but seeing the overall condition of the building that night, that, I would have to say, was a bit shocking. . . . I've been with the Architect of the Capitol for maybe twenty-two, twenty-three years. So I've seen a lot of the things that have gone on here, but I've never seen the building in such disarray.[13]

HOUSE CHAMBER

ABOUT 7:15 P.M.

REP. ERIC SWALWELL: I was among one of the first groups to go back. So a cleaning crew was sweeping up glass as you stepped into the chamber. And then when I stepped into the chamber, I noticed two individuals wearing a

---

★ The Architect of the Capitol is the division of staffers responsible for the physical maintenance of the Capitol campus.

blue FBI technician jacket, and they were taking photographs and conducting measurements on the House Floor. . . . I've never seen—photographs are not allowed on the House Floor, so odd. I don't know why but that was one of the first things I remember thinking, like, *You're not allowed to take photos of the House Floor.* But, of course, it had become a crime scene.[14]

RICHARD: We were escorted back over to the chamber at about 7:15 or 7:30. That was kind of a surreal moment when we first got onto the second floor, and there was so much law enforcement from so many different agencies. There were [US] Marshalls, there was FBI, there was ATF [Bureau of Alcohol, Tobacco, Firearms and Explosives], there was Capitol Police, there was District of Columbia [Metropolitan] police. There was Secret Service. I mean, they were everywhere. You could still smell the tear gas throughout the building. At that point, we were told you couldn't go into the Speaker's Lobby because it was a crime scene.[15]

LISA DESJARDINS, PBS NewsHour *correspondent:* Police finally escorted me, a few reporters, and staff back into the Capitol around 7:30 or 8 p.m. But at that point, we still couldn't leave the building [due to the lockdown]. I gulped down some water, then I quickly ate the lunch I'd brought. I was really unhappy that I brought a very healthy lunch: hummus and carrots. I was like, *Why didn't I bring a hamburger?* But at that point, I also just really wanted to get back to covering the election. I felt it was clear that the rioters wanted to stop the election, and they wanted to stop Congress from certifying it. As a reporter, I really wanted to cover Congress finishing their job and finishing the election.[16]

HOUSE FLOOR

8:06 P.M.

VICE PRESIDENT PENCE: Today was a dark day in the history of the United States Capitol, but thanks to the swift efforts of US Capitol Police, federal, state and local law enforcement, the violence was quelled. The Capitol is secured, and the people's work continues. . . .

Those who wreaked havoc in our Capitol today . . . you did not win. Violence never wins. Freedom wins. And this is still the people's house. . . . Let's get back to work.[17]

ALEXANDRA PELOSI: We went back in after all of that, and then [the Republicans] challenged [the election results] again! Oh my. That, to me, was the breaking point. That was when you knew this whole little experiment called democracy is dead. Because after everything we've been through, you're still going to challenge the results? And at that point, everyone was just done, just done, just done. So, yeah, that was the worst.

NORTH CORRIDOR OF THE CAPITOL

ABOUT 10 P.M.

While the debate continued, US Capitol Police officer Brian Sicknick collapsed.

STEVEN SUND, *chief of the US Capitol Police*: [Sicknick] collapsed while walking with a group of officers to get something to eat. One of the officers in the group with him was Chris Grzelak, a Virginia state trooper and tactical medic. Grzelak immediately went to work on Brian, providing CPR and trying to resuscitate him until DC Fire and Emergency Services arrived on the scene.[18]

JON HOPE, *firefighter, DC FEMS*: We heard the radio traffic from Capitol Police that they had an officer in cardiac arrest in the north corridor in the stairwell.[19]

RADIO TRANSMISSION, DC FEMS: We have a medical local inside the Capitol. CPR on a Capitol Police officer.[20]

DAVID HOAGLAND, *DC FEMS Lieutenant*: Me and the rest of the crew got escorted down into the Capitol. The first time I went into the Capitol was as a three-year-old and I've been in there various times throughout my life, so it was kind of surreal to see it in this state after everything just happened, with trash everywhere. It smelled really bad, and there was just an absolute army of police officers everywhere and it was just—it was kind of just like after a battle. We found a downed officer.[21]

JON HOPE: The patient was lying on the ground on his side, had other officers around him. I asked what exactly had happened, and the other officer said they didn't know, that he had just collapsed.[22]

LIEUTENANT HOAGLAND: The other officers were trying to do CPR on him, but he was actually not in cardiac arrest so we kind of pulled everybody back and then the Capitol physicians got there and we started coordinating his care while we were waiting on [the vehicles that] were initially dispatched on the run to get down there.[23]

TIMOTHY BENNETT, *sergeant paramedic, DC FEMS*: My job was to determine where we were in the building and figure out what was the best entrance to get him out of. The elevators were all out of service. The Capitol Police officers and the guardsmen actually had him in a wheelchair and carried them up the spiral staircase to get to the floor we needed to be to get them out. It was not an easy effort, and they did an admirable job.[24]

JON HOPE: And then transported him up to the ambulance where we provided some additional care and treatment and then transported him to the hospital.[25]

CRAIG SICKNICK, *Brian Sicknick's brother*: I got a call from my mother, and I knew it wasn't a normal call, just from the tone in her voice. She's in DC and my brother was injured and it's not good. This was a complete shock, but I wasn't sure how bad it was yet. [My father, brother, and I] all hopped in one car and started driving to DC.

The last text I got from my brother was something along the lines of, "Great, now I smell like BO, pepper spray, and weed." That was the last text I got from him.

It was mayhem in the car. Absolutely horrific. All three of our phones were blowing up. Anybody who knew us was calling us. Reporters were calling us. Of course, we were just shocked. After a while, we just turned the phones off. It's like, we don't need this.

And then we finally get down to the hospital, and we had a couple officers waiting for us who escorted us in. This was during the height of COVID, so nobody was allowed in hospitals normally. Of course, we masked up and did whatever we're supposed to do to go in and then went in, and we were braced for the worst.

It wasn't a good thing seeing your kid brother lying on a hospital gurney with tubes hanging out of him, not moving, gray. That was one hell of a shock, and it put me in a bad mood that I haven't managed to shake.

| Roseanne Boyland's family also got a phone call.

CHERYL BOYLAND, *Rosanne Boyland's mother:* It wasn't until II something that night that I got a phone call saying, "My captain told me to call you because you've been checking all around. I think we have your daughter." And I knew right then she was dead.

LONNA CAVE, *Rosanne Boyland's older sister:* She didn't have her driver's license on her. She didn't have anything on her because they just took her back. Like half of her clothes weren't even on.

CHERYL BOYLAND: Only thing she had on, they said, were the leggings.

BLAIRE BOYLAND, *Rosanne Boyland's younger sister:* The leggings she was wearing underneath her jeans.

CHERYL BOYLAND: They took the jeans off, but not the leggings and a sports bra.

CHERYL BOYLAND: He was asking, "Is there any way I can for sure identify her?" And I said, "Yeah, she has a tattoo that says 'Beautiful Disaster' across her chest." He goes, "Yeah, she passed away."

The family of Kevin Greeson—the rioter who had collapsed near the west side of the Capitol at about 1 p.m.—was also receiving phone calls. He had been declared deceased from a heart attack at 2:05 p.m.

Officers continued to stand by in the Capitol building, just in case they were needed.

OFFICER HODGES: We were sitting around sneezing and stuff just covered in OC spray. But, yeah, we're sitting around waiting and we'd see fresh federal officers coming through with their tactical gear looking sweet and being like, [*mimics deep voice*] "Hey guys, what can we do?"

They finally told us we could leave around midnight or something. After that, we left the grounds. Anyone who needed to go to the hospital went to a local hospital. And then those of us who didn't need immediate medical attention had to stay on [duty] because even though these people were being cleared from the Capitol grounds, they were now in the city, which is our problem. So we went to the city center and waited to see if anything else would happen. We laid out our gear on the sidewalk and the fire department came through and hosed it down to try and clean off the worst of it.

SERGEANT GONELL: I didn't see my wife until 3 a.m. on January 7th.[26] I had to push away my wife from hugging me because of all the chemicals that covered my body. I couldn't sleep because the chemicals reactivated after I took a shower, and my skin was still burning. I finally fell asleep two hours later, completely physically and mentally exhausted.[27]

JANUARY 7, 2021

HOUSE FLOOR

3:32 A.M.

Congress finished counting the electoral votes.

FRANK LOCKWOOD, Arkansas Democrat-Gazette *reporter*: The final vote ended up not being till like 3:30 in the morning or something. This was traumatic. This was not a pleasant day. And how do you process this stress and this unpleasantness? And for me, I said, "I think the best thing I can do is to be there to the bitter end." It's important for me—not just as a reporter, but as an American—it's important for me to be there and watch every second of it. I'm going to watch every vote, I'm going to watch every bit of action that happens, and I will not leave until this is completed. So that was my mindset, and that's what I did. I was there until the final gavel came down.[28]

Vice President Pence affirmed the result, declaring Joe Biden the winner.

ALEXANDRA PELOSI, TO NANCY PELOSI: You're done with Donald Trump. How does it feel?[29]

SPEAKER NANCY PELOSI: I just feel sick that what he did to the Capitol and to the country today. He's got to pay a price for that.[30]

ALEXANDRA PELOSI: At that point, we were all just tired. We went home. I mean, she didn't sleep. She was sad. And it was just sad. I don't know how else to put it. Just sad.

IGOR BOBIC, HuffPost *reporter:* Walking around in the morning hours of January 7th, I thought for sure that things are going to be different. Everybody in the aftermath thought, *This is going to change everything. How could this happen? There's got to be accountability.*

OLIVIA BEAVERS, Politico *congressional reporter:* I remember having trouble getting to my car and the garage because certain exits were closed, and resources from the Capitol Police had been drained. And everyone was asking the police like, "Hey, are you okay? Are you all right?" Those sorts of questions. And some were like, "Oh yeah, that was a really tough day," or "I can't believe this happened," or "I actually was able to avoid it and come in after things had settled down"—they were off duty and they came in to just provide additional help.

Getting home was just so difficult. I couldn't go the typical way. There's trucks blocking off roads, and you're trying to drive, and I'm like, "Hey, I'm credentialed. I'm trying to get out of here. I was in the building." I kept on pulling up to the police officers and being like, "Hey, I'm just trying to go home. I was in the Capitol. Where do I go?" And they're like, "Oh, you have to go this way," or "I don't know."

FRANK LOCKWOOD: I walked around and looked at some of the damage and took pictures. I think I probably left a little after 4 a.m. Well, there's a curfew. You are not supposed to be out. So I try to find a taxi—no taxis. There's a curfew. Uber? No Uber. Lyft? No Lyft. Subways don't start running for a while longer.[31] So I could either walk twelve miles home in the dark during a curfew, or I could stay on Capitol Hill. They were busy setting up barricades at 4:30 in the morning. Crews are out there. They're getting more security, more barricades. They're putting up the things on January 7th that they should have had in place before January 6. It seemed like too little, too late. It seemed like they were taking steps after the disaster that should have been taken before the disaster.

I don't know how you bring in a crew at three, four, five and get them set up, and where you get all those barriers and where you get the crews to do it and everything. That must've been an enormous undertaking.

Lockwood waited for the Metro to start running again and then took it home.

FRANK LOCKWOOD: By the time I got back to Vienna, Virginia, it was dawn. The sky is beginning to brighten. And my dog was not happy with me. She stuck right by my side the rest of the entire day.

BORIS SANCHEZ, *CNN correspondent*: I remember walking over to my apartment and there being sort of waves of people and again, sort of having my head on a swivel. I was alone. I just remember being like, *It would be my luck that I escaped them and then getting home, somebody throws a brick at my head. They've seen me on CNN or something.* And so fortunately none of that happened. I got home and I remember my face was so red and my eyes were bloodshot and I just remember—it's so stressful. But I took that letter [I'd written to my girlfriend in case I died] and I ripped it up and threw it in the trash.

LOUIE PALU: I lied in bed awake all night. I didn't sleep a single minute the whole night. I couldn't sleep. I was so—I'll just say I'm pretty sure I was traumatized. I was so anxiety ridden by so many things. *Like what just happened? What just happened?* And I lied in bed and I was afraid. *Did anyone follow me home? Are people going to find out where I live?*

OLIVIA BEAVERS: I was at home and I was extremely paranoid. White nationalists . . . were being like, "Oh, reporters are soft targets too." And so that sort of reinforced a fear of ours too, that we would've been targets of the attack if they had figured out our identity.

JACOB GLICK, *investigative counsel for the House Select Committee to Investigate the January 6th Attack on the United States Capitol*: That night they came back.

Many of the rioters were staying at a hotel across the street from Glick's apartment.

JACOB GLICK: They came back and they were still screaming and shouting. And I remember thinking, *Why are the police not here?* They were walking around freely, seemingly without a care in the world that the law would find them.

PART THREE

"IT'S GOING TO REQUIRE A NATIONAL RECKONING"

CHAPTER 15

"DO I FEAR ANOTHER ONE OF THESE HAPPENING? ABSOLUTELY"

JANUARY 7

4 A.M.

In the quiet overnight hours, the mostly Black and Latino custodial staff cleaned the Capitol building from top to bottom, scrubbing blood stains out of carpet and wiping human feces off walls.

BLACK SERVICE WORKER: It was degrading. If it was Black people, we never would have made it, but I think we know better not to attack the Capitol.[1]

SEN. SHERROD BROWN (D-OH): White supremacists make a mess, Black workers clean it up.[2]

CIERRA STEWART, *aide to Sen. Sherrod Brown*: The Capitol was built by people of color, and all the January 6th insurrectionists were white, and it was upholding a certain value system. They came in and destroyed everything, and then the people who had to come in and clean up after them were the same people that would've been harmed most by the policies that would've been implemented by Trump if he'd been reelected.

MAJ. GEN. WILLIAM WALKER, *DC National Guard commander*: I'm African American, child of the sixties. I think it would have been a vastly different response if those were African Americans trying to breach the Capitol. As a career law enforcement officer, the response would have been different. You're looking at someone who would be stopped by the police for driving a high-value government vehicle. As a human being, as an African American,

171

I think it would have been a different response by law enforcement on January 6. I know that from experience. It would have been . . . a lot more heavy-handed. I think it would have been a lot more bloodshed if the composition had been different.[3]

CIERRA STEWART: Most of the Capitol Police, custodial staff, people who work in the kitchen, in the cafeteria, in all pretty much service-level positions are, to my observation, disproportionately people of color and specifically Black. And I think that is also, in my eyes, an injustice. It seems like the people who are at the lowest or the bottom rung of an institution like the United States government or the United States Congress, the people who are the essential workers of the US government, are the same people who have always disproportionately been relegated to those jobs because that's all a lot of them have access to.

As a staffer of color, it upheld or it made very clear to me what kind of institution we were working in and how it didn't take into consideration the needs of minority staffers. Our lives were more in danger.

I know a lot of my peers and mentors who were on the Hill on January 6th didn't stay on the Hill for much longer. There was a lot, from what I saw, a lot of turnover of Black staff. People have told me that that was their catalyzing moment of realizing maybe this is not for me, or maybe this is my jumpstart for the next chapter of my life, or maybe this is the moment where I start to become jaded and have no more passion for continuing to work in a job like this where my safety is compromised and maybe my values are compromised, or my perspective is not taken into account.

SENIOR BLACK DEMOCRATIC AIDE: I am planning to leave. . . . I'm exhausted from this battle. Wednesday was like a nail in the coffin.[4]

6 A.M.

The curfew for the city of DC lifted, as ordered by mayor Muriel Bowser.

LOUIE PALU, *freelance photojournalist on assignment for* National Geographic: So the next morning, I thought I'd go to go back to Capitol. I got on my bicycle. At least it's downhill this time. I rode over there, locked up my bike. Now there's two fences around the Capitol with razor wire. There are Humvees with checkpoints, and it looks like Baghdad. The National Guard has assault rifles and they have camo on and combat boots. And no one is in the streets now.

And I showed my pass. I went into the Capitol and they had already started cleaning up and I took photographs. I remember walking into Dirksen and there was lines of National Guard lined up [like] in a dystopian movie. It [was] like science fiction had come to life—art imitates life or life imitates art—and they had assault rifles. And it was just like all those movies that we watch. Now there's senators in the hallway talking, there's lines of soldiers.

And I remember I went into Statuary Hall and there were two National Guard members reading a copy of the Declaration of Independence over a fireplace with their assault rifles on their back with a statue of the vice president of the Confederacy [Alexander Hamilton Stephens] beside them. And the [after]math of the day, it just kept unwinding into the more disturbing and unexplainable. I can't believe how these narratives just keep unfolding.

I remember walking through the visitor center and it was like a sea of National Guard sleeping on the floor. You can't even see the end of them. Riot shields, guns sleeping all over the floor.

CONGRESSIONAL FOOD SERVICE EMPLOYEE: That next day, I didn't go because I'm like, my nerve was messed up. My son was like, "Mom, see I told you, you shouldn't have went to work."[5]

CHERYL BOYLAND, *Rosanne Boyland's mother*: The next morning they told us, "Expect that she died of a fentanyl overdose." I said, "No way. There is no way on God's green Earth that girl did fentanyl." And they said, "Well, her lungs were in bad shape and that's usually a sign of fentanyl use." And I said, "Well, do you think maybe it could be tear gas? And some of the other things that were being sprayed all around her. They sprayed her in the face an awful lot of times." But anyway, they didn't even take any of that into consideration. They just said, "Expect it to be a drug overdose."

LONNA CAVE, *Rosanne Boyland's older sister*: So we had to wait for the toxicology report. And so then it's been like seventy-five days or some shit, and I called, they weren't responding.

So finally I reached someone and she was like, "Oh yeah, we got the toxicology report. She had caffeine, nicotine, and Adderall in her system."

And I said, "Okay, so there wasn't a drug overdose."

Then she was like, "Well, we don't know. But she didn't have any fentanyl in her system." So then it was another fifteen days and she called and she said, "I just want to let you know that we're ruling this as an amphetamine overdose."

CHERYL BOYLAND: She had taken a couple extra [Adderalls] than normal when she drove through the night and probably one in the morning.

LONNA CAVE: I asked them on the phone, I said, "Can you at least say that it was prescription medication?" Because everybody's going to see amphetamine and they're going to automatically assume methamphetamine and not her prescription Adderall that she's been taking for ten years. And they're like, "Well, people should know the difference." And I was like, "People don't know the difference."

BLAIRE BOYLAND, *Roseanne Boyland's younger sister*: And still to this day, just like last week, I was on Reddit and we were talking about—people were talking about January 6th and anytime Roseanne's name gets mentioned on social media, usually the response is, "Oh, the chick that died of a meth overdose," still to this day. Years later, that's what the general public thinks is her cause of death.

| **Capitol Police officer Brian Sicknick died at 9:30 p.m. on January 7.**

CRAIG SICKNICK, *Brian Sicknick's brother*: He managed to hang on until the 7th, so technically he didn't die on the 6th.

We waited outside the hospital for them to do what they had to do, to pick up my brother and put him in the ambulance to take [his body], and we were waiting. We were quietly talking to a couple officers who were there who were also in shock from just the events of that day.

And we were escorted by police, and it seemed like almost every police officer in that entire region was lined up along the street.

At that point, I was completely numb. I was overwhelmed. I'm watching it. It almost didn't compute seeing what was going on, and most of them saluted us as we went by, my family. We saw cars from Washington, DC Metro and Capitol. We saw Virginia Police, Maryland, you name it, we saw it, the various county officers.

Meanwhile, Capitol Police officer Caroline Edwards was diagnosed with a traumatic brain injury. Her symptoms included severe ear pain and ear ringing, chemical burns on her face, hands, and vocal cords, severe balance issues, and vertigo.[6]

MICHAEL FANONE, *DC Metropolitan Police officer:* At the hospital, doctors told me that I suffered a heart attack, and I was later diagnosed with a concussion, traumatic brain injury, and post-traumatic stress disorder.[7] Looking back, I held on to that [body camera] video like a security blanket. It was proof that I wasn't crazy. Despite all the noise, the riot was real, and so were my injuries.[8]

As my physical injuries gradually subsided and the adrenaline that had stayed with me for weeks waned, I have been left with the psychological trauma and the emotional anxiety of having survived such a horrifying event.[9]

The death toll among responding officers continued to rise. Three days after the riot, fifty-one-year-old Capitol Police officer Howard "Howie" Liebengood died by suicide.

About a week later, on January 15, thirty-five-year-old MPD officer Jeffrey Smith was scheduled to return to work after having been on sick leave since January 6. He'd been hit in the head with a metal pole during the riot. According to his wife, Erin Smith, he had been struggling ever since.

THE *WASHINGTON POST*: In the days that followed, Erin said, her husband seemed in constant pain, unable to turn his head. He did not leave the house, even to walk their dog. He refused to talk to other people or watch television. She sometimes woke during the night to find him sitting up in bed or pacing.[10]

ERIN SMITH: He wasn't the same Jeff that left on the 6th. I just tried to comfort him and let him know that I loved him. I told him I'd be there if he needed anything, that no matter what, we'll get through it. I tried to do the best I could.[11]

When Officer Smith was ordered back to work, Erin packed him ham and turkey sandwiches, trail mix, and cookies. He set off on his commute to DC, but never arrived at his shift. Police would later

find his body in his beloved Ford Mustang. He had shot himself in the head.

Within the week, President Trump was impeached a second time for his role in stoking the insurrection.

Within the month, President Joe Biden was inaugurated as the forty-sixth president of the United States of America.

JULIO CORTEZ, *Associated Press photojournalist*: Two weeks later, I had to go back to cover the inauguration of President Biden. I was afraid [a] man who yelled he'd be back with his big guns would make good on his threat. It took me more than two hours to say goodbye to my wife and kids before heading to Washington to prepare for inauguration coverage. I cried. I thought I would never come home.[12]

LOUIE PALU: I remember the day before inauguration, I just took a walk around the Capitol. I'm like, *I have to get something here.* The White House marine was at the doors, and he was practicing opening the door where the president and the vice president elect were going to walk through to go get inaugurated. And he was practicing, and the glass was smashed right in the middle. And there was all this powder from pepper balls shot at the door. And I thought, *What a dystopian end to this whole thing.* And it was a really dark inauguration.

In July, two more responding officers died by suicide: Gunther Hashida and Kyle DeFreytag.

All told, at least 140 officers who had been at the Capitol on January 6 reported physical injuries, though the true number is likely much higher.

GUS PAPATHANASIOU, *US Capitol Police officer*: There hasn't been any accountability. At the top, the [police] chiefs were the ones that let us down and hung us out to dry that day. So I think it was because of their failures, lack of communication, lack of preparation for that day.

I think it's a lot more than just Capitol Police leadership; political leadership failed us that day too. They all failed us that day.

January 6th should have never happened. It could have been prevented. It should have been prevented with the intel that they had.

The National Guard occupied the nation's capital for four months.[13] **At least 153 Capitol Police officers quit within one year of the attack, and many who have stayed have mixed feelings about their jobs.**[14]

LARRY, *US Capitol Police officer*: An officer of our tenure, we can't go anywhere. We have wives, we have kids. We've been in the department for over fifteen years, so where are we going to go? We're too old. So all these young officers saw this department and said, "You know what? We can't do twenty-five years here." We still have officers to this day that just want to get past January 6th because of what happened that day. I try to move past it. I did my job that day as well as every other officer. So I don't feel any remorse from what I did that day or moving forward, what I will do from now on.

DANIEL HODGES, *DC Metropolitan Police officer*: [I stay] 'cause I got a mortgage to pay, I don't know what—'cause it's my job. 'Cause yeah, I could still work. 'Cause I don't know what else I would do. 'Cause I'm not going to let these insurrectionists take that from me if I can help it.

Complicating Hodges's physical and mental recovery was the fact that a video of him being attacked went viral almost immediately after the assault.

OFFICER HODGES: It was actually one of my academy classmates who initially told me about it. She sent me this link and said, "Hey, heads up." And I think it was in the *New York Post* or something that I first saw it. And yeah, I watched and I was like, *Oh, geez.* It's a little embarrassing because you don't want to want your fifteen minutes of fame to be screaming for help getting beaten up, especially if you're supposed to be this big, tough police guy. But I'm glad it got out there because it communicated the level of violence that day and the stakes and what we went through in a way that words and even photos are not always capable of doing.

HuffPost **reporter Igor Bobic's footage of Officer Goodman luring the rioters up the Capitol stairs went viral as well.**

IGOR BOBIC, HuffPost *reporter*: I didn't even realize what I had. I think my caption on the tweet was like, "Here's a scary-looking video of what had happened," with me not processing just the gravity of what I had caught on video and Goodman's actions and all that. That all came later. I dunno.

I always just felt very uncomfortable with the idea of profiting personally off of it. People reached out to me. They were like, "You should monetize this." People offered me money for it. And I was always like, "Just take it for free, post it wherever." I dunno, it's not for me to cash in on. At least it just felt ugly enough that I didn't want to do that.

So it's definitely helped my career, but at the same time, I feel like now-adays people are like, "Oh, this is the guy who filmed the video." And I'm like, *Oh God, here we go again.* I don't want to relive it every day.

I'm still covering the Senate. Every day I see Goodman . . . and we lock eyes and something brings it back. Right?

Bobic not only has complicated feelings about the video and about his job future but also about America as a whole. His family had fled to the United States from Bosnia when he was just seven years old.

IGOR BOBIC: America saved me and my family. We were political refugees. I'm proud to be American. People talk shit about America. I always say, "Listen, you didn't come up in a war in Europe, so there are plenty of bad things here, but it could always get worse." And then seeing what happened just sort of gave me a lot of disillusionment about what it means for it to happen here and how far our politics have gone down.

And I think the worst part about it is I know Republicans who know better, who say better in private, but yet can't do it in public. And I think that's the most tragic part about it. People who assisted in a crime, like Republican senators who had spewed a bunch of these lies, are now just walking about scot-free. Nothing happened. They didn't face accountability for anything that had taken place.

Just on a human level, you work daily with people who lie to you, have lied to you, so you've sort of become pissed off about that. And people who spewed lies about the election and voter fraud and all that are now walking around consequence-free.

I haven't decided yet whether I want to keep being a journalist or not. I don't know, maybe I shouldn't have said that, but we'll see. I still enjoy it. I love the Congress and I love the Senate. There's so many different characters and it's so easy to go up and put your microphone in somebody's face and get answers. So I think that's still a draw for me, but I don't know how long I'm going to keep doing it.

ALEXANDRA PELOSI, *Speaker Nancy Pelosi's daughter*: It radicalized my son. He had to—at fourteen, he had to come to terms with the fact that he lives in a country full of people that will always believe in a fiction that you're going to be fighting your whole life.

To him, he was just a kid who saw this stuff go down. He saw all the Republicans act responsibly and be grownups, and he saw nothing bad in Kevin McCarthy or Mitch McConnell or Steve Scalise or Chuck Grassley. He had not an ill word to say about those people. He thought that they were all grownups and responsible and everything.

They completely changed their tune after; later, when the political landscape changed, they changed with it. I can see why they weren't demanding all of Alexandra Pelosi's footage to be released to the public. I'm not sure they wanted the whole world to see exactly what they were saying about Donald Trump down in the bunker.

So I think for him, the heartbreak of being—I think the way he lost his innocence was watching Kevin McCarthy and Mitch McConnell flip months later. *Like, what? I saw you saying that Donald Trump shouldn't be invited to the inauguration. I saw you say that. He undermined our democracy. I saw that. And now you're what?* So I think for him, that's what radicalized him was watching them since.

Many of the reporters, even those with previous combat reporting experience, say they're still traumatized by what they witnessed on January 6.

JASON ANDREW, *freelance photojournalist on assignment for the* New York Times: I still struggle with that day a lot. I mean, I started marathon swimming after that and doing ultra [marathons], and part of the reason I swam Catalina was like, *Sweet, I'm going to swim twenty-two miles and think about nothing.*

LOUIE PALU: At the time, my head was shaved and after that, I don't know why, I never cut my hair again. My hair's long. I don't know. I don't know what it is, but just it's a life change. And I thought, *I'm not cutting my hair no more.*

| **Others still bear physical reminders.**

JON FARINA, *freelance journalist on assignment for* Status Coup News: I still have pain to this day from being crushed in that tunnel. I thought time would heal it, but if I try and do something physical or just random sitting down, I'll feel a sharp pain in my ribs. And that's always a reminder.

ALAN CHIN, *freelance photojournalist*: I feel like I've lost whatever illusions I still had before 2020 about America having any kind of exceptional qualities. I think that was a good national myth for a long time. It's the kind of thing that propels people like my parents, who were immigrants, to come to the US—this belief in American exceptionalism, that this is a place where you can do all these things, the American dream. I think the experience of 2020 and the four years since and where we're now has really kind of disabused me of that.

| **In the months and years that followed the insurrection, at least 1,240 rioters were charged in federal court related to crimes committed at the Capitol on January 6.[15] Some said they regretted their participation.**

STEPHEN AYRES, *rioter*: I feel like we were used and abused as, like, a pawn in the situation.[16] I felt like we were kind of led astray, for lack of better words. I kind of felt like we basically were kind of played on, from the president telling us we need to march down there. That is one of the things that bothers me the most.[17]

DANIEL HERENDEEN, *rioter*: I think it's a black mark on history. After that, I got off social media. I got out of politics. I don't really care anymore. It just—it messed up my life and it wasn't worth it. . . . I feel a little betrayed, a little abandoned, a little frustrated.[18]

JANET BUHLER, *rioter*: Well, it was a huge mistake for me to even go. If I could take it back, I would take it back. I never want to be in that situation again. I don't plan on even being involved in politics. They're not my world at all.

Like with my son-in-law, I trusted him. He's a former police officer. I trusted his knowledge about—I just assumed he would know it would be okay to go in, because he just acted like it was totally fine. And I should have just been, I don't know. I just beat myself up every day about it. It's just dumb, stupid.[19]

After January 6, the militias involved—including the Proud Boys and the Oath Keepers—entered a largely quiet period.

MARY MCCORD, *executive director of the Institute for Constitutional Advocacy and Protection at Georgetown University*: The trajectory post–January 6th reminds me a lot of the post–Unite the Right [in Charlottesville] trajectory. So in the immediate aftermath, you had this elation: "Look at what we did. Look at how great we are." And the same on January 6th: "Look what we did. We prevented the vote for—I mean, not forever, but for six hours." And people were bragging about it and videotaping themselves. And then just like in Charlottesville, in twenty-four hours, when the rain of universal condemnation from around the world—not just the US—started raining down on people, that's when you start seeing . . . those groups getting a lot more quiet.

It did lead to a quiet time in the militia community, in particular for 2021. But it also turned into a very big strategic shift into localized, decentralized involvement in politics by not only militias but also ideological extremists. So that's what started something that I think has continued and still continues to this day, which is [that] we don't necessarily need these big national events like January 6th. *Forget these national things. First, take over your county, then another, then maybe your state. What we need is a localized, decentralized Christian nationalist political movement.* And we've seen it, right? Taking over county boards, taking over school boards, taking over election officials' positions, poll worker positions, and even taking them over from Republicans, even kicking out Republicans that are perceived as being too moderate, moving into elected office themselves.

It's like a grassroots extremism that really has impacts all the way up the levels of democracy. And that's why I think we're, in many ways, in a worse place than we were in 2020.

JACOB GLICK, *investigative counsel for the House Select Committee to Investigate the January 6th Attack on the United States Capitol*: I think what we saw on January

6th was the culmination of far-right extremism becoming mainstreamed first and foremost by Donald Trump. And that allowed militia groups to enter the public square because they were being welcomed into the public square. But it also mainstreamed a lot of conspiracy theories that had racist elements, antisemitic elements, anti-LGBTQ elements, misogynistic elements, really, really prominently. That sort of allowed these extremist groups to glom onto them but also gave a lot of other individuals who have been marinating in online spaces and anti-Hillary [Clinton] propaganda and anti-Obama propaganda for decades to then believe that that could be taken a step further in the real world.

I think there was a lot of effort to whitewash January 6th. In the mainstream press, there was not always a willingness to reckon with January 6th as a symptom of an American fascist movement egged on by an authoritarian president.

The violent far right—the kind of MAGA movement and the violence it inspired—is not a simple question of right versus left, Republican versus Democrat, white versus non-white. It doesn't break down that easily. January 6th is first and foremost an assassination attempt on a conservative, evangelical, Republican, white, straight vice president.

On Tuesday, November 5, 2024, Donald Trump was elected to another term as president of the United States—with a greater margin of victory than in 2016.

JON FARINA: I kind of had a feeling that Trump was going to win. I knew that things were just going to get worse over time, and then that was going to lead to more people becoming radicalized and more people moving towards Trump. So I knew what was coming. I was not surprised or shocked at all.

BLAIRE BOYLAND: I ended up crying myself to sleep that night and again in the morning. I think I was just more disappointed and angry than I was shocked. I was really hoping people had changed their minds on Trump after everything that has happened these last several years, especially January 6th. It was a really hard pill to swallow that he won the popular vote too.

Trump was inaugurated on January 20, 2025, and he immediately granted "a full, complete and unconditional pardon to all . . .

individuals convicted of offenses related to events that occurred at or near the United States Capitol on January 6, 2021."

HARRY DUNN, *US Capitol Police officer:* I wasn't shocked. My shock and dismay or anger was [at] the people who are shocked about it now, because, like I said, y'all weren't paying attention. If you're surprised, you were not paying attention.[20]

LOUIE PALU: Well, since several people used death threats and threatened violence against me with weapons, . . . I had to reflect on this because it is hard to hear and accept. My parents were children during the Second World War in a region in Italy under Nazi control, which was contested by partisans fighting fascism. They hung people and burned down homes in their region for opposing the Third Reich. When you think of countries like Germany after the Second World War, many Nazis who began as prisoners of war went on to live as pardoned and/or unprosecuted criminals. But in the history books they will always be remembered as criminals.

BLAIRE BOYLAND: I had been seeing lots of talk in the media about the pardons leading up to the election, so I wasn't really shocked when it actually happened. I think that is part of why I was so upset on election night because I knew this was going to be the eventual outcome and any investigations into Trump's involvement with J6 would just abruptly end. Feeling pretty defeated by it. It felt like that was the final nail in the coffin for any kind of answers coming to light on J6 and my sister's death, or Trump ever being held accountable.

CRAIG SICKNICK, *Officer Brian Sicknick's brother:* Reaction is, all of us are depressed. We're angered. We can't figure out why in a supposedly decent country that a madman could be elected with millions of his fans saying that everything he's doing is right. We [had] kind of got ourselves back together again over the last four years, and this just ripped everything wide open again.[21]

About 1,500 people were pardoned, many leaving jail the same evening. Jon Farina and Jason Andrew were among the journalists gathered outside the DC jail when some pardoned rioters held there were released.

JON FARINA: [Trump supporters] actually called them hostages. They wouldn't call them prisoners or anything like that. They would call 'em J6 hostages. It was nice to see them be reunited with their family, but the fact that they don't have any remorse or feel bad for what they did, that just shows that they were in the same mindset. They were thanking Trump and still caught up in the propaganda and the bullshit, but they didn't have any remorse. They didn't feel bad for what they did.

JASON ANDREW: To see people that had stormed the Capitol getting released and being celebrated like rock stars is definitely off-putting. I mean, they truly, truly believe that they were innocent.

JON FARINA: It just goes along with the white privilege and the white supremacy of being able to beat up cops and do what they did and then get set free. Now that they're all free, they're the soldiers for Trump, or for whoever is going to be running the show. Now they've got their soldiers.

JASON ANDREW: He certified his own personal army of supporters. Like, *what you did was okay, and I'm here to support you.*

Pardoned rioters and other members of the far right vowed retribution.

UNNAMED USER VIA TWITTER: All their prosecutors deserve a rope!!!![22]

UNNAMED USER VIA TWITTER: YOU ARE NEXT[23]

ENRIQUE TARRIO, LEADER OF THE PROUD BOYS, ON INFOWARS: The people who did this, they need to feel the heat, they need to be put behind bars, and they need to be prosecuted. Success is gonna be retribution.[24]

The next morning, Aquilino Gonell received nine automated calls from the Justice Department informing him that the rioters who had attacked him were back on the street.[25]

SGT. AQUILINO GONELL, *US Capitol Police officer*: It's a miscarriage of justice, a betrayal, a mockery, and a desecration of the men and women that risked their lives defending our democracy.[26]

Michael Fanone got protective orders against five men who pleaded guilty to violently assaulting him.[27]

OFFICER FANONE: The fact that I have to do this, to try to afford my family some degree of protection, is outrageous. But we are in an age of government lawlessness. I feel betrayed. I feel betrayed by my country.

JASON ANDREW: January 6th fucked with me more than any day that I have photographed. And so I really struggle with the fact that he let them all go, but it's also more reason why I've got to put myself in the middle of it to try to make sense of it and understand it all. We are going through something in America that we've probably never witnessed, and now is the time to be a witness. There is hope that we will learn from all of this down the road.

JACOB WARE, *Council on Foreign Relations research fellow*: Where we're going from here, basically, we'll see. I mean, I'll borrow a cliché from the counter-terrorism field, which is I think the alarms are flashing red. There is no good reason to believe that violent far-right extremism will go away, will get less violent, will go dormant with an end to the MAGA movement.

JASON ANDREW: At this point, the truth doesn't matter. Their own reality and how the algorithm reconfirms their reality is what matters.

IGOR BOBIC: Do I fear another one of these happening? Absolutely.

FRANK LOCKWOOD, Arkansas Democrat-Gazette *reporter*: I guess I just hope this never, never happens again, because next time we may not be so lucky. We survived it this time, but it was closer than it should have been.[28]

BORIS SANCHEZ, *CNN correspondent*: To me, what happened that day was a tragedy, but it could be just a precursor to something much worse.

I became a journalist because of my grandfather. He was a political prisoner in Cuba who was sentenced—[*chokes up*] I get emotional talking about this shit—to twenty years in prison for speaking his mind, for being an anti-communist. He fought in the Cuban Revolution, believing that it would bring democracy to Cuba, that people would have a chance to determine their own future, to elect their leaders to speak and think freely without fear of retribution. And when the revolution didn't go that direction, he turned against it. And for that, he was punished. So my family was fortunate to flee Cuba and find asylum here in the United States. So I consider what we have in this country sacred because, say what you will about its failings, but democracy is the best organizing principle civilization has yet to configure.

ALEXANDRA PELOSI: And by the way, you're not going to get that genie back in the bottle. You're just not. These people are out there. They believe it. They'll never, ever—nothing you can say will convince them that he didn't win the election.

JACOB WARE: The genie is fully out of the bottle and it's hard to know how to put it back.

JON FARINA: I think the illusions of democracy, of freedom, that's all done. That's completely gone.

JANE, *staff photojournalist for a major mainstream outlet*: I think that people forget that January 6th is our floor now. This is where we're standing at. It's not this thing that happened that's just random. No. That is where our reality has moved to. It is our baseline for behavior that now has happened. It's like it's out of the bag, so that's why I think it's important to be truthful about it.

JACOB WARE: It's going to require a national reckoning to find our way out of this situation.

LOUIE PALU: January 6th, it might be the beginning. It's not the end.

ACKNOWLEDGMENTS

Thank you to my intern, Kayla Williams; my researcher, Aaron Klein; and especially to my editorial assistant and chief researcher, Samantha Zachar. Sam's dedication to this project shines through each of these pages. Her attention to detail, her sensitivity to individuals' stories, and her ability to find the nuggets of gold hidden in hundreds of pages of court filings have made this book stronger. Any author who works with her is very lucky.

I'm grateful for the life-changing teachers I've had the honor of learning from throughout my life, especially my high school history and government teacher (and debate coach extraordinaire) Gail Fair, who inspired me to pursue the career path I have.

This book—like every single one of my books so far—would not exist without my agent Wendi Gu. I'm so lucky to have you in my corner.

Thank you to my editor, Catherine Tung, for seeing the need for this follow-up book and for her enthusiasm to work with me again, and to the entire team at Beacon, including Bev Rivero, Christian Coleman, Beth Collins, Susan Lumenello, Louis Roe, Rebekah Cotton, Beth Richards, and Kim Arney.

Finally, I'm grateful, always, to my family: Mom, Dad, Jack, Julia, Kendal, Gerrit, and, of course, the love of my life, Lex.

NOTES

CHAPTER 1: "IT'S TIME FOR FUCKING WAR IF THEY STEAL THIS SHIT"

1. NPR, "January 6: Inside the Capitol Siege," *Embedded* (podcast), Jan. 15, 2021, https://www.npr.org/transcripts/957362053.

2. Donald Trump (@realDonaldTrump), Twitter, Sept. 29, 2019, https://Twitter.com /realDonaldTrump/status/1178477539653771264.

3. @Oathkeepers, Twitter, Sept. 29, 2019, https://Twitter.com/nickmartin/status /1178580499708698624.

4. Donald Trump (@realDonaldTrump), Twitter, Apr. 17, 2020, https://Twitter.com /realDonaldTrump/status/1251168994066944003?ref_src=twsrc%5Etfw%7Ctwcamp%5 Etweetembed%7Ctwterm%5E1251168994066944003%7Ctwgr%5E67ae2df86aeef0e43d 246abd9dabae4343fb3797%7Ctwcon%5Es1_&ref_url=https%3A%2F%2Fwww.the trumparchive.com%2F%3Fsearchbox%3D22liberate22.

5. Donald Trump (@realDonaldTrump), Twitter, Apr. 17, 2020, https://Twitter.com /realDonaldTrump/status/1251169217531056130?ref_src=twsrc%5Etfw%7Ctwcamp%5 Etweetembed%7Ctwterm%5E1251169217531056130%7Ctwgr%5E8b31f7b40829a94ce0a 83f16dcfe6fe92b4ee8fc%7Ctwcon%5Es1_&ref_url=https%3A%2F%2Fwww.thetrump archive.com%2F%3Fsearchbox%3D22liberatemichigan22.

6. Donald Trump (@realDonaldTrump), Twitter, Apr. 17, 2020, https://Twitter.com /realDonaldTrump/status/1251169987110330372?ref_src=twsrc%5Etfw%7Ctwcamp%5 Etweetembed%7Ctwterm%5E1251169987110330372%7Ctwgr%5E67ae2df86aeef0e43d 246abd9dabae4343fb3797%7Ctwcon%5Es1_&ref_url=https%3A%2F%2Fwww.the trumparchive.com%2F%3Fsearchbox%3D22liberate22.

7. Facebook post, quoted in Bruce Hoffman and Jacob Ware, *Gods, Guns, and Sedition: Far-Right Terrorism in America* (New York: Columbia University Press, 2024), 2.

8. Telegram message, quoted in Hoffman and Ware, *Gods, Guns, and Sedition*, 192.

9. CDC, "Timing of State and Territorial COVID-19 Stay-at-Home Orders and Changes in Population Movement—United States, March 1–May 31, 2020," Sept. 4, 2020, https://www.cdc.gov/mmwr/volumes/69/wr/mm6935a2.htm.

10. Kathleen Gray, "In Michigan, a Dress Rehearsal for the Chaos at the Capitol on Wednesday," *New York Times*, Jan. 9, 2021, https://www.nytimes.com/2021/01/09/us /politics/michigan-state-capitol.html.

11. Craig Mauger, "Protesters, Some Armed, Enter Michigan Capitol in Rally Against COVID-19 Limits," *Detroit News*, Apr. 30, 2020, https://www.detroitnews.com /story/news/local/michigan/2020/04/30/protesters-gathering-outside-capitol-amid -covid-19-restrictions/3054911001/.

12. Gray, "In Michigan, a Dress Rehearsal for the Chaos at the Capitol on Wednesday."

13. Andrew Solender, "Armed Protesters Storm Michigan State House Over COVID-19 Lockdown," *Forbes*, Apr. 30, 2020, https://www.forbes.com/sites/andrew solender/2020/04/30/armed-protesters-storm-michigan-state-house-over-covid-19 -lockdown/.

14. Sen. Dayna Polehanki (@SenPolehanki), X, Apr. 30, 2020, https://Twitter.com /SenPolehanki/status/1255899318210314241.

15. Mauger, "Protesters, Some Armed, Enter Michigan Capitol in Rally Against COVID-19 Limits."

16. Gray, "In Michigan, a Dress Rehearsal for the Chaos at the Capitol on Wednesday."

17. Gray, "In Michigan, a Dress Rehearsal for the Chaos at the Capitol on Wednesday."

18. Gini Gerbasi, Facebook post, June 1, 2020, https://www.facebook.com/gini .gerbasi/posts/10157575422089624.

19. Jeremy Diamond, "Trump: 'I'm Afraid the Election's Going to Be Rigged,'" CNN, Aug. 2, 2016, https://www.cnn.com/2016/08/01/politics/donald-trump -election-2016-rigged/index.html.

20. Sarah McCammon, "From Debate Stage, Trump Declines to Denounce White Supremacy," NPR, Sept. 30, 2020, https://www.npr.org/2020/09/30/918483794/from -debate-stage-trump-declines-to-denounce-white-supremacy.

21. Joe Biggs, Parler message, quoted in Hoffman and Ware, *Gods, Guns, and Sedition*, 204.

22. Telegram message, quoted in Hoffman and Ware, *Gods, Guns, and Sedition*, 204.

23. Telegram message, quoted in Hoffman and Ware, *Gods, Guns, and Sedition*, 204.

24. Jeremy Bertino, "Transcribed Interview with the January 6th Committee," conducted Apr. 26, 2022, 37–38, accessed online at https://www.govinfo.gov/content /pkg/GPO-J6-TRANSCRIPT-CTRL0000082294/pdf/GPO-J6-TRANSCRIPT -CTRL0000082294.pdf.

25. Third Superseding Indictment, *United States of America v. Nordean et al.*, Feb. 14, 2022, 5, accessed online at https://www.justice.gov/usao-dc/case-multi-defendant/file /1510966/dl.

26. Indictment, *United States v. Rhodes et al.*, Jan. 12, 2022, 10, accessed online at https://extremism.gwu.edu/sites/g/files/zaxdzs5746/files/Rhodes%20et%20al%20 Indictment.pdf.

27. Mike Pence (@Mike_Pence), Twitter, Nov. 9, 2020, https://Twitter.com/Mike _Pence/status/1325871164443545600.

28. Indictment, *United States v. Rhodes et al.*, 10.

CHAPTER 2: "WILL BE WILD"

1. Steven A. Sund, *Courage Under Fire: The Definitive Account from Inside the Capitol on January 6* (Ashland, OR: Blackstone Publishing, 2023), 51–52.

2. Sund, *Courage Under Fire*, 51–52.

3. "Pro-Trump Rallies in DC Attract Extremists & Erupt into Violence," Anti-Defamation League, Dec. 13, 2020, https://www.adl.org/resources/article/pro-trump -rallies-dc-attract-extremists-erupt-violence.

4. Sund, *Courage Under Fire*, 56–57.

5. Carol Leonnig and Philip Rucker, *I Alone Can Fix It: Donald J. Trump's Catastrophic Final Year* (New York: Penguin Random House, 2021), 419.

6. Christina Morales, "Man Is Arrested in Stabbing at D.C. Election Protest," *New York Times*, Dec. 13, 2020, https://www.nytimes.com/2020/12/13/us/politics/trump -election-protests-violence.html.

7. Morales, "Man Is Arrested in Stabbing at D.C. Election Protest."

8. Donald Trump (@realDonaldTrump), Twitter, Dec. 19, 2020, https://twitter .com/realDonaldTrump/status/1340185773220515840.

CHAPTER 3: "ONE MILLION PATRIOTS"

1. SITE Intelligence Group, quoted in *Washington Post*, "What Happened on Jan. 6: Bloodshed," Oct. 31, 2021, https://www.washingtonpost.com/politics/interactive/2021 /what-happened-trump-jan-6-insurrection/.

2. Telegram post, quoted in Bruce Hoffman and Jacob Ware, *Gods, Guns, and Sedition: Far-Right Terrorism in America* (New York: Columbia University Press, 2024), 207.

3. Eric Barber, "Transcribed Interview with the Select January 6th Committee," conducted Mar. 16, 2022, 29, accessed online at https://www.govinfo.gov/content /pkg/GPO-J6-TRANSCRIPT-CTRL0000055539/pdf/GPO-J6-TRANSCRIPT -CTRL0000055539.pdf.

4. Robert Schornak, "Transcribed Interview with the Select January 6th Committee," conducted Feb. 1, 2022, 23, accessed online at https://www.govinfo.gov/content /pkg/GPO-J6-TRANSCRIPT-CTRL0000040480/pdf/GPO-J6-TRANSCRIPT -CTRL0000040480.pdf.

5. Statement of Offense, *United States of America v. Robert Schornak*, Nov. 12, 2021, 3, accessed online, https://www.justice.gov/usao-dc/case-multi-defendant/file /1448091/dl.

6. Statement of Offense, *United States of America v. Robert Schornak*.

7. Federal Bureau of Investigation (FBI), "Statement of Facts: Daniel Herendeen and Robert Schornak," 2, accessed online at https://extremism.gwu.edu/sites/g/files /zaxdzs5746/files/Daniel%20Herendeen%20and%20Robert%20Schornak%20Statement %20of%20Facts.pdf.

8. FBI, "Statement of Facts: Daniel Herendeen and Robert Schornak," 2.

9. FBI, "Statement of Facts: Daniel Herendeen and Robert Schornak," 2.

10. FBI, "Statement of Facts: Daniel Herendeen and Robert Schornak," 2.

11. Daniel Herendeen, "Transcribed Interview with the Select January 6th Committee," conducted Mar. 16, 2022, 12, accessed online at https://www.govinfo.gov /content/pkg/GPO-J6-TRANSCRIPT-CTRL0000055540/pdf/GPO-J6-TRANSCRIPT-CTRL0000055540.pdf.

12. Stephen Ayres, "Transcribed Interview with the Select January 6th Committee," conducted June 17, 2022, 13–14, accessed online at https://www.govinfo.gov/content /pkg/GPO-J6-TRANSCRIPT-CTRL0000916061/pdf/GPO-J6-TRANSCRIPT -CTRL0000916061.pdf.

13. Janet Buhler, "Transcribed Interview with the Select January 6th Committee," conducted Feb. 28, 2022, 13, accessed online at https://www.govinfo.gov/content /pkg/GPO-J6-TRANSCRIPT-CTRL0000050985/pdf/GPO-J6-TRANSCRIPT-CTRL0000050985.pdf.

14. Buhler, "Transcribed Interview with the Select January 6th Committee," 25.

15. Indictment, *United States v. Rhodes et al.*, 14.

16. Indictment, *United States v. Rhodes et al.*, 16.

17. Indictment, *United States v. Rhodes et al.*, 17.

18. Indictment, *United States v. Rhodes et al.*, 18.

19. Third Superseding Indictment, *United States of America v. Nordean et al.*, Feb. 14, 2022, 13, accessed online at https://www.justice.gov/usao-dc/case-multi-defendant/file/1510966/dl.

20. Third Superseding Indictment, *United States of America v. Nordean et al.*, 13.

21. Claire Withycombe and Virginia Barreda, "4 Arrests Made After Protesters Attempt to Enter Oregon State Capitol During Session," *Statesman Journal*, Dec. 21, 2020, https://www.statesmanjournal.com/story/news/politics/2020/12/21/protesters-gather-oregon-legislature-starts-special-session/3993102001/.

22. Withycombe and Barreda, "4 Arrests Made After Protesters Attempt to Enter Oregon State Capitol During Session."

23. Mary McCord, screen capture in email message to Brian Gilhooly, "Flag: Conversation Getting Heated in Oath Keepers Members Chat," Dec. 22, 2020, accessed online at https://www.govinfo.gov/content/pkg/GPO-J6-DOC-CTRL0000930476/pdf/GPO-J6-DOC-CTRL0000930476.pdf.

24. McCord, email message to Gilhooly.

25. Special Agent of the United States Secret Service, email message to FBI, Dec. 27, 2020, accessed online at https://www.govinfo.gov/content/pkg/GPO-J6-DOC-USSS0000067420/pdf/GPO-J6-DOC-USSS0000067420.pdf.

26. Anonymous civilian, email message to US Capitol Police, Dec. 28, 2020, https://www.govinfo.gov/content/pkg/GPO-J6-DOC-CTRL0000000087/pdf/GPO-J6-DOC-CTRL0000000087.pdf.

27. Talking points prepared by Christopher Rodriguez, for a briefing with DC Mayor Bowser, Dec. 30, 2020, https://www.govinfo.gov/content/pkg/GPO-J6-DOC-CTRL0000926794/pdf/GPO-J6-DOC-CTRL0000926794.pdf.

28. "Mayor Bowser Continues Preparation for Upcoming First Amendment Demonstrations," Executive Office of the Mayor, Jan. 3, 2021, https://mayor.dc.gov/release/mayor-bowser-continues-preparation-upcoming-first-amendment-demonstrations.

29. Third Superseding Indictment, *United States of America v. Nordean et al.*, Feb. 14, 2022, 13, accessed online at https://www.justice.gov/usao-dc/case-multi-defendant/file/1510966/dl.

30. Andy Wang, screen capture in email message to Bryan Molnar and Lawrence Grasso, "Parler Posts," Jan. 4, 2021, accessed online at https://www.govinfo.gov/content/pkg/GPO-J6-DOC-CTRL0000001487/pdf/GPO-J6-DOC-CTRL0000001487.pdf.

31. Donald Trump (@realDonaldTrump), Twitter, Jan. 5, 2021, https://Twitter.com/realDonaldTrump/status/1346583537256976385?ref_src=twsrc%5Etfw%7Ctwcamp%5Etweetembed%7Ctwterm%5E1346583537256976385%7Ctwgr%5E7c7e94264b1715dob95dc2a2d520a86403721c02%7Ctwcon%5Es1_&ref_url=https%3A%2F%2Fwww.thetrumparchive.com%2F%3Fsearchbox%3D22AntifaisaTerrorist22.

32. FBI, Norfolk Division, *Situational Information Report, Potential Activity Alert*, Jan. 5, 2021, accessed online at https://www.govinfo.gov/content/pkg/GPO-J6-DOC-CTRL0000001532.0001/pdf/GPO-J6-DOC-CTRL0000001532.0001.pdf.

33. FBI, Norfolk Division, *Situational Information Report, Potential Activity Alert*.

34. Indictment, *United States v. Rhodes et al.*, 20.

35. FBI, "Seeking Information: Pipe Bombs in Washington, D.C.," Mar. 9, 2021, video, 2:21, https://youtu.be/YJ8oLJIOn3E?si=b8EzCqPNz-sJNs9y.

36. Marissa J. Lang et al., "Trump Supporters Pour into Washington to Begin Demonstrating Against Election," *Washington Post*, Jan. 5, 2021, https://www.washington post.com/dc-md-va/2021/01/05/dc-protest-trump-supporters-election/.

37. FBI, "Statement of Facts: John Douglas Wright," Apr. 2021, accessed online at https://www.justice.gov/usao-dc/case-multi-defendant/file/1391071/dl.

38. FBI, "Statement of Facts: John Douglas Wright."

39. FBI, "Statement of Facts: John Douglas Wright."

40. FBI, "Statement of Facts: John Douglas Wright."

41. NPR, "January 6: Inside the Capitol Siege," *Embedded* (podcast), Jan. 15, 2021, https://www.npr.org/transcripts/957362053.

CHAPTER 4: "THAT'S EXACTLY HOW CHARLOTTESVILLE BEGAN"

1. Kathleen Gray et al, "Washington Girds for a Pro-Trump Rally, as Local Officials Warn of Possible Violence," *New York Times*, Jan. 6, 2021, https://www.nytimes.com /2021/01/06/us/politics/washington-girds-for-a-pro-trump-rally-as-local-officials -warn-of-possible-violence.html?searchResultPosition=3.

2. Zolan Kanno-Youngs and Matthew Rosenberg, "Pro-Trump Protesters to Gather amid Fears of Violence," *New York Times*, Jan. 5, 2021, https://www.nytimes .com/2021/01/05/us/politics/dc-protests.html.

3. Boris Sanchez, "Georgia Senate Race; Pence Can't Block Biden's Win; Ossoff Widens Lead over Perdue; Protesters Clash with D.C. Police; Only 4.8 Million Vaccine Doses Administered in U.S.," CNN, Jan. 6, 2021, https://transcripts.cnn.com/show /nday/date/2021-01-06/segment/04.

4. MSNBC, "The Other Justin," *American Radical* (podcast), Feb. 10, 2022, https:// www.msnbc.com/msnbc-podcast/transcript-other-justin-n1288902.

5. Daniel Hodges, "Written Statement for Select Committee to Investigate the January 6th Attack on the United States Capitol Hearing," July 27, 2021, https:// www.congress.gov/117/meeting/house/113969/witnesses/HHRG-117-IJ00-Wstate -HodgesO-20210727.pdf.

6. Hodges, "Written Statement for Select Committee to Investigate the January 6th Attack on the United States Capitol Hearing."

7. Select Committee to Investigate the January 6th Attack on the United States Capitol, *Final Report*, Dec. 22, 2022, 68, https://www.govinfo.gov/content/pkg/GPO -J6-REPORT/pdf/GPO-J6-REPORT.pdf.

8. Anonymous, "Account from a Food Service Employee," Co-Equal, Oral History Project, Oral History #12, https://www.co-equal.org/jan-6.

9. Eric Swalwell, interview with the author, Sept. 27, 2024.

10. Swalwell, interview.

11. Opening Brief of Petitioners, *Anderson v. Griswold*, Nov. 30, 2023, 137, accessed online at https://www.courts.state.co.us/userfiles/file/Court_Probation/02nd_Judicial _District/Denver_District_Court/Cases%20of%20Interest/20CV32577/SC/4%20-%20 Opening%20Brief%20of%20Petitioners.pdf.

12. Aquilino Gonell and Susan Shapiro, *American Shield: The Immigrant Sergeant Who Defended Democracy* (Berkeley, CA: Counterpoint Press, 2023), 156–57.

13. Erin Burnett, "The Presidential Election: Congress Counts the Votes," CNN, Jan. 6, 2021, https://archive.org/details/CNNW_20210106_140000_The_Presidential _Election_Congress_Counts_the_Vote/start/60/end/120.

14. Donald Trump, "Jan. 6 Rally Speech," Washington, DC, Jan. 6, 2021, https:// www.c-span.org/video/?507744-1/trumps-jan-6-rally-speech.

15. Boris Sanchez, "The Presidential Election: Congress Counts the Votes," CNN, Jan. 6, 2021, https://archive.org/details/CNNW_20210106_140000_The_Presidential _Election_Congress_Counts_the_Vote/start/900/end/960.

16. Sanchez, "The Presidential Election."

17. Rudy Giuliani, "Jan. 6 Rally Speech," Washington, DC, Jan. 6, 2021, https:// www.rev.com/blog/transcripts/rudy-giuliani-speech-transcript-at-trumps-washington -d-c-rally-wants-trial-by-combat.

18. Aquilino Gonell, US Capitol Historical Society (USCHS) interview, May 11, 2022.

19. Gonell, USCHS interview.

20. Office of Inspector General, "The Secret Service's Preparation for, and Response to, the Events of January 6, 2021," July 31, 2024, 49–50, https://www.oig .dhs.gov/sites/default/files/assets/2024-08/OIG-24-42-Aug24-Redacted.pdf.

21. "Never Before Seen January 6 Riot Footage Shows Lawmakers Taking Shelter," CNN, video, Oct. 13, 2022, https://www.cnn.com/videos/politics/2022/10/13/jan -6-riot-video-pelosi-fort-mcnair-full-ac360-vpx-sot.cnn.

22. Maggie Haberman, "Trump Told Crowd 'You Will Never Take Back Our Country with Weakness,'" New York Times, Jan. 6, 2021, https://www.nytimes.com /2021/01/06/us/politics/trump-speech-capitol.html?searchResultPosition=7.

23. Trump, "Jan. 6 Rally Speech."

24. Janet Buhler, "Transcribed Interview with the Select January 6th Committee," conducted Feb. 28, 2022, 33, accessed online at https://www.govinfo.gov/content /pkg/GPO-J6-TRANSCRIPT-CTRL0000050985/pdf/GPO-J6-TRANSCRIPT -CTRL0000050985.pdf.

25. Buhler, "Transcribed Interview with the Select January 6th Committee," 30.

26. Karlin Younger, "'You're Not Expecting to See It': Madison Native Finds DC Pipe Bomb, Thwarts Attack on RNC," FOX47, Jan. 13, 2021, https://fox47.com/news /local/youre-not-expecting-to-see-it-madison-native-finds-dc-pipe-bomb-thwarts -attack-on-rnc.

27. Business Insider, "The January 6 Insurrection, in All Its Heart-Pounding Detail, from 34 People Who Lived Through It," Oct. 28, 2021, https://www.businessinsider .com/january-6-oral-history-capitol-attack-insurrection-timeline-investigation -2021-10.

28. Younger, "'You're Not Expecting to See It.'"

29. Karlin Younger, "Wisconsin Woman Credits 'Infamous Load of Laundry' with Discovery of D.C. Pipe Bomb," WISN, Jan. 14, 2021, https://www.wisn.com/article /wisconsin-woman-credits-infamous-load-of-laundry-with-discovery-of-dc-pipe -bomb/35221177.

30. Business Insider, "The January 6 Insurrection."

31. Doug Moe, "A Madison Woman Found the RNC Pipe Bomb in D.C.," Madison Magazine, Jan. 12, 2021, https://www.channel3000.com/madison-magazine/columns

/a-madison-woman-found-the-rnc-pipe-bomb-in-d-c/article_a92152fa-04f0-5c93-a537
-02700c75e560.html.

32. Frank Lockwood (@LockwoodFrank), Twitter, Jan. 6, 2021, https://twitter.com
/LockwoodFrank/status/1346877836200718338.

CHAPTER 5: "THINGS STARTED TO GET REALLY VIOLENT"

1. Caroline Edwards, US Congress, House, Select Committee to Investigate the
January 6th Attack on the United States Capitol, 117th Cong., 2nd sess., June 9, 2021,
34, accessed online at https://www.govinfo.gov/content/pkg/CHRG-117hhrg48998
/pdf/CHRG-117hhrg48998.pdf.

2. Edwards, US Congress, House, Select Committee to Investigate the January 6th
Attack on the United States Capitol, 35.

3. Edwards, US Congress, House, Select Committee to Investigate the January 6th
Attack on the United States Capitol, 37.

4. Steven A. Sund, *Courage Under Fire: The Definitive Account from Inside the Capitol
on January 6* (Ashland, OR: Blackstone Publishing, 2023), 117.

5. Aquilino Gonell and Susan Shapiro, *American Shield: The Immigrant Sergeant Who
Defended Democracy* (Berkeley, CA: Counterpoint Press, 2023), 158.

6. Gonell and Shapiro, *American Shield*, 158.

7. Gonell and Shapiro, *American Shield*, 158.

8. Aquilino Gonell, USCHS interview, May 11, 2022.

9. Edwards, US Congress, House, Select Committee to Investigate the January 6th
Attack on the United States Capitol, 44.

10. Edwards, US Congress, House, Select Committee to Investigate the January 6th
Attack on the United States Capitol, 46.

11. Gonell and Shapiro, *American Shield*, 158.

12. Gonell, USCHS interview.

13. Anthony Brooks, host, "A Former Capitol Police Sergeant on the Personal and
Political Consequences of Jan. 6," interview with Aquilino Gonell, *On Point* (podcast),
Jan. 8, 2024, https://www.wbur.org/onpoint/2024/01/08/a-former-capitol-police
-sergeant-on-the-personal-and-political-consequences-of-jan-insurrection.

14. Gonell, USCHS interview.

15. Edwards, US Congress, House, Select Committee to Investigate the January 6th
Attack on the United States Capitol, 23.

16. Raw footage provided by Jon Farina.

17. Gonell, USCHS interview.

18. DC FEMS, "Jan. 6 2021: Events at the U.S. Capitol, as told by DC FEMS,"
video, 51:14, Sept. 2, 2021, https://www.youtube.com/watch?v=vw5pfgUxARw.

19. DC FEMS video.

20. Adam Goldman, "An Alabama Man Who Suffered a Heart Attack Outside the
Capitol Is Among the Dead," *New York Times*, Jan. 7, 2021, https://www.nytimes.com
/2021/01/07/us/politics/an-alabama-man-who-suffered-a-heart-attack-outside-the
-capitol-is-among-the-dead.html.

21. DC FEMS video.

22. DC FEMS video.

23. DC FEMS video.

24. Mike Pence (@Mike_Pence), Twitter, Jan. 6, 2021, https://Twitter.com/Mike_Pence/status/1346879811151605762.

25. Opening Brief of Petitioners, *Anderson v. Griswold*, Nov. 30, 2023, 131, accessed online at https://www.courts.state.co.us/userfiles/file/Court_Probation/02nd_Judicial_District/Denver_District_Court/Cases%20of%20Interest/20CV32577/SC/4%20-%20Opening%20Brief%20of%20Petitioners.pdf.

26. Opening Brief of Petitioners, *Anderson v. Griswold*, 131–32.

27. "Never Before Seen January 6 Riot Footage Shows Lawmakers Taking Shelter," CNN, video, Oct. 13, 2022, https://www.cnn.com/videos/politics/2022/10/13/jan-6-riot-video-pelosi-fort-mcnair-full-ac360-vpx-sot.cnn.

28. "Never Before Seen January 6 Riot Footage Shows Lawmakers Taking Shelter."

29. Donald Trump, "Jan. 6 Rally Speech," Jan. 6, 2021, Washington, DC, https://www.c-span.org/video/?507744-1/trumps-jan-6-rally-speech.

30. Select Committee to Investigate the January 6th Attack on the US Capitol, *Final Report*, Dec. 22, 2022, 68, accessed online at https://www.govinfo.gov/content/pkg/GPO-J6-REPORT/pdf/GPO-J6-REPORT.pdf.

31. Select Committee to Investigate the January 6th Attack on the US Capitol, *Final Report*, 77.

32. Daniel Herendeen, "Transcribed Interview with the Select January 6th Committee," conducted Mar. 16, 2022, 24, https://www.govinfo.gov/content/pkg/GPO-J6-TRANSCRIPT-CTRL0000055540/pdf/GPO-J6-TRANSCRIPT-CTRL0000055540.pdf.

33. Barber, interview with Select Committee, 24.

34. House Administration Subcommittee on Oversight, *Initial Findings Report: On the Failures and Politicization of the January 6th Select Committee and the Activities on and Leading Up to January 6, 2021*, Mar. 11, 2024, https://cha.house.gov/_cache/files/d/9/d96ba6ce-03fb-4fc8-a4a7-5b5daf19d064/4F510144C1F427873D3298D955C8E19F.initial-findings-report.pdf.

35. Jamie Roberts, *Four Hours at the Capitol*, HBO, Oct. 20, 2021.

36. Shane Smith, USCHS interview, Jan. 14, 2022.

37. DC FEMS video.

38. DC FEMS video.

39. DC FEMS video.

40. DC FEMS video.

41. DC FEMS video.

42. DC FEMS video.

43. DC FEMS video.

44. DC FEMS video.

CHAPTER 6: "HAND-TO-HAND BATTLE"

1. Select Committee to Investigate the January 6th Attack on the United States Capitol, *Final Report*, Dec. 22, 2022, 77, accessed online at https://www.govinfo.gov/content/pkg/GPO-J6-REPORT/pdf/GPO-J6-REPORT.pdf.

2. Michael Fanone, "Testimony of Officer Michael Fanone of the District of Columbia Metropolitan Police Department," July 27, 2021, 2, accessed online at https://www.congress.gov/117/meeting/house/113969/witnesses/HHRG-117-IJ00-Wstate-FanoneO-20210727.pdf.

3. Daniel Hodges, "Written Statement for Select Committee to Investigate the January 6th Attack on the United States Capitol Hearing," July 27, 2021, accessed online at https://www.congress.gov/117/meeting/house/113969/witnesses/HHRG -117-IJoo-Wstate-HodgesO-20210727.pdf.

4. Hodges, "Written Statement for Select Committee to Investigate the January 6th Attack on the United States Capitol Hearing."

5. Hodges, "Written Statement for Select Committee to Investigate the January 6th Attack on the United States Capitol Hearing."

6. Hodges, "Written Statement for Select Committee to Investigate the January 6th Attack on the United States Capitol Hearing."

7. Daniel Hodges, interview with the author, Sept. 19, 2024.

8. Hodges, interview.

9. Daniel Hodges, US Congress, House, Select Committee to Investigate the January 6th Attack on the United States Capitol, *The Law Enforcement Experience on January 6th*, 117th Cong., 1st sess., July 27, 2021, 40, https://www.govinfo.gov/content/pkg /CHRG-117hhrg45472/pdf/CHRG-117hhrg45472.pdf.

10. Hodges, interview.

CHAPTER 7: "THEN ALL OF A SUDDEN WE WERE INSIDE"

1. Daniel Hodges, "Written Statement for Select Committee to Investigate the January 6th Attack on the United States Capitol Hearing," July 27, 2021, accessed online at https://www.congress.gov/117/meeting/house/113969/witnesses/HHRG-117-IJoo -Wstate-HodgesO-20210727.pdf.

2. US Congress, House, Select Committee to Investigate the January 6th Attack on the United States Capitol, *The Law Enforcement Experience on January 6th*, 117th Cong., 1st sess., 2021, 56, https://www.govinfo.gov/content/pkg/CHRG-117hhrg45472/pdf /CHRG-117hhrg45472.pdf.

3. Hodges, "Written Statement for Select Committee to Investigate the January 6th Attack on the United States Capitol Hearing."

4. Hodges, "Written Statement for Select Committee to Investigate the January 6th Attack on the United States Capitol Hearing."

5. Hodges, "Written Statement for Select Committee to Investigate the January 6th Attack on the United States Capitol Hearing."

6. Third Superseding Indictment, *United States of America v. Nordean et al.*, Feb. 14, 2022, 21, accessed online at https://www.justice.gov/usao-dc/case-multi-defendant /file/1510966/dl.

7. FBI, "Affidavit in Support of a Criminal Complaint: Dominic Pezzola," Jan. 13, 2021, 4, https://www.justice.gov/opa/page/file/1355186/dl.

8. *Washington Post*, "What Happened on Jan. 6: Bloodshed," Oct. 31, 2021, https:// www.washingtonpost.com/politics/interactive/2021/what-happened-trump-jan-6 -insurrection/.

9. Eugene Goodman, "Testimony of Eugene Goodman," *United States of America v. Kevin Seefried and Hunter Seefried*, 17.

10. Goodman, "Testimony of Eugene Goodman," 17.

11. *Washington Post*, "What Happened on Jan. 6."

12. Goodman, "Testimony of Eugene Goodman," 18.

13. Goodman, "Testimony of Eugene Goodman," 21.

14. Eugene Goodman, "An Interview with Eugene Goodman," *3 Brothers No Sense* (podcast), Jan. 24, 2022, https://podcasters.spotify.com/pod/show/threebrothers nosense/episodes/An-interview-with-Eugene-Goodman-e1dc6c5.

15. Goodman, "Testimony of Eugene Goodman," 24.

16. Goodman, "Testimony of Eugene Goodman," 25.

17. Goodman, "Testimony of Eugene Goodman," 36.

18. Goodman, "Testimony of Eugene Goodman," 32.

19. Goodman, "Testimony of Eugene Goodman," 38–39.

20. Goodman, "Testimony of Eugene Goodman," 42–43.

21. Dalton Bennett et al., "41 Minutes of Fear: A Video Timeline from Inside the Capitol Siege," *Washington Post*, Jan. 16, 2021, https://www.washingtonpost.com /investigations/2021/01/16/video-timeline-capitol-siege/?itid=sf_national-security _jan-6-insurrection_pulitzer_p008_f002.

22. Goodman, "Testimony of Eugene Goodman," 51.

23. Goodman, "Testimony of Eugene Goodman," 43.

CHAPTER 8: "IF THEY STOP THE PROCEEDINGS, THEY WILL HAVE SUCCEEDED IN STOPPING THE VALIDATION OF THE PRESIDENT OF THE UNITED STATES"

1. Frank Lockwood, USCHS interview, Nov. 21, 2022.

2. Anonymous, "Account from the House Floor: A Congressional Staff Member Recounts House Floor Activity as the Capitol was Breached, Sheltering, and Returning to the Capitol," Co-Equal, Oral History Project, https://www.co-equal.org/jan-6.

3. "Never Before Seen January 6 Riot Footage Shows Lawmakers Taking Shelter," CNN, video, Oct. 13, 2022, https://www.cnn.com/videos/politics/2022/10/13/jan-6 -riot-video-pelosi-fort-mcnair-full-ac360-vpx-sot.cnn.

4. *Washington Post*, "What Happened on Jan. 6: Bloodshed," Oct. 31, 2021, https:// www.washingtonpost.com/politics/interactive/2021/what-happened-trump-jan-6 -insurrection/.

5. Shane Smith, USCHS interview, Jan. 14, 2022.

6. Julio Cortez and Andrew Harnik, "Images of Chaos: AP Photographers Capture US Capitol Riot," Associated Press, Jan. 5, 2022, https://apnews.com/article/photos -election-jan6-trump-washington-f69b5f03316eaef2044d520bc7ffe49a.

7. Olivia Nuzzi, "Eric Swalwell on Impeaching Trump, Surviving the Capitol Riot, and Being Linked to a Chinese Spy," *New York Magazine*, Feb. 4, 2021, https://nymag .com/intelligencer/2021/02/swalwell-on-impeachment-capitol-riot-and-that-chinese -spy.html.

8. Robert Schornak, "Transcribed Interview with the Select January 6th Committee," conducted Feb. 1, 2022, 34, accessed online at https://www.govinfo.gov/content /pkg/GPO-J6-TRANSCRIPT-CTRL0000040480/pdf/GPO-J6-TRANSCRIPT -CTRL0000040480.pdf.

9. Caroline Edwards, "Transcribed Interview with the Select January 6th Committee," conducted Apr. 18, 2022, 47, https://www.govinfo.gov/content/pkg/GPO-J6 -TRANSCRIPT-CTRL0000082302/pdf/GPO-J6-TRANSCRIPT-CTRL00000 82302.pdf.

10. Caroline Edwards, US Congress, House, Select Committee to Investigate the January 6th Attack on the United States Capitol, 117th Cong., 2nd sess., June 9, 2021, 47–49, accessed online at https://www.govinfo.gov/content/pkg/CHRG-117hhrg48998 /pdf/CHRG-117hhrg48998.pdf.

11. Edwards, US Congress, House, Select Committee to Investigate the January 6th Attack on the United States Capitol, 47–49.

12. Daniel Herendeen, "Transcribed Interview with the Select January 6th Committee," conducted Mar. 16, 2022, 25–27, accessed online at https://www.govinfo.gov /content/pkg/GPO-J6-TRANSCRIPT-CTRL0000055540/pdf/GPO-J6-TRANSCRIPT -CTRL0000055540.pdf.

13. Schornak, "Transcribed Interview with the Select January 6th Committee," 34.

14. "Never Before Seen January 6 Riot Footage Shows Lawmakers Taking Shelter."

15. "Never Before Seen January 6 Riot Footage Shows Lawmakers Taking Shelter."

16. Jamie Roberts, *Four Hours at the Capitol*, HBO, Oct. 20, 2021.

17. "Never Before Seen January 6 Riot Footage Shows Lawmakers Taking Shelter."

18. "Never Before Seen January 6 Riot Footage Shows Lawmakers Taking Shelter."

19. "Never Before Seen January 6 Riot Footage Shows Lawmakers Taking Shelter."

20. "Never Before Seen January 6 Riot Footage Shows Lawmakers Taking Shelter."

21. "Never Before Seen January 6 Riot Footage Shows Lawmakers Taking Shelter."

22. Roberts, *Four Hours at the Capitol*.

23. Roberts, *Four Hours at the Capitol*.

24. Roberts, *Four Hours at the Capitol*.

25. Roberts, *Four Hours at the Capitol*.

26. Select Committee to Investigate the January 6th Attack on the United States Capitol, *Final Report*, Dec. 22, 2022, 68, https://www.govinfo.gov/content/pkg/GPO -J6-REPORT/pdf/GPO-J6-REPORT.pdf.

27. Select Committee to Investigate the January 6th Attack on the United States Capitol, *Final Report*.

28. Select Committee to Investigate the January 6th Attack on the United States Capitol, *Final Report*.

29. "Tweets of January 6, 2021," American Presidency Project, https://www .presidency.ucsb.edu/documents/tweets-january-6-2021.

30. *Washington Post*, "What Happened on Jan. 6: Bloodshed," Oct. 31, 2021, https://www.washingtonpost.com/politics/interactive/2021/what-happened-trump -jan-6-insurrection/.

31. *Washington Post*, "What Happened on Jan. 6."

32. *Washington Post*, "What Happened on Jan. 6."

33. Select Committee to Investigate the January 6th Attack on the United States Capitol, *Final Report*.

34. Jake Tapper, "Live Footage as Protesters Enter Statuary Hall," CNN, Jan. 6, 2021, https://transcripts.cnn.com/show/se/date/2021-01-06/segment/11.

35. Donald Trump (@realDonaldTrump), Twitter post, Jan. 6, 2021, https://Twitter .com/realDonaldTrump/status/1346904110969315332?ref_src=twsrc%5Etfw%7Ctwcamp %5Etweetembed%7Ctwterm%5E1346904110969315332%7Ctwgr%5E8bb0fea2eb83fa6ce 09e149345794c50f0fc6446%7Ctwcon%5Es1_&ref_url=https%3A%2F%2Fwww.the trumparchive.com%2F%3Fsearchbox%3D22pleasesupportour22.

CHAPTER 9: "YOU CAN SEE THE LINE OF LOSS. THE TERRITORY IS THEIRS"

1. Michael Fanone and John Shiffman, *Hold the Line: The Insurrection and One Cop's Battle for America's Soul* (New York: Atria Books, 2022), 92.

2. Aquilino Gonell, USCHS interview, May 11, 2022.

3. DC FEMS video.

4. "Two Officers Died of Suicide After Capitol Riot," *Washington Post*, Feb. 12, 2021, https://www.washingtonpost.com/local/public-safety/police-officer-suicides-capitol-riot/2021/02/11/94804ee2-665c-11eb-886d-5264d4ceb46d_story.html.

5. Gonell, USCHS interview.

6. Gonell, USCHS interview.

7. Gonell, USCHS interview.

8. Frank Lockwood (@LockwoodFrank), Twitter post, Jan. 6, 2021, https://twitter.com/LockwoodFrank/status/1346903433320792069.

9. Opening Brief of Petitioners, *Anderson v. Griswold*, Nov. 30, 2023, 143, accessed online at https://www.courts.state.co.us/userfiles/file/Court_Probation/02nd_Judicial_District/Denver_District_Court/Cases%20of%20Interest/20CV32577/SC/4%20-%20Opening%20Brief%20of%20Petitioners.pdf.

10. Anonymous, "Account from the House Floor: A Congressional Staff Member Recounts Evacuation from the House Floor, Sheltering, and Returning to the Capitol," Co-Equal, Oral History Project, accessed online at https://www.co-equal.org/jan-6.

11. Opening Brief of Petitioners, *Anderson v. Griswold*, 144.

12. Anonymous, "Account from the House Floor."

13. Anonymous, "Account from the House Floor."

14. Anonymous, "Account from the House Floor."

15. Frank Lockwood (@LockwoodFrank), Twitter post, Jan. 6, 2021, https://Twitter.com/LockwoodFrank/status/1346904232860020741.

16. Frank Lockwood (@LockwoodFrank), Twitter post, Jan. 6, 2021, https://twitter.com/LockwoodFrank/status/1346904458647777285.

17. Frank Lockwood, USCHS interview, Nov. 21, 2022.

18. Opening Brief of Petitioners, *Anderson v. Griswold*, 143.

19. Ryan Lizza, "Politico Playbook," as quoted in Warren Rojas and Brent D. Griffiths, "Democratic Rep. Ruben Gallego, an Iraq War Vet, Said He Was Prepared to 'Kill Somebody' on January 6," *Business Insider*, Apr. 22, 2022, https://www.businessinsider.com/ruben-gallego-january-6-capitol-riot-prepared-to-kill-somebody-2022-4.

20. Opening Brief of Petitioners, *Anderson v. Griswold*, 143.

21. Bennett et al., "41 Minutes of Fear: A Video Timeline from Inside the Capitol Siege," *Washington Post*, Jan. 16, 2021, https://www.washingtonpost.com/investigations/2021/01/16/video-timeline-capitol-siege/?itid=sf_national-security_jan-6-insurrection_pulitzer_p008_f002.

22. Daniel Herendeen, "Transcribed Interview with the Select January 6th Committee," conducted Mar. 16, 2022, 29, https://www.govinfo.gov/content/pkg/GPO-J6-TRANSCRIPT-CTRL0000055540/pdf/GPO-J6-TRANSCRIPT-CTRL0000055540.pdf.

23. Robert Schornak, "Transcribed Interview with the Select January 6th Committee," conducted Feb. 1, 2022, 34, https://www.govinfo.gov/content/pkg/GPO-J6-TRANSCRIPT-CTRL0000040480/pdf/GPO-J6-TRANSCRIPT-CTRL0000040480.pdf.

24. Herendeen, "Transcribed Interview with the Select January 6th Committee," 29.

25. Statement of Offense, *United States of America v. Robert Schornak*, Nov. 12, 2021, 3, accessed online, https://www.justice.gov/usao-dc/case-multi-defendant/file/1448091/dl.

26. Statement of Offense, *United States of America v. Robert Schornak*.

27. Indictment, *United States v. Rhodes et al.*, Jan. 12, 2022, 27, accessed online at https://extremism.gwu.edu/sites/g/files/zaxdzs5746/files/Rhodes%20et%20al%20 Indictment.pdf.

28. Indictment, *United States v. Rhodes et al.*, 27.

29. Indictment, *United States v. Rhodes et al.*, 24–25.

30. Indictment, *United States v. Rhodes et al.*, 25.

31. Indictment, *United States v. Rhodes et al.*, 26.

32. Indictment, *United States v. Rhodes et al.*, 26.

33. Bennett et al., "41 Minutes of Fear."

34. Anonymous, "Account from the House Floor."

35. Opening Brief of Petitioners, *Anderson v. Griswold*, 145–46.

36. Anonymous, "Account from the House Floor."

37. Opening Brief of Petitioners, *Anderson v. Griswold*, 152–54.

38. Julio Cortez and Andrew Harnik, "Images of Chaos: AP Photographers Capture US Capitol Riot," Associated Press, Jan. 5, 2022, https://apnews.com/article /photos-election-jan6-trump-washington-f69b5f03316eaef2044d520bc7ffe49a.

39. Anonymous, "Account from the House Floor."

40. Cortez and Harnik, "Images of Chaos."

41. Lockwood, interview with the author.

42. Lockwood, USCHS interview.

43. Opening Brief of Petitioners, *Anderson v. Griswold*, Nov. 30, 2023, 137, https:// www.courts.state.co.us/userfiles/file/Court_Probation/02nd_Judicial_District/Denver _District_Court/Cases%20of%20Interest/20CV32577/SC/4%20-%20Opening%20 Brief%20of%20Petitioners.pdf, 154.

44. Rich Schapiro, Anna Schecter, and Chelsea Damberg, "Officer Who Shot Ashli Babbitt During Capitol Riot Breaks Silence: 'I Saved Countless Lives,'" NBC News, Aug. 26, 2021, https://www.nbcnews.com/news/us-news/officer-who-shot-ashli -babbitt-during-capitol-riot-breaks-silence-n1277736.

45. Schapiro et al., "Officer Who Shot Ashli Babbitt During Capitol Riot Breaks Silence."

CHAPTER 10: "THEY JUST KILLED A GIRL"

1. Frank Lockwood (@LockwoodFrank), Twitter posts, Jan. 6, 2021, https:// twitter.com/LockwoodFrank/status/1346906114311548928.

2. DC FEMS video.

3. DC FEMS video.

4. DC FEMS video.

5. DC FEMS video.

6. DC FEMS video.

7. DC FEMS video.

8. DC FEMS video.

9. DC FEMS video.

10. DC FEMS video.

11. DC FEMS video.

12. Jamie Raskin, *Unthinkable: Trauma, Truth, and the Trials of American Democracy* (New York: HarperCollins, 2022), 149.

13. Shane Smith, USCHS interview, Jan. 14, 2022.

14. Smith, USCHS interview.

15. Cameron Joseph, "'So, So Angry': Reporters Who Survived the Capitol Riot Are Still Struggling," *Vice*, July 6, 2021, https://www.vice.com/en/article/reporters -survived-capitol-riot-struggling/.

16. Joseph, "So, So Angry."

17. "WATCH: Lisa Desjardins Reports from Inside U.S. Capitol Where Pro-Trump Mob Interrupts Vote Count," *PBS NewsHour*, Jan. 6, 2021, accessed online at https:// www.youtube.com/watch?v=4E72MIiS8UM.

18. Smith, USCHS interview.

19. Frank Lockwood, USCHS interview, Nov. 21, 2022.

20. Lockwood, USCHS interview.

21. Smith, USCHS interview.

22. "WATCH: Lisa Desjardins Reports from Inside U.S. Capitol Where Pro-Trump Mob Interrupts Vote Count."

23. Olivia Beavers (@Olivia_Beavers), Twitter post, Jan. 6, 2021, https://Twitter .com/Olivia_Beavers/status/1346907520506474497.

24. Lockwood, USCHS interview.

25. Video released by January 6 committee, accessed online at https://customer -uh7tqhki3bpanql6.cloudflarestream.com/01a631018ce51f48560d5cf9b762568c /watch.

26. Daniel Hodges, US Congress, House, Select Committee to Investigate the January 6th Attack on the United States Capitol, *The Law Enforcement Experience on January 6th*, 117th Cong., 1st sess., July 27, 2021, 44, https://www.govinfo.gov/content /pkg/CHRG-117hhrg45472/pdf/CHRG-117hhrg45472.pdf.

27. Daniel Hodges, "Written Statement for Select Committee to Investigate the January 6th Attack on the United States Capitol Hearing," July 27, 2021, accessed online at https://www.congress.gov/117/meeting/house/113969/witnesses/HHRG -117-IJ00-Wstate-HodgesO-20210727.pdf.

28. Hodges, US Congress, House, Select Committee to Investigate the January 6th Attack on the United States Capitol, 44.

29. Hodges, "Written Statement for Select Committee to Investigate the January 6th Attack on the United States Capitol Hearing."

30. Hodges, US Congress, House, Select Committee to Investigate the January 6th Attack on the United States Capitol, 44.

31. Hodges, "Written Statement for Select Committee to Investigate the January 6th Attack on the United States Capitol Hearing."

32. Hodges, "Written Statement for Select Committee to Investigate the January 6th Attack on the United States Capitol Hearing."

33. Hodges, "Written Statement for Select Committee to Investigate the January 6th Attack on the United States Capitol Hearing."

34. Aquilino Gonell, USCHS interview, May 11, 2022.

35. US Congress, House, Select Committee to Investigate the January 6th Attack on the United States Capitol, *The Law Enforcement Experience on January 6th*, 117th Cong., 1st sess., 2021, 56, accessed online at https://www.govinfo.gov/content/pkg /CHRG-117hhrg45472/pdf/CHRG-117hhrg45472.pdf.

36. Hodges, "Written Statement for Select Committee to Investigate the January 6th Attack on the United States Capitol Hearing."

CHAPTER 11: "KILL HIM WITH HIS OWN GUN"

1. Daniel Hodges, "Written Statement for Select Committee to Investigate the January 6th Attack on the United States Capitol Hearing," July 27, 2021, https://www .congress.gov/117/meeting/house/113969/witnesses/HHRG-117-IJ00-Wstate-HodgesO -20210727.pdf

2. Jon Farina footage.

3. Jon Farina footage.

4. "Tweets of January 6, 2021," American Presidency Project, https://www .presidency.ucsb.edu/documents/tweets-january-6-2021.

5. Michael Fanone and John Shiffman, *Hold the Line: The Insurrection and One Cop's Battle for America's Soul* (New York: Atria Books, 2022), 100.

6. Michael Fanone, "Testimony of Officer Michael Fanone of the District of Columbia Metropolitan Police Department," July 27, 2021, 4, https://www.congress .gov/117/meeting/house/113969/witnesses/HHRG-117-IJ00-Wstate-FanoneO -20210727.pdf.

7. Fanone, "Testimony of Officer Michael Fanone of the District of Columbia Metropolitan Police Department," 4.

8. Fanone, "Testimony of Officer Michael Fanone of the District of Columbia Metropolitan Police Department."

9. Fanone, "Testimony of Officer Michael Fanone of the District of Columbia Metropolitan Police Department," 5.

10. Fanone, "Testimony of Officer Michael Fanone of the District of Columbia Metropolitan Police Department," 5.

11. Aquilino Gonell, USCHS interview, May 11, 2022.

12. Aquilino Gonell and Susan Shapiro, *American Shield: The Immigrant Sergeant Who Defended Democracy* (Berkeley, CA: Counterpoint Press, 2023), 168.

13. Gonell, USCHS interview.

14. Ryan J. Reilly, "Mike Fanone's Body Camera Footage from Jan. 6," video, Oct. 21, 2022, https://www.youtube.com/watch?v=UE7W66gsvjA.

15. Reilly, "Mike Fanone's Body Camera Footage from Jan. 6."

16. Fanone and Shiffman, *Hold the Line*, 109.

17. Reilly, "Mike Fanone's Body Camera Footage from Jan. 6."

CHAPTER 12: "IT JUST WAS ANOTHER LEVEL INTO DANTE'S INFERNO"

1. Alex Burns and Jonathan Martin, *This Will Not Pass: Trump, Biden, and the Battle for America's Future* (New York: Simon & Schuster, 2022), 203.

2. "Never Before Seen January 6 Riot Footage Shows Lawmakers Taking Shelter," CNN, video, Oct. 13, 2022, https://www.cnn.com/videos/politics/2022/10/13/jan -6-riot-video-pelosi-fort-mcnair-full-ac360-vpx-sot.cnn.

3. "Never Before Seen January 6 Riot Footage Shows Lawmakers Taking Shelter."

4. DC FEMS video.

5. Select Committee to Investigate the January 6th Attack on the United States Capitol, *Final Report*, Dec. 22, 2022, 68, https://www.govinfo.gov/content/pkg/GPO -J6-REPORT/pdf/GPO-J6-REPORT.pdf..

6. Stephen Ayres, "Transcribed Interview with the Select January 6th Committee," conducted June 17, 2022, 31–32, https://www.govinfo.gov/content/pkg/GPO-J6 -TRANSCRIPT-CTRL0000916061/pdf/GPO-J6-TRANSCRIPT-CTRL0000916061.pdf.

CHAPTER 13: "THE MOB KEPT ATTACKING EVEN WHILE
WE TENDED TO THEIR WOUNDED"

1. "Never Before Seen January 6 Riot Footage Shows Lawmakers Taking Shelter," CNN, video, Oct. 13, 2022, https://www.cnn.com/videos/politics/2022/10/13/jan -6-riot-video-pelosi-fort-mcnair-full-ac360-vpx-sot.cnn.

2. MSNBC, "The Other Justin," *American Radical* (podcast), Feb. 10, 2022, https:// www.msnbc.com/msnbc-podcast/transcript-other-justin-n1288902.

3. MSNBC, "The Other Justin."

4. MSNBC, "The Other Justin."

5. Aquilino Gonell and Susan Shapiro, *American Shield: The Immigrant Sergeant Who Defended Democracy* (Berkeley, CA: Counterpoint Press, 2023), 169.

6. DC FEMS video.

7. DC FEMS video.

8. DC FEMS video.

9. DC FEMS video.

10. Gonell and Shapiro, *American Shield*, 169.

11. DC FEMS video.

12. Gonell and Shapiro, *American Shield*, 170.

13. Aquilino Gonell, USCHS interview, May 11, 2022.

14. DC FEMS video.

15. Gonell, USCHS interview.

16. DC FEMS video.

17. DC FEMS video.

CHAPTER 14: "YOU STARTED TO SEE THE POLICE OFFICERS MAKE PROGRESS"

1. Michael Bender, *Frankly, We Did Win This Election: The Inside Story of How Trump Lost* (New York: Hachette Book Group, 2021), 377.

2. Aquilino Gonell, USCHS interview, May 11, 2022.

3. Daniel Hodges, US Congress, House, Select Committee to Investigate the January 6th Attack on the United States Capitol, *The Law Enforcement Experience on January 6th*, 117th Cong., 1st sess., July 27, 2021, 40, https://www.govinfo.gov/content/pkg /CHRG-117hhrg45472/pdf/CHRG-117hhrg45472.pdf.

4. Peter Hermann, "Two Officers Who Helped Fight the Capitol Mob Died by Suicide. Many More Are Hurting," *Washington Post*, Feb. 12, 2021, https://www .washingtonpost.com/local/public-safety/police-officer-suicides-capitol-riot/2021 /02/11/94804ee2-665c-11eb-886d-5264d4ceb46d_story.html.

5. Video released by January 6 committee, accessed online at https://customer -uh7tqhki3bpanql6.cloudflarestream.com/01a631018ce51f48560d5cf9b762568c/watch.

6. Anonymous, "Account from the House Floor: A Congressional Staff Member Recounts Evacuation from the House Floor, Sheltering, and Returning to the Capitol," Co-Equal, Oral History Project, 06:54–07:43, https://www.co-equal.org/jan-6.

7. "Tweets of January 6, 2021," American Presidency Project, https://www .presidency.ucsb.edu/documents/tweets-january-6-2021.

8. Anonymous, "Account from the House Floor."

9. Shane Smith, USCHS interview, Jan. 14, 2022.

10. Anonymous, "Account from the House Floor."

11. Smith, USCHS interview.

12. AOC Staff, "U.S. Capitol Clean-Up," Architect of the Capitol, Jan. 15, 2021, https://www.aoc.gov/explore-capitol-campus/blog/us-capitol-clean-up.

13. AOC Staff, "U.S. Capitol Clean-Up."

14. Opening Brief of Petitioners, *Anderson v. Griswold*, Nov. 30, 2023, 167, accessed online at https://www.courts.state.co.us/userfiles/file/Court_Probation/02nd_Judicial _District/Denver_District_Court/Cases%20of%20Interest/20CV32577/SC/4%20-%20 Opening%20Brief%20of%20Petitioners.pdf.

15. Anonymous, "Account from the House Floor."

16. Rachel Epstein, "18 Hours of Chaos and Uncertainty," *Marie Claire*, Jan. 8, 2021, https://www.marieclaire.com/politics/a35152166/lisa-desjardins-reporting-inside -us-capitol-breach/.

17. Mike Pence as quoted in Select Committee to Investigate the January 6th Attack on the United States Capitol, *Final Report*, Dec. 22, 2022, 68, https://www .govinfo.gov/content/pkg/GPO-J6-REPORT/pdf/GPO-J6-REPORT.pdf.

18. Steven A. Sund, *Courage Under Fire: The Definitive Account from Inside the Capitol on January 6* (Ashland, OR: Blackstone Publishing, 2023), 175.

19. DC FEMS video.

20. DC FEMS video.

21. DC FEMS video.

22. DC FEMS video.

23. DC FEMS video.

24. DC FEMS video.

25. DC FEMS video.

26. Aquilino Gonell, USCHS interview, May 11, 2022.

27. Aquilino Gonell, US Congress, House, Select Committee to Investigate the January 6th Attack on the United States Capitol, 117th Cong., 1st sess., July 27, 2021, 56, accessed online at https://www.govinfo.gov/content/pkg/CHRG-117hhrg45472 /pdf/CHRG-117hhrg45472.pdf.

28. Frank Lockwood, USCHS interview, Nov. 21, 2022.

29. "'He's got to pay a price': Unaired Footage Reveals Nancy Pelosi's Jan. 6 Fury," *Politico*, Aug. 27, 2024, https://www.politico.com/news/2024/08/27/nancy-pelosi-jan -6-fury-00176529.

30. "'He's got to pay a price': Unaired Footage Reveals Nancy Pelosi's Jan. 6 Fury," *Politico*.

31. Lockwood, USCHS interview.

CHAPTER 15: "DO I FEAR ANOTHER ONE OF THESE HAPPENING? ABSOLUTELY"

1. Elvina Nawaguna and Rachel Epstein, "'It Was Degrading': Black Capitol Custodial Staff Talk About What It Felt Like to Clean Up the Mess Left on January 6 by Violent Pro-Trump White Supremacists," *Business Insider*, Jan. 13, 2021, https:// www.businessinsider.com/capitol-riot-custodial-staff-cleanup-janitors-maga-trump -white-supremacists-2021-1.

2. Nawaguna and Epstein, "'It Was Degrading'."

3. Gen. William Walker, "Transcribed Interview with the Select January 6th Committee," conducted Apr. 21, 2022, 76, accessed online at https://www.govinfo .gov/content/pkg/GPO-J6-TRANSCRIPT-CTRL0000086314/pdf/GPO-J6 -TRANSCRIPT-CTRL0000086314.pdf.

4. Aishvarya Kavi, "Rampage Weighs on Congressional Staff Members and Capitol Workers," *New York Times*, Jan. 8, 2021, https://www.nytimes.com/2021/01/08/us/politics/capitol-rampage-congressional-staff.html.

5. Anonymous, "Account from a Food Service Employee," Co-Equal, Oral History Project, accessed online at https://www.co-equal.org/jan-6.

6. Caroline Edwards, US Congress, House, Select Committee to Investigate the January 6th Attack on the United States Capitol, 117th Cong., 2nd sess., June 9, 2021, 54–55, accessed online at https://www.govinfo.gov/content/pkg/CHRG-117hhrg48998/pdf/CHRG-117hhrg48998.pdf.

7. Michael Fanone, "Testimony of Officer Michael Fanone of the District of Columbia Metropolitan Police Department," July 27, 2021, 5, accessed online at https://www.congress.gov/117/meeting/house/113969/witnesses/HHRG-117-IJ00-Wstate-FanoneO-20210727.pdf.

8. Michael Fanone and John Shiffman, *Hold the Line: The Insurrection and One Cop's Battle for America's Soul* (New York: Atria Books, 2022), 130.

9. Fanone, "Testimony of Officer Michael Fanone of the District of Columbia Metropolitan Police Department," 5.

10. Peter Hermann, "Two Officers Who Helped Fight the Capitol Mob Died by Suicide. Many More Are Hurting," *Washington Post*, Feb. 12, 2021, https://www.washingtonpost.com/local/public-safety/police-officer-suicides-capitol-riot/2021/02/11/94804ee2-665c-11eb-886d-5264d4ceb46d_story.html.

11. Hermann, "Two Officers Who Helped Fight the Capitol Mob Died by Suicide."

12. Julio Cortez and Andrew Harnik, "Images of Chaos: AP Photographers Capture US Capitol Riot," Associated Press, Jan. 5, 2022, https://apnews.com/article/photos-election-jan6-trump-washington-f69b5f03316eaef2044d520bc7ffe49a.

13. Amanda Macias, "National Guard Troops Leave Capitol Months After Deadly Jan. 6 Insurrection," CNBC, May 24, 2021, https://www.cnbc.com/2021/05/24/national-guard-leaves-capitol-after-january-6-insurrection.html.

14. Bart Jansen, "US Capitol Police Chief: 153 Officers Have Left Force Since Jan. 6; Hiring Is Imperative," *USA Today*, Jan. 5, 2022, https://www.usatoday.com/story/news/politics/2022/01/05/capitol-police-officers-left-since-jan-6/9104403002/.

15. US Attorney's Officer, District of Columbia, "Capitol Breach Cases," Justice Department, https://www.justice.gov/usao-dc/capitol-breach-cases.

16. Stephen Ayres, "Transcribed Interview with the Select January 6th Committee," conducted June 17, 2022, 39, accessed online at https://www.govinfo.gov/content/pkg/GPO-J6-TRANSCRIPT-CTRL0000916061/pdf/GPO-J6-TRANSCRIPT-CTRL0000916061.pdf.

17. Ayres, "Transcribed Interview with the Select January 6th Committee," 38.

18. Daniel Herendeen, "Transcribed Interview with the Select January 6th Committee," conducted Mar. 16, 2022, 30, accessed online at https://www.govinfo.gov/content/pkg/GPO-J6-TRANSCRIPT-CTRL0000055540/pdf/GPO-J6-TRANSCRIPT-CTRL0000055540.pdf.

19. Janet Buhler, "Transcribed Interview with the Select January 6th Committee," conducted Feb. 28, 2022, 55–56, accessed online at https://www.govinfo.gov/content/pkg/GPO-J6-TRANSCRIPT-CTRL0000050985/pdf/GPO-J6-TRANSCRIPT-CTRL0000050985.pdf.

20. Evan Casey, "Former US Capitol Officer Calls Out Trump's Jan. 6 Pardons During Wisconsin Visit," *Wisconsin Public Radio*, Jan. 28, 2025, https://www.wpr.org /news/former-us-capitol-officer-trump-jan-6-pardons-wisconsin-milwaukee-visit.

21. Briana Vannozzi, "Brian Sicknick's Family 'Angered' After Trump Pardons Jan. 6 Rioters," *NJ Spotlight News*, Jan. 22, 2025, https://www.njspotlightnews.org/video /brian-sicknicks-family-angered-after-trump-pardons-jan-6-rioters/.

22. Tom Dreisback, "FBI Agents, Prosecutors Fear Retribution from Jan. 6 Rioters Pardoned by Trump," *NPR*, Feb. 6, 2025, https://www.npr.org/2025/02/06/nx-s1 -5287708/trump-pardoned-jan-6-rioters-prosecutors-fbi-police.

23. Dreisback, "FBI Agents, Prosecutors Fear Retribution from Jan. 6 Rioters Pardoned by Trump."

24. Dreisback, "FBI Agents, Prosecutors Fear Retribution from Jan. 6 Rioters Pardoned by Trump."

25. Luke Broadwater, "'A Betrayal, a Mockery': Police Express Outrage Over Trump's Jan. 6 Pardons," *New York Times,* Jan. 21, 2025, https://www.nytimes.com /2025/01/21/us/politics/jan-6-pardons-police.html.

26. Broadwater, "'A Betrayal, a Mockery.'"

27. Drew Wilder, "'Betrayed': Former DC Officer Seeks Protection After Jan. 6 Attackers Pardoned," *News 4 Washington*, Jan. 21, 2025, https://www.nbcwashington .com/news/local/betrayed-former-dc-officer-seeks-protection-after-jan-6-attackers -pardoned/3821489/.

28. Frank Lockwood, USCHS interview, Nov. 21, 2022.

INDEX